ANCIENT AMERICAS

THE GREAT CIVILISATIONS

Nicholas J. Saunders

SUTTON PUBLISHING

First published in the United Kingdom in 2004 by
Sutton Publishing Limited · Phoenix Mill
Thrupp · Stroud · Gloucestershire · GL5 2BU

British Library Cataloguing in Publication Data
A catalogue record for this book is available from the British Library.

ISBN 0-7509-3340-2

Typeset in 11/13.5 Sabon.
Typesetting and origination by
Sutton Publishing Limited.
Printed and bound in England by
J.H. Haynes & Co. Ltd, Sparkford.

Contents

List of Illustrations

Puquio wells at Nazca
Quechua woman and llama at Sacsahuaman
Machu Picchu

BLACK AND WHITE PLATES between pages 120 and 121

Amerindian petroglyph from Trinidad
Carib church at Salybia, Dominica
Olmec crying baby ceramic figurine
La Venta female figurine
Danzante figure at Monte Albán
Teotihuacan funerary urn
The ball court at Monte Albán
Teotihuacan mural figure
Teotihuacan, Quetzalcoatl head
Aztec Calendar Stone
Jade burial mask of Pacal from Palenque
Aztec carved-stone jaguar heart container
Aztec god Xipe Totec, 'Our Lord the Flayed One'
Jaguar men fighting at Acatlán
Chavín-style pottery vessel
Moche Sacrifice Scene from Pañamarca
Nasca ceramic trophy head
Nasca desert drawing of a Hummingbird
Wari polychrome ceramic
Gateway of the Sun at Tiwanaku
Pyramid at El Purgatorio (Tucumé)
Ponce Stela at Tiwanaku
Adobe frieze at Huaca del Dragon, Moche Valley
Coricancha Sun Temple in Cuzco
Inka terraces at Pisac
Inka ceramic showing man carrying an aryballus

Chronological Chart

MESOAMERICA

Olmec	1250–400 BC
Zapotec	500 BC–AD 750
Teotihuacán	150 BC–AD 750
Classic Maya	AD 250–900
Toltecs	AD 900–1200
Aztecs	AD 1350–1521

SOUTH AMERICA

Chavín	850–400 BC
Paracas	300 BC–AD 150
Nasca	AD 150–600
Moche	AD 100–750
Wari	AD 400–800
Tiwanaku	AD 100–900
Sicán	AD 800–1375
Chimú	AD 1200–1476
Inka	AD 1438–1532

Acknowledgements

This book is one result of thirty years' involvement in the archaeology and anthropology of pre-Columbian America, during which time I have been engaged in teaching, research, and academic publication in the United Kingdom, Mexico, Peru, and the Caribbean. This period has seen dramatic changes not only in the quantity of our knowledge of the ancient Americas, but also qualitatively in the sophistication of the ways in which we interpret and understand what we discover. In one sense, as archaeology has been increasingly influenced by anthropology, our ability to 'interrogate' the past has become sensitised to issues and ideas that would have been considered impossible three decades ago.

As the chapters in this book illustrate, archaeology has not only become more scientific and technological – DNA profiling of ancient remains being an outstanding example – but also more philosophical and reflexive. We are now more interested than before in why ancient Americans did certain things in particular ways, how they made their choices, and what they believed about the natural world and their place within it. Bearing in mind all the people from many different disciplines who have influenced my thinking over thirty years I would like to thank the following for their advice, criticisms, support and friendship – though they of course bear no responsibility for what I have made of this.

I am especially grateful to Elizabeth P. Benson, Jeffrey Quilter, Clive Ruggles, Peter Ucko, Michael Coe, Gustavo Politis, Gerardo Reichel-Dolmatoff, Tom Dillehay, Stephen Hugh-Jones, Danny Miller, Suzanne Küchler, Jay Kettle-Williams, Marion Oettinger, Peter Roe, Arie Boomert, Mary Helms, John Carlson, Sonia Rivero and Michael Roth. The following institutions have greatly facilitated my research: Southampton University, Sheffield Univerity, Cambridge University, Dumbarton Oaks (Washington DC), University of the West Indies (Trinidad and Jamaica), Mexican

National Autonomous University, National University of La Plata (Argentina), University College London, and the British Museum.

On a personal note, the support of my wife Pauline, and of my children Roxanne and Alexander, as well as my parents Geoff and Pat, has been invaluable. And for the long march, the friends of decades include Bill Chandler, John Wyatt, Phil Reeve, Steve Cunliffe, Gerry O'Connell, Barry O'Shea, and Bob Craig. Finally I would like to thank my editors at Sutton who have done such a wonderful job in bringing this book to life!

Nicholas J. Saunders

PART ONE

Ancient America
– A New World

ONE

Alien Encounters: America and Europe

Imagine a world full of mirrors in which everything seems strangely familiar yet subtly and inexplicably different. For an instant everything appears fixed and real, then splinters into a thousand broken images, shifting in and out of focus. People materialise, and they too seem familiar but unknown. They are part of this place, yet move and talk in unfamiliar ways, sliding between the brilliant reflections of this strange reality – a reality that for all its otherness will change the shape of world history.

The year AD 1492 was the time and the Caribbean the place for this otherworldly experience – an experience shared by Amerindians and Europeans. When Christopher Columbus came face to face with an unknown Amerindian on a small Caribbean island it was akin to an encounter with alien species in our own time. Here was an unsuspected land, discovered in the middle of the ocean and inhabited by human beings who seemed to experience things differently – to live, love, worship and die according to a different sense of the world. Here were a land and a people who simultaneously confirmed and subverted the medieval European view of how the world should be. This was an encounter in which not only enormous differences in language and technology collided, but one with a civilisation whose ideas about disease, natural philosophy, morality, spirituality and the human experience of the natural world had evolved along a profoundly 'other' trajectory.

Amerindians and Europeans were mutually confused and misled by their early encounters with each other – how could it have been otherwise? Two worldviews had come into contact and not a single word was shared between them. And yet this was only the beginning. Within thirty years the Aztec kingdom of Mexico would be conquered, and a decade or so later the Inka empire of South America would follow. Cultural traditions that had been shaped by thousands of years of isolation from the rest of the world would come to an end in little more than a generation.

Yet, while brilliant civilisations fell and Europeans fought over the spoils, indigenous beliefs proved more resilient and malleable. Militarily, economically and politically Europeans had wrested the Americas from its own people – yet in everyday life and belief it seems as if a part of the Amerindian spirit had in its own way colonised the faith of its own conquerors. Today, native traditions endure from Mexico to Chile and Argentina. The old ways, sometimes mixed with the historically recent and new, continue to give meaning to indigenous peoples and places, the living and the dead. This is one part of their story, and it begins with a man who some believed was about to sail off the edge of the world.

FIRST ENCOUNTERS

On 3 August 1492, Christopher Columbus set sail from Palos on Spain's Atlantic coast with three ships – the *Santa Maria*, *Niña* and *Pinta*. He sailed west, expecting to find a shortcut route to the spice-rich Orient, and for which reason he had brought along a Jewish linguist who spoke Chaldean and Arabic as well as Hebrew. There were some, however, who believed that he would simply drop off the world's rim and never be heard of again. After a brief sojourn in the Canary Islands, the little fleet set sail again on 6 September, running before the north-east trade winds that blew westward from Africa.

Land was sighted at 2 o'clock on the morning of Friday 10 October, and when the sun rose, Columbus waded ashore to take possession of a small island for King Ferdinand and Queen Isabella of Spain. He christened it San Salvador, though later learnt that its native name was Guanahaní. Columbus noticed the shiny gold ornaments the natives wore in their noses and, though neither the Spanish nor the natives could speak each other's language, he endeavoured to discover the source of the precious metal. He then made a move that established an enduring template for such meetings by offering glass beads in exchange for food, water, information and local goods. Such were the first manoeuvres in one of the most momentous chains of events in history.

Columbus noted the timid nature of the natives and added that they would be easy to enslave and convert to Christianity. To illustrate his point, he abducted seven of the Amerindians to take back to Spain. On leaving San Salvador, the three Spanish ships cruised the Bahamas, hearing more rumours of a gold-rich island called Cipangu. On 28 October, Columbus believed he had finally reached Cathay (China), although in fact he was off the coast of Cuba. Expeditions inland proved unrewarding, and by 5 December he was offshore of the island known to its Taíno inhabitants as Bohío, and which he named La Española (i.e. Hispaniola – modern Haiti and Dominican Republic).

Disaster struck as he was sailing along Hispaniola's northern coast. The *Santa Maria* ran aground and only the timely help of the local Taíno chief Guacanagarí enabled the Spanish to salvage their valuables from Columbus's wrecked flagship. In meetings between the two leaders, Columbus repeated his previous act of exchanging low-value European goods for Amerindian gold jewellery. Conversations, such as they were, soon came around again to the source of the precious metal, and Columbus was heartened to learn that there was a gold-rich land known as Cibao in the centre of the island.

Ever the opportunist, Columbus made a virtue of necessity. His two remaining ships could not transport all his men back to Spain and so he decided to build La Navidad as the first European settlement in the Americas. The thirty-eight men whom he left behind were charged with finding and collecting gold ready for his return. And so, on 16 January 1493, the *Niña* and *Pinta* set sail for Spain with the momentous news of Columbus's discoveries.

Such are the bare bones of the tale of this first encounter between Europeans and the indigenous peoples of the Americas. Yet, they conceal far more than they reveal. In the real life experiences framed by these events lay hidden worlds of meaning that would shape the European experience of the Americas and change world history for ever.

Columbus's accidental discovery of the Americas was full of irony, not least of which was the collision between two mutually incomprehensible worldviews. In the Caribbean itself there was an immediate confusion of real and imagined landscapes, illustrated by Columbus's belief that he had reached the East Indies and his consequent labelling of the native peoples as Indians – a term still used some five hundred years later.

Along with trade trinkets, Columbus took with him the intellectual baggage of late medieval Europe, much of it derived from classical antiquity, which conceived of strange and foreign places as inhabited by equally exotic creatures such as Amazons and cannibals. These represented the polar opposites of European social and moral norms. Amazon societies were controlled by women, and cannibals were people whose habit of eating human flesh was the antithesis of civilised Christian behaviour. Amerindians walked about naked and, even worse, appeared to be unashamed of the fact, in defiance of Biblical injunction.

Columbus, and those who travelled in his wake, heard rumours of monsters – people without heads, with only one eye, or who spent their lives carrying trees around. Ideas from medieval alchemy also influenced the Europeans, such as the belief that gold was produced by warm climates. At first the Caribbean and then Central and South America, along with their inhabitants, were understood as definitively 'other', a mythical landscape and people constructed in European minds, and into which Columbus's discoveries were forced, as if into a straitjacket.

Apart from these preconceptions and misconceptions, there were problems of translation and interpretation. Columbus quickly classified the Taíno as peaceful and the Carib as warlike. From the outset, the cultural geography of the Caribbean was drafted by Europeans in terms of docile, co-operative but simple-minded Indians and savage, warlike and troublesome sub-human cannibals. The richly varied and endlessly fascinating complexity of Caribbean Amerindian peoples was thereby reduced almost immediately to bizarre stereotypes – a typical outsider's view which is still taught in many of the region's schools.

In fact, Columbus's first voyage saw him stumbling not into a world of savagery, but rather into a sophisticated universe where mythology had the force of history and humans, animals, plants and even the weather were inextricably and eternally connected to the powerful spirit forces of ancestors and gods.

When the Taíno of Hispaniola and Puerto Rico first met the Spanish, they recognised a powerful ally against their Carib enemies, accusing the latter of eating their men and stealing their women. These accusations appeared to be supported by Columbus's subsequent experiences in Dominica and Guadeloupe where he rescued captured Taíno women and encountered human bones hanging inside Carib houses. The Spanish misunderstood these traditional Amerindian customs of respect for the dead and humiliation of defeated enemies, customs that included the ritual display of human bones, the tasting of small strips of flesh and the drinking of manioc beer mixed with powdered human bone.

This 'evidence' of bestial behaviour clearly suited the desire of Columbus and his successors to justify continued attacks on and enslavement of the Caribs. Carib and cannibal quickly became synonymous, with the term cannibalism replacing the older Greek word anthropophagy as a universal term for the ultimate crime of consuming human flesh. It was another irony that the region would soon come to be known as the Caribbean.

Such were some of the complex issues that surrounded Columbus's first encounter with the native peoples of the Caribbean, and that helped shape the idea of the Americas in the European imagination. But what of the people themselves? Who were they? Where did they come from? And when?

THE PREHISTORIC CARIBBEAN

The islands of the Caribbean offered a bewildering variety of landscapes and resources to early prehistoric peoples. The diversity of their interactions with local environments led to different kinds of lifeways, dwellings and material culture that are often difficult for archaeologists to interpret. One consequence of this has been different ways of classifying cultural remains, and of trying to build an overall picture of cultural development from the scattered, fragmentary and often ambiguous evidence.

The earliest Caribbean peoples belonged to the so-called Archaic Period and appear around 5500 BC at the sites of Banwari Trace and St John Oropuche in Trinidad, opposite the South American mainland. They were hunters, fishers, and gatherers who lived a transient existence probably in small family groups. They did not make or use pottery but did have spears tipped with bone, roughly shaped stone tools and *manos* and *metates* for grinding. From the archaeological remains it appears they gathered vast quantities of shellfish whose empty shells they discarded on to huge heaps known today as shell middens. These sites are typically located near mangrove swamps and beaches.

Slightly later, around 4000 BC, comes the earliest evidence for the human occupation of Cuba, far to the north. Sites such as Seboruco are often rockshelters or caves with flaked-stone tools scattered on the floor. Some sites are thought to date back even earlier, possibly to 6000 BC. However, around 2000 BC these early pre-ceramic sites become more frequent and are divided into a number of different, if not universally accepted, subdivisions of the Archaic Period. Such places include Painted Cave in Cuba, Barrera-Mordan in the Dominican Republic, and Angostura in Puerto Rico which also had human burials. Some sites, such as Cayo Redondo on Cuba, had a long life, inhabitation spanning the period 2000 BC to AD 1300, and include shell middens and painted caves. On Antigua, the site of Jolly Beach flourished around 1800 BC as a workshop area where stone flakes were struck from the abundant local pebbles. Similarly, at Hope Estate on St Martin, flint flakes and shell artefacts have been dated to between 2350 and 1800 BC. On St Thomas, the site of Krum Bay has yielded stone tools and jewellery made from bone and shell produced between 880 and 225 BC.

Making archaeological sense of this early evidence continues to be problematic. Some sites that lack pottery have been called pre-ceramic and assigned to the Archaic Period rather than more accurately being called aceramic and thus potentially of a much later date. Arguably the most notorious problem has been identifying the first pre-ceramic inhabitants of Cuba. These people, called the Ciboney, lived in caves with lifeways defined by simple stone tools. They were assumed to be the ancestors of the primitive Guanahatabey people who occupied the same area when Europeans arrived. The thorny question remains whether the Guanahatabeys should be considered a surviving relic of the Archaic Period surrounded by more sophisticated pottery-using peoples, or the creation of our inability to make sense of a patchy archaeological record.

Somewhere between 500 and 200 BC, a new and different kind of people arrived in the Caribbean. These were the pottery-using, village-dwelling Saladoid peoples who had left their South American homeland for Trinidad and then sailed north in seagoing canoes to colonise the Greater Antilles. Their advent isolated, marginalised and possibly absorbed the earlier hunter-gatherers of the Archaic Period.

The Saladoid peoples originated from the mouth of the Orinoco river in Venezuela. They brought with them a settled village life, agriculture and a shamanic religion typical of tropical rainforest societies in lowland Amazonia. They grew manioc, sweet potato, cotton and tobacco, and introduced pottery making in the form of distinctive white-on-red decorated ceramics which take their name, Saladoid, from the type-site of Saladero in Venezuela. Their stone-tools were more varied and efficient than those of their predecessors, and they were able to fell larger trees and clear more extensive areas for their fields and villages.

By about AD 300, Saladoid peoples had spread throughout the Caribbean and most islands probably had some variation of Saladoid culture. The sea continued to play an important role in everyday and spiritual life as canoe travel connected the islands with each other and also with mainland South America. For the Saladoid era and later periods, there is a strong argument for looking at the Caribbean islands and South America as an integrated unit – an 'interaction sphere' of diverse but connected peoples and landscapes, rather than the separate political entities they became after Europeans arrived.

Saladoid cultures eventually developed in different ways on different islands into what archaeologists call the Ostionoid cultural tradition, named after the Ostiones culture on the island of Hispaniola dated to around AD 500. Local developments of the Ostionoid tradition are known as Meillacan in Hispaniola, Cuba and Jamaica; Elenan in the Leeward and Virgin Islands; and Palmetto in the Bahamas. By around AD 1200 on Hispaniola, local developments led to the Chican Ostionoid culture – the name given by archaeologists to the remains of the Taíno peoples, those people first encountered by Columbus in AD 1492.

The Taíno

Like their Saladoid predecessors, the Taíno – sometimes also called the Arawak – lived a settled village life and practised agriculture, growing so many of those foods that would, in time, colonise the world: maize, manioc, sweet potatoes, guava, papaya, pineapple and tobacco. They grew cotton from which they made clothing, collected clams, oysters and crabs, and hunted birds, snakes, manatees and sea turtles.

Their arts and crafts included body painting and the fashioning of earrings, nose ornaments, lip plugs and colourful feather headdresses. Carved-stone beads and ornaments known as *çibas* were worn with gold ornaments which were in fact usually a gold–copper–silver alloy known as *guanín*. For the Taíno, *guanín*'s sacredness was due partly to its smell, which recalled sexuality and fertility and which they encountered also in European brass – a strange similarity that led to exchanges of what Europeans misunderstood to be pure Amerindian gold for worthless European scrap.

The Taíno were expert woodworkers and carved distinctive ceremonial stools known as *duhos*, often decorated with shell and *guanín*. Shamans (*behiques*) and chiefs (*caciques*) sat on these stools and connected to the supernatural realm of ancestors and spirits. The Taíno built large elaborate canoes, travelling regularly between islands and maintaining a network of trade relationships. Many of their sophisticated *guanín* items were obtained in down-the-line maritime trade between islands from their original source in South America. Regarded as high-class possessions, these objects embodied supernatural power and as such were ceremonially exchanged between Taíno chiefs. It is no surprise that such valuable items were among those offered to Columbus in 1492 by chief Guacanagarí on Hispaniola.

Taíno society was ruled by hereditary chiefs, their status inherited through the mother's line. Consequently, highborn women could have great status in Taíno society. Chiefs could have many wives, an indication that many marriages were often little more than strategic political alliances. This tight social organisation is reflected in the size and sophistication of Taíno villages. The larger ones could have hundreds of communal houses occupied by extended families, built around a central plaza which was used for social and religious events such as ceremonial dances and music called *areítos* and rubber ball-games known as *batey*.

Hidden away in the mountainous area of central Puerto Rico, Caguana has the densest and most elaborate grouping of ballcourts and plazas of any Taíno site. At its peak around AD 1350, Caguana was a ceremonial and probably political centre, dominated by its specialised plaza architecture which included images of mythological creatures and figures engraved on to stone slabs that flanked the central plaza. Caguana is thought to have been the seat of the powerful Taíno chief Guarionex.

Taíno religion was based on the shamanic tradition inherited from their Saladoid ancestors. In keeping with all Amerindian peoples of the Americas, they saw plants, animals and landscapes as infused with spirit force derived from the ancestors and the natural world. It was the Taíno chiefs and shamans who controlled these forces of life and death through their active interpretation of a philosophy founded on symbolism and analogy – ideas that will surface time and again as we explore ancient Mesoamerica and South America. In such a spiritually animated universe, all things possessed sacred and secular dimensions and blended into each other in ways which we today, as well as the first European conquerors, find difficult to comprehend.

Taíno belief that spirits inhabited sacred places is revealed at the site of La Aleta in the Dominican Republic (the eastern half of Hispaniola). Here, between AD 1035 and AD 1420, a flooded cavern was used by the Taíno and the watery conditions have preserved such normally fragile items as basketry, gourds and carved wooden artefacts. La Aleta appears to have been a ritual and ceremonial location and not a heavily populated town, an impression reinforced by the presence of four ceremonial plazas.

The Taíno considered caves to be entrances to the underworld and they feature in myths of origin as places of emergence and as the homes of the spirits of the dead – the *opía* – who, transformed into bats, flew out of their cave-roosts at night to feed on guava fruit. At the bottom of the La Aleta cavern, archaeologists found an underwater hill upon which were scattered stone tools, pottery, wooden items and baskets, seemingly having been placed there deliberately as offerings to gods and ancestral spirits. A small *duho*, decorated bowls, a crocodile figurine and a war club were among the items retrieved, along with a 'vomiting spatula' used to purify the body during religious rituals.

The main focus of Taíno religion was the veneration of gods and spirits known as *zemís* whose supernatural powers were embodied in sacred images – three-dimensional objects fashioned from stone, bone, wood, shell, clay and cotton, sometimes in combination. Zoomorphic examples took the form of birds, frogs, turtles and sometimes vegetable foods like cassava. Others are more abstract with geometric designs carved or painted on rocks and artefacts. Some were anthropomorphic carved wooden containers in which the remains of dead chiefs were kept, while others were doll-like cotton figures decorated with stone beads. However, *zemís* were also personifications of spiritual forces which resided in trees, rocks, caves, rivers and other features of the landscape.

This connection with the sacred landscape of myth was embodied in the most common form of *zemí* – the three-pointed stones whose triangular shape has been interpreted as a miniature mountain or volcano, but perhaps also was representative of women's breasts, conical seashells or the shoots of the manioc plant. Some depict stylised human faces, animals or fantastical half-human half-animal creatures which recall the startling imagery experienced during shamanistic trances. *Zemís* were well looked after, given food and drink and rubbed with cassava; each had different powers, ranging from promoting successful childbirth to guaranteeing victory in war or enhancing agricultural fertility when buried in the manioc fields known as *conucos*.

Wooden *zemís* demonstrated the shaman's or chief's ability to link everyday life and the spirit realm in the *cohoba* ceremony. Taíno chiefs and shamans inhaled this hallucinogenic powder in order to commune with spirits, especially those of their venerated ancestors. Columbus himself witnessed such a ritual in 1495, commenting on the paraphernalia used and the resulting intoxication of the participants. *Zemís* were a vital and integral part of Taíno spiritual and social life. Uniquely Caribbean, each possessed its own powers and symbolism depending on its material, shape and the stories attached to it by its owner. *Zemí* objects were associated with the cosmic powers of the universe, ancestral spirits and the acquisition and maintenance of political power by the elite. *Zemí* designs bestowed supernatural power on artefacts and landscape alike.

The Taíno had several important gods such as Yúcahu – the invisible lord of fertility and 'spirit of cassava'. His female counterpart was Atabey, 'Mother of Waters', who was associated with rivers and the rain needed to nourish the cassava crops. She was also responsible for women's fertility and childbirth. The relationship between the Taíno, their gods and the universe was enshrined in myths which emphasised the belief in metamorphosis. Here, heroes had superhuman animal strength and animals possessed uncannily human qualities. Some animals were tribal ancestors, some trees the spirits of dead chiefs. Taíno myths accounted for the origins of the world, of women, and of tobacco; one myth tells how women were created when woodpeckers pecked a hole in strange sexless creatures where female sexual parts are now located.

Although the evidence for warfare in Taíno society is ambiguous, undoubtedly battles took place between different chiefdoms to resolve disputes. Nevertheless, it was the Carib peoples of the Lesser Antilles to the east and south who were the common enemy, possibly because they raided Taíno islands, mainly for marriageable women. Whether or not such accusations were true, the Taíno initially saw the Spanish as powerful potential allies against the traditional foe – only too late did they realise their mistake.

The Caribs

The Caribs, unlike the Taíno, were late arrivals in the Caribbean. They sailed large sea-going canoes from South America perhaps around AD 1400, and began colonising the Lesser Antilles, especially Dominica, Martinique, St Vincent and Guadeloupe. They maintained close trading relationships with their mainland cousins up to and beyond the period of European colonisation.

Carib society was primarily agricultural, though not as intensive as that of the Taíno. They grew and consumed manioc, making it into cassava bread, and also ate a stew known as pepper-pot. These were supplemented by sweet potatoes, yams, beans and tobacco. Fishing was also important and the Carib used nets, hooks and harpoons to catch a variety of fish. They also collected shellfish, hunted sea turtles and the agouti (*Dasyprocta aguti*) which had been introduced from South America.

Carib society was less hierarchical and sophisticated than that of the Taíno. There were no major chiefs, though each village had its own headman. Wider alliances seem only to have formed during war, at which time outstanding war leaders exercised temporary authority. Carib villages were small and focused on the men's house or *carbet*, which also served as the communal meeting place within which a special men-only language was spoken. This phenomenon was misunderstood for many years, having given rise to the erroneous belief that Carib men spoke one language and their wives another.

Carib arts and crafts were also basic when compared to those of the Taíno. Their pottery was undecorated, though basketry was highly prized, and cotton weaving was used to make hammocks and jewellery. Their canoes were especially valued due to the economic importance of long-distance maritime trade, which provided luxury items from South America such as the *caracoli*, a crescent-shaped *guanín* object worn as jewellery.

As with the Taíno, Carib religion followed the shamanic traditions of South America, where plants, animals and landscapes were infused with the spirituality of ancestors and nature. There were few recognisable gods, and no evidence of the elaborate *zemí* figures of the Taíno. Nevertheless, they made and wore figurines of stone and wood to protect against evil spirits known as *mabouya*, and used these images to decorate their war clubs and canoes. Good spirits were called *akamboue*, and each Carib was believed to have their own guardian spirit. Zoomorphic and geometric designs of these supernatural beings were carved as petroglyphs on boulders and rockfaces throughout the Carib region.

Carib culture is dramatically and endlessly misrepresented by the emphasis on cannibalism. Taíno accusations of Carib cannibalism made to Columbus became a defining feature of savage behaviour perpetrated by indigenous Caribbean peoples.

Unlike the Taíno, the Caribs survived well into the European period in the Caribbean. It was not until the seventeenth century that French missionaries in Dominica, Guadeloupe and Martinique began to observe and record Carib cultural traditions. The most influential of these missionaries was the Dominican Father Raymond Guillaume Breton, the 'Apostle to the Caribs'. Carib society as we know it today is in many respects a seventeenth-century creation, and is clearly entangled with European propaganda and misunderstandings, and further confused by the comparatively little archaeological research which has been carried out to date.

LEGACY AND HERITAGE

The prehistoric Caribbean was a region of unique cultural development and diversity – as much a mosaic of peoples and places as it was to become after the arrival of Europeans and the introduction of slavery and plantations. The Caribbean and its indigenous peoples also represented the first European experience of the hitherto unsuspected continent of the Americas. Many of the impressions, tragedies and misunderstandings that occurred between Amerindians and Europeans throughout the Americas happened first in the Caribbean.

Here, Amerindians initially considered Europeans powerful gods, or their representatives, and Europeans regarded the Taíno as gullible and child-like, and the Carib as pagan savages suitable only for enslavement. The *encomienda* system, which gave Amerindians to Spanish colonists for whom they were expected to provide food, goods and labour for no pay but instruction in the Christian faith, was invented in the Caribbean and exported to the rest of Spanish America.

Today, the Caribbean remains a vibrant mix of peoples, religions and cultures, and one of the world's most famous holiday destinations. Beneath the silver sands, however, lies a rich pre-Columbian heritage. Among the living descendants of the Taíno and Carib too things are changing. There is a resurgence of interest in their own indigenous past – a long-overdue claim is being made to a unique cultural heritage. Yet, despite its important archaeological remains and the pivotal role it played during the European encounter, the Caribbean was never home to pre-Columbian America's great civilisations. These belong to Mesoamerica and South America, and it is to them that we now turn.

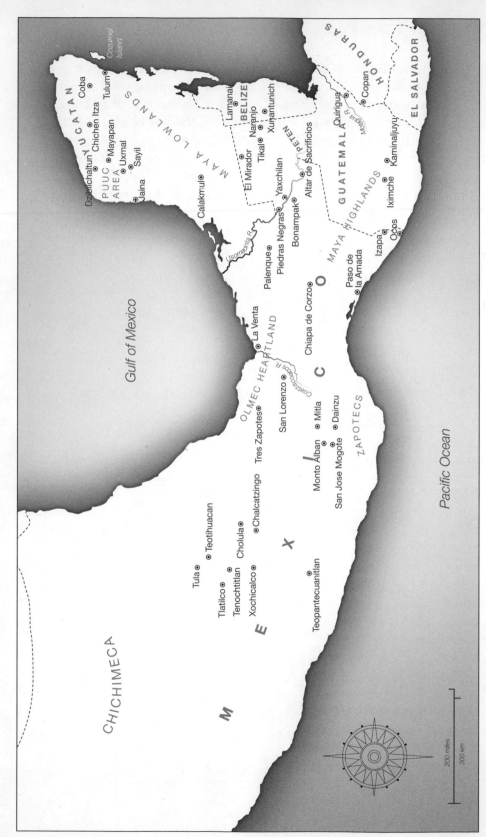

Mesoamerica

PART TWO

Mesoamerica –
the Classic Cultures

TWO

Mesoamerican Beginnings and the Olmec

The origins of civilisation in Mesoamerica are later than in South America and are associated mainly with the rise of the precocious Olmec civilisation around 1250 BC. Building on the advent of agriculture and settled village life which preceded them, the Olmec created Mesoamerica's first major art style and organised religion and constructed the region's first ceremonial architecture during the late part of the Early Formative Period (1200–900 BC). The Olmec were thus Mesoamerica's first civilisation, but were not necessarily the first or only people to show signs of sophisticated culture based on hereditary inequalities; this development in social organisation was a pan-Mesoamerican phenomenon.

Sometime around 1600 BC in the Soconusco region of Meso-america's southern Pacific coastal area, Early Formative-Period culture had become increasingly sophisticated. The site of La Victoria has yielded the technically advanced Ocós pottery, a well-fired and polished kind of ceramic decorated with rocker stamping and cord impressions and finished with iridescent paint. In the nearby Mazatán area, sites such as Paso de la Amada had emerged as chiefdoms, with this site functioning as a ceremonial centre and containing a population of some two thousand people, a ballcourt and large plaza capable of holding perhaps ten thousand people. More generally throughout this area there developed a distinctive ceramic tradition depicting such varied animals as duck, rabbit, dog, monkey and fish. Around 1000 BC a change occurred and these local groups seem to have become organised into a larger chiefdom, a change reflected in the appearance of typically Olmec motifs on their ceramics. Some sites, such as Paso de la Amada, disappeared for ever while others flourished.

Further north, in the valley of Mexico, early cultural development also took place. Around 1400 BC at Zohapilco/Tlapacoya, on an island in the south-eastern part of the valley's lake system, there is evidence for the region's first use of simple gourd-like pottery followed within two centuries by more sophisticated kinds and baby-faced ceramic figurines. At the same site have been found ceramic figurines wearing the elaborate paraphernalia of the ball-game player dated to *c.* 1250 BC. Further north, at the site of Tlatilco, along the margins of the ancient lake there is evidence of a 65 hectare village flourishing around 1200 BC. Excavation of storage pits revealed animal bones and fragments of pottery and sophisticated ceramic figurines still bearing the traces of red, yellow and white paint.

Over three hundred burials were excavated at Tlatilco and each was accompanied by grave goods that included figurines sometimes of monstrous figures with three eyes, two heads, or wearing masks. Tlatilco pottery was masterful and included polished jars and plates as well as a beautiful effigy vessel in the shape of a fish. In among this distinctive ceramic repertoire were examples of Olmec style ceramics that suggested some contact with the Olmec heartland to the southeast.

In the Oaxaca Valley to the south, between 1900 and 1400 BC, small rural villages appeared, as did the first ceramics in the region. San José Mogote is the best known of these early villages, and some time around 1350 BC public architecture appeared there alongside pottery with increasingly complex decoration. Between 1150 and 850 BC, craft specialisation had embraced the manufacture of shiny mirrors from locally available magnetite (iron ore), examples of which found their way to the great Olmec centre of San Lorenzo. It is becoming increasingly clear to archaeologists that the development of Mesoamerican civilisation was a complex and multi-regional process but that within that process the culture known as Olmec played a unique and pivotal role.

THE OLMEC

The Olmec came as a surprise and an enigma to archaeologists who specialised in ancient Mexico. Until their discovery, and the realisation of their antiquity, no one suspected that a hitherto unknown civilisation lurked in the swampy jungles of eastern Mexico.

The story began in 1862 when the explorer José María Melgar, who was travelling through the eastern Mexican state of Veracruz, investigated rumours of a giant sculpture near the small town of

Hueyapan. What he discovered was to change the course of Mexican and, indeed, wider Mesoamerican prehistory. Melgar unearthed a giant stone head with no trace of an accompanying body. In his opinion, it looked like an Ethiopian – a comment that led to a rush of outlandish explanations as to its possible origin. This was followed in 1886 by the publication of a picture of an intricately carved piece of jade which appeared as a half-human, half-feline creature, and which was labelled a 'votive axe'. At the time, there was no obvious connection between these two apparently quite different objects.

In 1900, Marshall Saville published an illustration of what is now called the Kunze Axe, noting its feline characteristics and making the prescient comment that its sophistication indicated the existence of a hitherto unknown art style. A quarter of a century later, the Danish archaeologist Frans Blom and his companion the ethnographer Oliver La Farge discovered a second colossal stone head, quickly followed by the finding of a stone figure on the peak of the volcano known as San Martín Pajapan in the Tuxtla highlands of coastal Veracruz. This was a momentous discovery for in a pit beneath the sculpture were found pieces of pottery and several items of carved green jade – providing a secure archaeological link between the two previously separate kinds of object.

Blom and La Farge continued their odyssey southeastwards across the low-lying riverine area and made a second major discovery – an archaeological site now known as La Venta appearing as an 'island' in the middle of a swamp. Here they discovered Mexico's oldest pyramid – an earthen mound some 25m high – and a variety of elaborately carved stone monuments. It was clear to both men that they were wandering around in the midst of a huge and previously unsuspected archaeological site. With hindsight, it is obvious that the two men had discovered what we now call the Olmec culture, though at the time such was the pre-eminence and fame of the Classic Maya civilisation that both they and the archaeological community assigned these new discoveries to that culture.

The name Olmec was first used by the German scholar Hermann Beyer who recognised a similarity between the stone sculpture of San Martín Pajapan and a jade figurine he had previously owned. In many ways, this name was a misnomer. During Aztec times, the Gulf Coast region was a major producer of rubber, paid as tribute to the Aztecs, and from which balls were made for the ceremonial ball-game. To the Aztecs this country was *Olman* or 'rubber country' and its inhabitants the *Olmeca* or 'people of the rubber country'. Thus the naming of what was to become one of Mexico's most famous civilisations was an accident of history, not an accurate reflection of what the people would have called themselves. Once used, the name Olmec became impossible to dislodge.

Despite further Olmec objects coming to light during the 1930s, and Marshall Saville christening the zoomorphic votive axes as 'tiger-faces' or 'were-jaguars', it was not until 1938 that any serious archaeological attempt was made to identify and investigate the culture which had produced these striking images. It was Matthew Stirling, an archaeologist working for the Smithsonian Institution in Washington D.C., who, with the support of the National Geographic Society and Mexico's National Institute of History and Anthropology, began work at Hueyapan (now renamed as the archaeological site of Tres Zapotes). He discovered an extraordinary monument called Stela C inscribed with a precociously early and typically Maya Long Count date of 31 BC. This angered those archaeologists who championed the Maya cause, and they refused to recognise the Olmec as a pre-Maya civilisation. It was not until 1955 that the new technique of radiocarbon dating confirmed that the Olmec were indeed a separate and earlier civilisation, flourishing a thousand years before the Classic Maya.

Stirling went on to excavate La Venta, retrieving more colossal stone heads, carved stone sculptures with images from Olmec mythology, caches of buried serpentine blocks, jadework and polished mirrors of magnetite. Human remains, however, were almost non-existent due to the tropical conditions of the region. It was not long before the Mexican archaeologist Alfonso Caso was referring to the Olmec as the 'Mother Culture' of Mexican civilisation. As if to reinforce this view, Stirling continued to make groundbreaking discoveries. In 1945, he found and excavated the Olmec site of San Lorenzo, recovering five more colossal heads and fifteen other carved stone sculptures. By the late 1950s, the Olmec had emerged from the shadows of Mexican prehistory – their enigmatic feline imagery, huge stone heads and delicate jadework had finally coalesced into a real archaeological culture.

San Lorenzo

A plateau rising 50m above the meandering River Coatzacoalcos is home to the archaeological site of San Lorenzo – in fact a group of three smaller sites: Potrero Nuevo, Tenochtitlán and San Lorenzo itself. According to Michael Coe who excavated there during the 1960s, and Ann Cyphers who worked there in the 1990s, this plateau may in fact be artificial – shaped into a giant stylised bird of prey flying eastward. If true, this is the first known example in Mesoamerica of a 'sacred mountain'.

Originally, Olmec sites were regarded as ceremonial centres largely devoid of permanent occupation or craft specialisation and used solely for religious purposes. This view has been altered radically during recent years and we have a much more accurate picture of such sites. San Lorenzo is now known to have been not only a huge regional centre extending over at least 7sq. km, but also the largest known centre in Mesoamerica at the time. Locally, San Lorenzo's traders took advantage of the network of rivers that criss-crossed the region. The discovery of causeways that probably served as riverside docking areas indicates the importance of canoe transportation.

San Lorenzo's prehistoric mounds are arranged along a north–south axis on top of the plateau and one of these is thought to be Mesoamerica's first ball-court. Earlier than La Venta, San Lorenzo dates to *c.* 1500 BC at which time the earliest occupation phases of Ojochi and Bajío are regarded as non-Olmec. San Lorenzo took on a distinctly Olmec appearance around 1200 BC during the so-called Chicharras phase (1250–1150 BC) – though where the Chicharras people came from remains a mystery. In the past, various explanations have been offered – they invaded from the highlands of Mexico or travelled across the Atlantic from Africa; in fact, they almost certainly developed *in situ* from the peoples who already lived there and knew the area and its resources well.

In any event, at this time typically Olmec material culture appears – white kaolin pottery and figurines, ceramics known as Mojonera Black, and the beginnings of a monumental stone-carving tradition. Exotic materials and minerals also appear in San Lorenzo at this time, indicating the forging of long-distance trade relationships with other parts of Mesoamerica. Particulalrly well documented are its relations with the early village of San José Mogote in the Oaxaca

Valley from where it seems it obtained small highly polished magnetite mirrors and left elements of its distinctive art style in return.

Recent investigations have thrown much light on the way the San Lorenzo Olmec organised their society. Excavations have revealed a series of palaces and high-status houses on the higher parts of the site, with less prestigious buildings on the lower slopes. The so-called Red Palace investigated by Ann Cyphers reveals what she calls the ostentatious use of carved stone features such as aqueducts, cylindrical columns and steps. The economic and possibly ritual significance of the 'expensive' basalt was highlighted by the discovery of a basalt workshop and an area used for recycling monuments made from the stone – both in close proximity to the Red Palace. In one example, a large monument was being broken up and used to make *metates* and other smaller practical items.

The high value set on basalt was apparent also in ordinary houses where fragments of sculptures were apparently being kept for future re-use. Obsidian tools seem also to have been produced on a household basis, with blades and scrapers being made from cores imported from the highland sources at Otumba in Mexico and El Chayal in Guatemala. It is becoming clear that San Lorenzo was a thriving centre of craft specialisation; apart from the previously unsuspected recycling of basalt statues and the manufacture of obsidian implements, huge quantities of ilmenite were also being worked, with one area yielding 6 tonnes of ilmenite blocks marked with traces of drilling.

The site's stone monuments include colossal stone heads and monuments called 'altars' – many if not all appear to have been carved from the basalt quarries of Cerro Cintepec in the Tuxtla mountains some 70km away. The investment of time and effort in stone-working which had a ritual purpose is seen clearly in the fascinating discovery that beneath San Lorenzo's ceremonial centre was an elaborate drainage system composed of U-shaped basalt blocks, and that was traced by archaeologists for some 170m. The drainage channels seem to have been associated with supplying water to a number of stone-lined depressions around the site's centre, and have been interpreted as having a ritual purpose linked to the worship of rain gods.

Recently, it has been suggested that monumental Olmec sculptures may not have been intended for use as single monuments but rather

Olmec colossal head.
(© Author's collection)

Olmec were-jaguar jade figurine.
(© Werner Forman and The Trustees of the British Museum)

View over Monte Albán. *(© Author's collection)*

The 'Street of the Dead' at Teotihuacán. *(© Author's collection)*

View of Uxmal, with the Pyramid of the Magician on the right and the Nunnery quadrangle in the centre. (© *Author's collection*)

The Temple of Inscriptions at Palenque. (© *Author's collection*)

Toltec warrior statues at Tula.
(© *Author's collection*)

Aztec stone statues at The Great
Aztec Temple. (© *Author's
collection*)

were arranged as ensemble pieces associated not only with each other, but also with ritual space, sacrificial offerings and even the ritual flow of water, perhaps as backdrops for ceremonies. One spectacular example of such an ensemble still *in situ* was discovered at the site of Loma del Zapote. On the site's acropolis, known as El Azuzul, two Olmec-style kneeling male figures with elaborate headdresses were found facing two squatting felines. Possibly this arrangement of sculptures represented some act or episode from Olmec mythology, and also may be associated with myths of the heroic actions of primordial cosmic twins, as is well documented for later Mesoamerican civilisations.

Although the humidity and acidic soils of the Olmec region has often militated against the preservation of more fragile remains such as wood, textile or significant amounts of human bone, there are occasional exceptions. Perhaps the most spectacular is El Manatí, a small hill on the other side of the Coatzacoalcos river from San Lorenzo. Ancient freshwater springs gush forth from the base of the hill which also has natural hematite deposits.

El Manatí appears to have been a sacred place for the Olmec between 1600 and 1000 BC, as springs still are today throughout Mexico and beyond. The Olmec made ritual offerings of unique wooden busts in typical Olmec style that have been preserved by the anaerobic watery conditions. Some were interred wrapped in straw matting, treated the same way as human corpses in later Aztec times when they were referred to as 'death bundles'. Along with the carved-wood heads, greenstone beads and celts, seeds and human bones – probably of newborn children – were also deposited, though whether the latter were sacrificed or placed there after dying a natural death is not known. Lumps of copal resin and no less than fourteen rubber balls used in the Mesoamerican ball-game were also found.

San Lorenzo reached its peak during the San Lorenzo Phase (1150–900 BC), whose two pottery types, Calzadas Carved and Límon Carved-Incised, are considered reliable archaeological markers for the period, and also carry typical Olmec designs. The distinctive pottery from this period is found in other parts of Mexico, such as the Olmec-influenced site of Chalcatzingo in the highlands, and so may be the period at which the Olmec changed from a purely local culture to one of pan-Mesoamerican signifi-cance, though the nature of this significance is hotly debated (see

below). The succeeding Nacaste phase (900–700 BC) saw the end of
Olmec society at San Lorenzo – the giant heads were defaced and
buried, and new kinds of pottery appeared that seem to have
nothing to do with previous types. Whatever happened at San
Lorenzo, the flame of Olmec civilisation did not die, it simply
moved to the other great Olmec site of La Venta.

La Venta

La Venta, like San Lorenzo, was once thought to be a ceremonial
centre devoid of resident population. Recent investigations have
proven this a false assumption, revealing a sizeable population living
around the civic and religious architecture at the heart of the site.
Today, as presumably at its height, La Venta is dominated by its
volcano-shaped pyramid – the first such structure in Mesoamerica,
though built of earth not stone. The site itself stretches northward
from the pyramid and includes two long narrow mounds, smaller
mounds and a plaza which was originally surrounded by a row of
2m high basalt columns. The extraordinary range of stone sculptures found scattered around the site is on display at a specially built
archaeological park in the nearby city of Villahermosa.

While San Lorenzo has yielded a small amount of greenstone
objects, La Venta has produced vast quantities. If this is an accurate
reflection of contemporary reality rather than of archaeological
sampling, it indicates a technological, economic and presumably
political shift in the nature of Olmec society and ideology. The time
and effort involved in obtaining (via trade) and making polished
figurines, slabs and celts of jade and serpentine must have been
immense. This is especially significant inasmuch as many, perhaps
most, of these items were then buried in so-called dedicatory caches
at least nineteen of which have been discovered in the area north of
the earthen pyramid alone. These offerings included greenstone slabs
arranged in the shape of a stylised jaguar face, and greenstone axes
together with jewellery made from jade and serpentine. The effort
required to make then bury such valuable objects is indicated by the
fact that one cache had no less than 1,180 individual items.

Apart from such burials, the La Venta Olmec also followed the
intriguing practice of designing then burying huge mosaics of
serpentine blocks in layers of olive-coloured clay. One of these was
discovered in 1955 by the archaeologist Philip Drucker who

described it as laid out in the shape of a jaguar mask with a head-dress, plumed eyebrows and fangs. Beneath this was another layer of coloured clays and more serpentine blocks arranged in twenty-eight levels. The multi-level burial lay beneath a platform of adobe bricks which itself was capped with a covering of red clay and flanked by basalt columns. Altogether, there was over 1,000 tons of stone in this single location – all of which had to be brought from great distances.

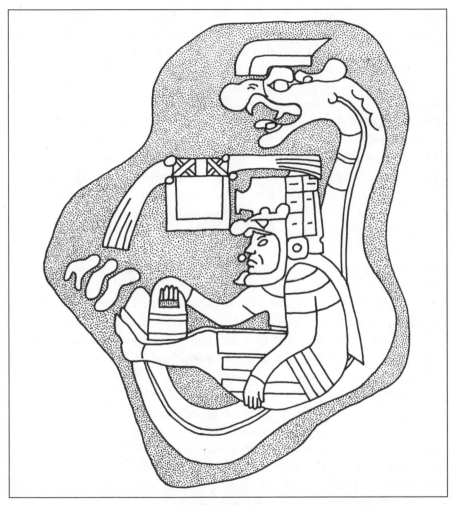

La Venta, Monument 19, showing Olmec person wearing jaguar helmet and sitting cradled by a giant serpent. (© *Pauline Stringfellow, after P. Drucker, R. Heizer and R. Squier.* Excavations at La Venta, *Tabasco, 1955. 1959, Bureau of American Ethnology Bulletin 170, Fig. 55. Washington DC)*

Perhaps the most extraordinary of the buried caches was also one of the smallest. Offering 4 consisted of a carefully arranged ensemble scene – 16 carved and polished Olmec-style figurines, 2 of jade, 13 of serpentine and, mysteriously, 1 of red sandstone standing in front of a row of 6 jade celts. All the figurines had a typical Olmec appearance and intriguingly were already weathered when deposited. Over the centre of the cache was a 'check shaft' which had been dug through the multi-coloured clay layers of the original burial, perhaps to see if the figures were still there. Whoever made this cut was apparently satisfied as it was filled in during prehistoric times.

While the humid and lush conditions of La Venta and the whole Olmec area are not favourable for the survival of human bones, one major tomb was discovered at La Venta. Tomb A had been built just to the north of the pyramid and consisted of large basalt columns covered with earth. Hardly any human bones remained, but the surviving fragments suggested that two children had been interred here, covered with red ochre and accompanied by luxury items, notably a female figurine wearing a shiny haematite mirror on her breast and a jade pendant. This discovery indicated that Olmec society was organised in such a way that status could be inherited (as well as achieved), as these young children could never have accomplished deeds worthy of such a burial in their own short lifetimes.

Of the many superb stone sculptures discovered at La Venta arguably the most intriguing is a group misleadingly called 'altars'. These are monolithic basalt blocks carved with various scenes from what may have been Olmec mythology. Some depict a seated figure emerging from a niche, and several are cradling babies in their arms. The so-called 'baby theme' is most prominent on Altar 5 which has a central figure holding a baby and two more adults each cradling an infant on each of the sides. The niches themselves have been interpreted as cave entrances represented as stylised jaguar-monster mouths. The term altar has also been replaced by the description of these monuments as thrones on which La Venta's (royal?) elite sat, surrounded by the symbols of their mythological origins.

Equally sophisticated in their production were other stone sculptures found at the site. Stela 1 shows an Olmec figure wearing a helmet, earrings and a skirt watched over by a stylised jaguar mask. Most famous, however, as at San Lorenzo, are the colossal heads found at the site. Weighing between 11 and 24 tons each, these giant sculptures are unique inasmuch as they do not depict the typical stylised Olmec forms but rather make every attempt to portray their subjects as lifelike as possible. In other words, it seems as if they represent real people – possibly the rulers of La Venta.

Each of these heads wears a skull cap style of headdress, quite unlike the elaborate tiered headdresses found on other stone sculptures or depicted in jade carvings and cave paintings. Each one is different, possessing a unique emblem which may have identified the name or status of the individual concerned. Whatever the reality of Olmec politics, and whatever the nature of their official art, these individualised monuments clearly had a different purpose – to identify political and sacred power with recognisable individuals. Given the sacred nature of Amerindian politics, and the clear need for accurate physical likeness and technical perfection in the production of these monumental heads, it is probably significant that when La Venta went into decline between 450 and 300 BC, some of these monuments were laboriously defaced with surface pitting. Interestingly, unlike modern vandalism, the defacing of the Olmec heads left their identity untouched; what it did achieve was to destroy the perfection of the monument. Perhaps it was the Olmec themselves who defaced their own monuments in some now long forgotten ritual of royal succession.

Beyond the heartland

San Lorenzo and La Venta are the best-known Olmec centres but there are other and usually less well-known sites beyond the Gulf Coast heartland. The Olmec journeyed, traded and exchanged with other peoples who inhabited regions rich in the raw materials the Olmec needed to define and maintain their society and produce their startling works of art. While the Olmec region had clay for pottery and plentiful animal and food resources, and fortuitously a source of basalt in the nearby Tuxtla highlands, other raw materials were not locally available. The black volcanic glass obsidian, the 'steel of prehistory', jade, serpentine and magnetite belonged to different geologies and to different peoples.

Originally it was thought that the Olmec had conquered the resource-rich highland areas, spreading their idea of civilisation far and wide and thus becoming the 'Mother Culture' of Mesoamerican civilisation. Today, the picture is less clear and it seems that complex

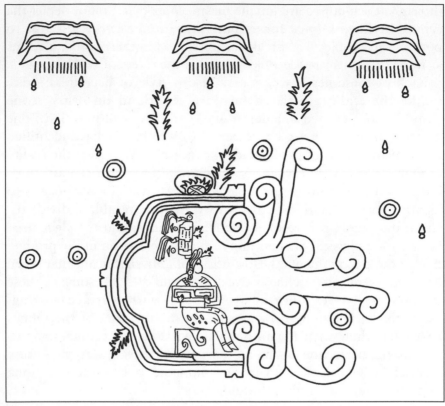

Chalcatzingo, the 'El Rey' carving. *(© Pauline Stringfellow, after D. Grove. Chalcatzingo, Thames and Hudson, London, 1984, Fig. 5)*

interactions with different peoples took place, with Olmec influence adopted and adapted to local cultural conditions – in other words, a mosaic of interaction is emerging, one not amenable to a single or simple explanation.

Of the many places in highland Mesoamerica that show evidence of Olmec influence none has been so well investigated as Chalcatzingo. Situated south of the valley of Mexico in the modern state of Morelos, Chalcatzingo existed before the arrival of Olmec influence. It has been called a Gateway Community, strategically placed between the lowland Olmec area and the highlands of Central Mexico. It was located to take advantage of different vegetation zones and mineral sources, perhaps for the collection of obsidian, greenstones and kaolin clay (used to make the white ceramic baby figures) from its hinterland and, with the help of Olmec intermediaries, funnelling them into the Olmec area in exchange for Olmec prestige-by-association reflected in Olmec influence in its monumental art.

By *c.* 700 BC this trade was in full flow – the dating and style of art at Chalcatzingo suggest that the relationship was mainly with La Venta. The evidence for Olmec presence or at least influence around this time are the large bas-reliefs carved on to the rock face of Chalcatzingo's prominent twin hills. Monument 1, known as El Rey (the King), depicts an elaborately dressed figure seated on a throne inside what has variously been called a cave or stylised jaguar mouth (the two being synonymous by later Aztec times). From rainclouds hovering above, jade droplets fall, and curling smoke billows from the cave entrance. Other simpler carvings show humans reeling under the attack of rampant felines, warriors with weapons standing over a naked and bound prisoner, and a feline curiously licking a plant.

Deeper into the mountain country of central Mexico are other sites which reveal Olmec presence. In the cave shelter of Oxtotitlán in the modern state of Guerrero are the weathered remains of colourful paintings, the most impressive showing an Olmec figure with an eagle-shaped headdress sitting on a throne shaped like a stylised jaguar-monster. Nearby and standing behind a large jaguar is a startling image of an Olmec figure painted in black with a prominent penis. Some 30km away, almost 0.6km inside the cave of Juxtlahuaca is the painting of an Olmec figure wearing a feathered headdress and jaguar skin. The reason for these Olmec images in remote mountain locations is unknown other than that their creators were possibly here seeking the precious greenstones needed back in La Venta.

In 1983, in eastern Guerrero an Olmec-period city was found which is now known as Teopantecuanitlán (Temple of the Jaguar Gods). As with the better-known centres in the Olmec heartland, Teopantecuanitlán had monumental architecture and was located near the confluence of several rivers. It covered an area of 160ha and flourished between *c.* 1400 and 600 BC. The ceremonial heart of the site had a series of platforms as well as large stone sculptures including a 1m tall human head. Dominating the area was a huge sunken court whose staircases led to a sculpture of a stylised feline head. The enclosure itself revealed four great T-shaped stone sculptures, each decorated with an Olmec-style anthropomorphic feline face, and apparently associated with the cardinal directions. Some

experts believe it served as a ballcourt and/or a place where the
natural and supernatural worlds met. Elaborate water conduits
drained the enclosure and another hydraulic system directed water
to irrigate nearby fields.

It seems clear that Teopantecuanitlán served as a large regional
centre far from the Olmec heartland – a place of sacred rituals but
also of economic power. The excavation of various house remains
indicates local diet (mainly dogs), and items from everyday life,
including ceramics and ceramic figurines, iron-ore mirrors and
jewellery fragments of onyx, serpentine and Pacific-coast seashells
including Spondylus. Obsidian, too, was found. Clearly the city was
at the hub of an extensive interregional trade network though the
exact nature of its relationship with far distant Gulf Coast Olmec
centres to the east is unknown.

In such a wild and inaccessible area as Guerrero many other
Olmec-period sites probably await discovery, whether impressive
centres like Teopantecuanitlán or small cave sites such as
Juxtlahuaca. In recent years other sites have been found, large ones
such as the huge but heavily looted Xochipala, or the accidental
discoveries such as burials in the town of Chilpancingo – the latter's
construction, dating to *c.* 600 BC, suggesting that the architectural
development of the corbelled vault may have been developed here
rather than, as traditionally believed, by the Maya.

Art, politics and religion

The Olmec did not invent the pan-Amerindian worldview, or even
those elements of Mesoamerican worldview that were an integral
part of it. What they did achieve was to give systematic physical
expression to age-old ideas and beliefs in a unique and distinctive
repertoire of large- and small-scale art in what has come to be called
the Olmec style. The content of most Olmec art deals with ideas,
beliefs and issues that are typically Amerindian: ideas of transformation, sacred landscapes, and the power of ancestors – and through
this a concept of the spiritual nature of political power. This was a
natural philosophy built on analogy and symbolic reasoning not
amenable to Western scientific ideas of cause and event. How could
it have been otherwise?

Olmec art deals head on with indigenous notions of a world
infused with spirituality, where people and animals could shape-shift

into each other, and where shiny minerals could embody ideas of cosmic energy represented by the sun. It was a supernaturally animated world, where weather, mountains, animals and plants had identities, shared spiritual essences between their varied forms, and could exercise power over the fate of humans.

For the first time in Mesoamerica, ancient beliefs about the nature of human life (and death) that had been shaped by millennia of a hunting and gathering existence moved beyond the realm of oral tradition, an individual's lifetime and memory, and fragile material culture. Now, mythology and religious beliefs became tangible and permanent, carved in durable stone and jade. The pre-eminence of the Olmec elite was inextricably linked to stone and jade images whose striking visual appearance combined with the new quality of 'permanence' to convey the power of ancestors, the presence in this world of human-animal beings, and the control of natural forces and cosmic myth – all of which were exercised by the rulers themselves. It was the rulers' connections with and influence over omnipotent and ambivalent supernatural forces that bestowed on them their political power.

It is partly for these reasons that so much Olmec art deals with what we might consider the impossible and fantastic – the extremes of human imagination – in visualising so clearly and dramatically creatures and connections for which the modern world finds no evidence. For the Olmec elite, however, such images manifested their lineage, status and power as representations that worked – whose very existence spoke of previously unknown and unimaginable technologies and abilities that must have seemed as magical and awe-inspiring to the Olmec farmer as did the arrival of the Spanish to the Aztec emperor Moctezuma II in AD 1519.

Olmec artists and craftsmen were supported by the elite, their skills and techniques used to create objects that supported their patrons' views and desires, that is artworks that represented and justified their exalted social positions. Given the spiritual nature of political power in Amerindian societies, it was important that monumental and miniature art – however novel its shape and presence – integrated and honoured long-established and widely held concepts that organised the world. One of the main concepts was that of transformation, where powerful people, whether shamans, priests, chiefs or kings, were identified with powerful animals. So intimate were these associations thought to be that there appears to have been an unshakeable belief in the deep cosmological connection between the souls of high-ranking individuals and those of the (usually fierce and aggressive) animals with whom they shared an identity.

These relationships are seen most clearly, though by no means exclusively, in the Olmec fascination with feline imagery, as has been noted in various descriptions given above. These images are usually identified with the jaguar (*Panthera onca*), America's largest cat and most widespread and successful predator (apart from humans). In the early years of Olmec archaeology, it was thought that most Olmec art was inspired by the jaguar, though today a more complex picture has emerged, reflecting the fact that serpents, birds, caymans and even spiders are also represented in what was evidently a rich artistic tradition.

In smaller hunter-gatherer societies in Central and South America, the jaguar is the most common spirit-companion of pre-eminent individuals, following the logic that as the jaguar is prominent in the natural world so shamans and chiefs mirror that prominence in the social world. Some Amazonian chiefs have titles that incorporate the local name for jaguar, and some even claim to be descended from jaguar ancestors and to have inherently jaguar features or characteristics. Looking at much Olmec art, it seems that such ideas may have been current also in their society. Monument 3 from Potrero Nuevo at San Lorenzo depicts a scene, albeit damaged, which could have come directly from Amazonian mythology – a huge jaguar-monster apparently copulating with a human female. While biologically barren, in human imagination the result of such a union would be a race of half-jaguar, half-human creatures – with features matching those seen in so many Olmec artworks – caught, as it were, between the human and the animal. Recent investigations have shown that San Lorenzo possessed the largest number of feline images of any Olmec site excavated to date.

Such hybrid creatures may have represented the essence of the Olmec elite – an official origin myth that accorded with widespread beliefs about transformation but which capitalised on the psychological effect of seeing imagination become real in permanent artworks. Monument 52 at San Lorenzo shows another example, a hybrid feline-human basalt statue with a snarling were-jaguar mouth and paws resting on its knees. Its association with an elaborate drainage system has been interpreted as signifying that it represents a possible Olmec rain deity.

Similarly stylised feline imagery is also found in the delicately carved jade and serpentine objects that today are scattered throughout the world's museums. The so-called votive axes such as that in the British Museum and famous Kunz Axe mentioned above, werejaguar figurines in the collection of Dumbarton Oaks in Washington, DC, and the greenstone carvings of Olmec figures holding 'jaguarised babies' all speak of an Olmec religion and ideology that materialised ancient beliefs in jaguar-human associations in new and startling ways.

While most Olmec artworks deal in some way with stylised feline or human images in which an ideological message is encoded in the concept of human-animal co-equivalence, the monumental basalt heads are a clear exception – and an unusual occurrence in Mesoamerican (and pan-Amerindian) art. As we have already seen, these giant heads were carved as presumably accurate portraits of real people. The supernatural power of tradition may have been represented in the anonymous stylised artworks, but the identity of those who wielded that power was made plain to all by the psychologically disorientating effect of colossal heads that portrayed real people at many times their natural size.

Olmec legacy

The Olmec have understandably dominated much debate concerning the origins of Mesoamerican civilisation since Matthew Stirling began excavating San Lorenzo and La Venta during the 1940s, debates which became sharper with radiocarbon dating's confirmation of the chronological primacy of this 'new' culture. However, while the 'Mother Culture' tag has been increasingly disputed if not ridiculed in recent years, there is a powerful sense in which it still has something to teach us.

Few would argue today that the Olmec conquered or forced their cultural ideas and styles on ancient Mesoamerica and therefore inspired or somehow created Mesoamerican civilisation. Nevertheless, for the most part, the phenomenon of monumental and iconographically complex artwork set in a sophisticated architectural framework did begin with the Gulf Coast Olmec. Something happened in the area of San Lorenzo and La Venta before it occurred elsewhere, at least in terms that are archaeologically visible. Clearly also, the Olmec's desire for exotic raw materials, which they decided could help define and maintain their social structure, brought them into contact (directly and indirectly) with other Mesoamerican groups.

Equally clear is that these other regions of Mesoamerica were not merely passive recipients of Olmec enlightenment but were actively engaged in selecting and adapting whatever it was the Olmec offered according to their own cultural ideas and what they themselves could offer in return – whether obsidian, kaolin clay, greenstone minerals, or other less durable or identifiable goods and services such as local knowledge, food and drink, and acting as porters. So-called Olmec art at Chalcatzingo, Xochipala, Oxtotitlán, and most spectacularly at Teopantecuanitlán, indicates not a slavish imitation of Gulf Coast canons but a locally appropriate interpretation of its style.

It is important to emphasise that while style and material were distinctively Gulf Coast Olmec, the ideas they expressed were not. As we have already seen, the content of most Olmec art emanated from a pan-Mesoamerican, probably pan-Amerindian, worldview, whose basic assumptions would have been understood by all Mesoamerican peoples whatever their level of social and political organisation. What was new, perhaps shockingly so at the time, was to see these ideas transformed into physical objects, objects that were visually and psychologically seductive and that embodied such potential for political manipulation via their adaptation and integration into local social systems.

In other words, the undeniable Gulf Coast Olmec influence on Mesoamerica was not achieved by inventing a new worldview or religious outlook – there were no Old World-style proselytising movements here, but rather by giving it form and presence in the physical world. Olmec pottery, jadework, sculpture and painting, as well as less durable items such as woodwork and textiles, gave physical expression to age old beliefs in a way which made them available for ritual and ideological manipulation and elaboration by existing or emerging elites.

Olmec civilisation began in the Gulf Coast region, but its full-blown zenith was a hybrid affair, the result of contact, trade, compromise and exchange with Mesoamerica's varied peoples and the natural resources they possessed.

THREE

Zapotec

Zapotec civilisation was one of Mesoamerica's most precocious and distinctive cultural achievements. Situated in the rich Oaxaca Valley region of southern-central Mexico, the Zapotecs created their political capital of Monte Albán. For over a thousand years, between 500 BC and AD 750, Zapotec civilisation flourished, developing an early writing and mathematical system based on glyphs, building in a distinctive architectural style and maintaining superpower relations with the great city of Teotihuacán. This chapter explores the uniqueness of Zapotec civilisation and illustrates how, at one and the same time, it was culturally distinct yet also typically Mesoamerican.

BEGINNINGS OF ZAPOTEC CIVILISATION

Between 1400 and 1150 BC, called by archaeologists the Tierras Largas phase, small rural villages appeared in the Etla Valley in Oaxaca, probably drawn by the rich agricultural land of the area. At this time, an unusual development took place at San José Mogote – a site seven times larger than the typical hamlet and with a population of around two hundred. Unusual burials occur in which middle-aged men were interred in a seated position, perhaps regarded as venerable family ancestors. The presence of clay figurines depicting women may represent female ancestors at this time.

Situated above the floodplain of the Atoyac river, the large community of San José Mogote was in fact a grouping of nine living residential units with an apparent ritual focus in a building interpreted as a 'Men's House', which was rebuilt on the same spot many times. This was to become a common Mesoamerican practice suggestive of the sacred nature of particular places in the cultural landscape. Excavation revealed that floors and walls had been covered with gleaming white plaster, and floor pits contained deposits of powdered lime – a substance known from the later sixteenth-century Zapotec practice to have been mixed with tobacco as a ritual intoxicant. The Men's House building indicates organisation and co-operation, and the probable presence of a group of influential, perhaps charismatic men. These individuals were probably involved with long-distance trade of obsidian, marine shells and other items.

Sometime around 1150 BC there occurred what the scholars of Zapotec culture, Kent Flannery and Joyce Marcus, refer to as a turning point in the development of Zapotec civilisation. Dating from the San José phase (1150–850 BC), there appears the first archaeological evidence for inherited rather than achieved social status, and thus the social inequalities of what is termed a ranked society. One of the features of such a society is the claim of community leaders to have supernatural ancestors, thereby sanctifying and justifying their own elite status and tying it to the social and natural worlds through elaborate ritual events.

In what was probably already a time-honoured Mesoamerican tradition (and, if not, would soon become so) the supernatural beings invoked by this emerging elite appear to have been the Earth and the Sky. In this tectonically active region, Earth manifested his presence through earthquakes, and Sky by thunder and lightning. It is no coincidence that as these developments were being assimilated into their culture, Zapotec symbolic conceptions of Earth and Sky found their way into art – notably as decorative motifs on the sophisticated ceramics that appeared around this time. In one view, Earth was represented as a grimacing feline mouth and cleft skull, and Lightning as flaming eyebrows on a serpent head. So far, pottery decorated with these motifs has been found only in burials of males.

Different kinds of burial goods and different burial positions have been interpreted as further evidence of the inherited social inequalities of the time. While the majority of burials saw bodies laid out flat and often with few luxury items such as jade beads or pottery, a select few seem to have been interred in a kneeling position, accompanied by more jade jewellery and ceramics bearing the lightning motif. The evidence is not clearcut, however, and imported luxury items such as seashells and sheets of gleaming mica seem to have been less an indication of social status than were the small polished mirrors made of locally mined iron ores. It may be, as some authorities have speculated, that these mirrors (some of which found their way to the Olmec region) were highly restricted symbols of leadership, albeit they were worn in combination with jade and seashells.

Burial evidence does seem to support the idea that at this time social status was ascribed rather than achieved – in other words at least some degree of inequality was due to the lineage into which an individual was born. The discovery of fine pottery decorated with lightning motifs in burials of children who were clearly too young to have achieved high status through their own actions supports this idea, as does the presence of skulls which have been artificially shaped by binding from a very young age. In later Mesoamerican civilisations, cranial deformation was a sign of noble status.

Other evidence points to increasingly sophisticated and effective strategies of social control by the emerging elite. The leaders of San José Mogote attracted ever more people and satellite settlements to their immediate area – there were around two hundred such individuals in 1150 BC, but over a thousand by 850 BC. New architecture was also being built, monumental and public in conception, and the result of labour drawn and organised from different communities, each of which contributed their own building materials to the construction. These structures were pyramidal platforms designed to support public buildings and, significantly, appear to have been decorated with carved-stone images including a feline and a raptorial bird – the symbolic animals *par excellence* in Mesoamerica.

Between 850 and 700 BC, a period called by archaeologists the Guadalupe phase, social differences in society continued to increase and rival centres to San José Mogote such as Huitzo sprang up. Nevertheless, San José Mogote was still the largest population centre with some two thousand people occupying an area of about 70ha. Evidence from elite female burials in nearby hamlets suggests the possibility that high-ranking San José Mogote women were being married into such satellite communities as a way of building a network of political alliances, if not outright control. Elite women's importance is apparent in the elaborate costume of female figurines that became common at this time.

In the years that followed, called the Rosario phase (700–500 BC), social organisation in the valley of Oaxaca becomes sophisticated enough for archaeologists to refer to it as a complex chiefdom. High-status grey pottery appears and was possibly used in feasting

between the leaders of different communities. Population grows –
there are now perhaps as many as eighty-five villages in the valley –
an expansion made possible by increasingly elaborate irrigation
schemes. Public architecture at San José Mogote and elsewhere is
ever more prolific, suggesting perhaps chiefly rivalry between competing communities, an impression reinforced by the evidence for
the deliberate burning of temples, something which may have
occurred during military raids.

Even more graphic is Monument 3 at San José Mogote which
depicts an individual with a complex scroll-motif on his chest
suggestive of heart sacrifice, and whose name, derived from the sacred
260-day calendar (see below), appears as 1-Earthquake in the glyphs
carved at his feet. It is considered that the Zapotec glyphic writing
system had its origin in the chaos of war and in the propaganda-
driven desires of the victor to commemorate his triumph.

The Oaxaca Valley's population had increased dramatically
between 700 and 500 BC, and warfare between paramount chiefs
was commemorated in art and in Oaxaca's first hieroglyphic
writing. Sometime between 600–500 BC, a crucial political decision
seems to have been made by the leaders of San José Mogote and
other communities, which saw their villages and expensive ceremonial buildings all but abandoned within a few years. In effect,
there occurred a unique, rapid and spectacular population shift
away from the villages of the Etla Valley and elsewhere to a new
centre of political dominance in the strategic heart of the Oaxaca
Valley. This was the birth of the great Zapotec city of Monte Albán
which would rule the area for a thousand years.

MONTE ALBAN, THE ZAPOTEC CAPITAL

The early city

At this earliest time, called by archaeologists Monte Albán I
(500–150 BC), small communities began establishing themselves on
the hills of Monte Albán. Although we do not know from whence
they came, San José Mogote itself and nearby villages such as
Tierras Largas are likely candidates for the reasons given above.
This new strategic position, itself surrounded by rich agricultural
land in the river valleys below, was ideal as a market centre, drawing
in and facilitating the production and exchange of a diversity of

items, from pottery to salt, obsidian to foodstuffs. If market exchange was the engine that drove this development it was remarkably successful. While there were no inhabitants on Monte Albán's dry ridges in 600 BC, there were approximately five thousand by 400 BC and possibly seventeen thousand by 200 BC.

By this time, perhaps one third of the Oaxaca Valley's entire population had moved from their river-valley villages to live in Monte Albán and within its 3km of defensive walls. The city was now an urban phenomenon, with dynastic families, palaces and a state religion in place, and all the trappings of an aggressive militaristic society. In the valley lowlands below the city the number of small satellite villages also increased greatly, from around 5 at the beginning of Period I to perhaps 744 at the end of the period. Archaeologically, this unprecedented expansion of population is identifiable through extensive irrigation projects and the appearance of mass-produced pottery griddles (*comales*) used to bake maize tortillas in vast quantities to feed the inhabitants of the city and its environs. Everything, it seemed, was now revolving around the new city.

There is little doubt that the rulers of Monte Albán had an aggressive approach to Oaxacan politics, and displayed this in typical Mesoamerican fashion in their monumental art. Nowhere is this more gruesomely visible than in the human figures known as the *danzantes* (dancers) and *nadadores* (swimmers). Some three hundred of these carved-stone figures are known and show men in various positions – hence their misleading Spanish names. It appears that they were originally part of a great wall in the south-west part of the city's main plaza, though later many were removed and re-used in other buildings. The surviving section of the Danzante Wall still stands several metres tall, indicating how visually stunning this earliest of Mesoamerican war-propaganda monuments must have been when complete.

The *danzantes* seem to portray real people rather than stylised figures, and they wear different kinds of jewellery such as jade necklaces, ear discs, and also have distinctive individualising hairstyles. Some have glyphs in front of their mouths that may be name glyphs. Others have what is called the 'genital scroll', a design composed of wavy lines and having a quasi-floral appearance. These intriguing motifs have been interpreted as evidence for ritual mutilation of male genitals associated perhaps with the imagery of flowing blood or semen as symbols of fertility.

It is unclear what these figures represent. While they were probably not dancers or priests, might they have been honoured ancestors from the inception of Monte Albán, or perhaps high-ranking captives who were sacrificed? There is certainly a strong case for thinking that they may have been slain high-status enemies subjected to ritual humiliation and disfigurement, portrayed for the glory of the emerging Zapotec state in typical Mesoamerican fashion. Even their naked appearance would have been humiliation for leaders who took so much trouble to depict themselves dressed in elaborate costumes, and concealed behind dramatic ceremonial masks. More prosaically, perhaps the larger vertical *danzantes* represent the elite and the smaller horizontal *nadadores* the commoners. Some believe the figures represent contemporary individuals, although the widespread appearance of the eyes as shut suggests otherwise.

It may be that the later re-use of some of these carved-stone figures as steps in the ceremonial stairway that led to the summit of the city's Building L gives a clue to at least one of their meanings. Anyone ascending the stairway would have stepped on the figures, a further ritual humiliation and one known as a metaphor for conquest elsewhere in Mesoamerica. As honoured ancestors would not have been treated this way, this re-use suggests the *danzantes* were indeed representations of sacrificed war prisoners. If so, then the original Danzante Wall with its 300 grotesquely mutilated figures was a powerful and intimidating expression of Zapotec power.

This early period of Monte Albán's history has also yielded evidence for the use of what was to become one of the defining features of Mesoamerican civilisation – the dual calendar system, tied intimately to the development of glyphs that could be used for recording mathematical information and for writing. The dual calendar system is composed of an everyday or solar calendar which had 365 days, and was divided into 18 months of 20 days each, the extra 5 days being regarded as particularly unlucky. The smaller religious calendar had 260 days and was divided into 13 months of 20 days each. These two calendars fitted together like cog-wheels, and produced a different date every day for 52 years before starting again. This is called the calendar round.

While glyphs had already been discovered at San José Mogote, suggesting the presence of the 260-day calendar, it is only now at

Monte Albán that there is glyphic evidence for the 365-day calendar as well. Almost two thousand years later, during the sixteenth century, the Spanish recorded that the Zapotec were still using their two interlocking calendars, the solar one being called *yza* and the sacred one the *piye*.

At Monte Albán, Stelae 12 and 14 are considered some of the earliest examples of Mesoamerican glyphic texts and incorporate what is arguably the first reference to a named month in the 365-day calendar. Other glyphs on these two stelae apparently make reference to a leader called 10-Jaguar, a year-sign, a day from the 260-day sacred calendar called 8-Water, and a sign indicating 'first born'. Although our understanding of Zapotec glyphs is still in its early stages, the placement of these two stelae next to the Danzante Wall suggests that its glyphic text and dates are related to the victorious Zapotec lord who commissioned the monument.

By the end of Period I, *c.* 150 BC, it appears that most if not all the valley area was under Monte Albán's control. The city itself covered more than 400ha, and the defining features of Classic Zapotec state-level civilisation were in place.

The classic city

It was during the succeeding periods, known as Monte Albán II (150 BC–AD 100) and Monte Albán III (AD 200–750), that the city finally became a true state and enjoyed its golden age. By the beginning of Period II, Monte Albán had spread across some 416ha and had perhaps as many as nineteen thousand inhabitants. Interestingly, the population of the valley of Oaxaca as a whole seems to have declined somewhat, perhaps indicating a deliberate colonisation of areas further from the political centre.

Nevertheless, this great city was a definitive break with what had gone before. Strategically sited some 400m above the valley bottom, Monte Albán's civic architecture was built of stone and its houses of adobe brick rather than the fragile wattle and daub construction of earlier times. A planned ceremonial centre, monumental architecture and a glyphic writing system accompanying a sophisticated repertoire of art all heralded a new era of urbanism for the Oaxaca region.

At this time, the great plaza was cleared at the centre of the city and paved with white stucco. It measured some 300m north to south, and 200m east to west. Around it would soon be built ceremonial architecture in the form of two-roomed temples which defined Zapotec civilisation. Interestingly, the previously important site of San José Mogote, which had largely fallen into disuse, was now reinvigorated and given a central plaza almost identical to that at Monte Albán. In both places, secret tunnels led to the flanking temples, allowing priests and functionaries to appear and depart unseen.

The distinctive twin-roomed temples, known as *yohopèe* ('house of the vital force' known as *pèe*) in the Zapotec language of the later sixteenth century, had developed out of earlier single-roomed structures. The extra room may have accommodated the priests who were becoming ever more specialised and full-time as Zapotec culture developed. Typical of these temples is Building X, which has a wide and large entrance room whose roof was supported by two columns and through which one had to pass in order to ascend to a much smaller room at the back that was supported by two smaller columns. It is thought that it was this inner sanctum which received sacrificial offerings in the swirling smoke of incense burners. These temples were clearly sacred places, a fact marked by ritual deposits found beneath their floors and that typically include offerings of greenstone jewellery, shell mosaics and sometimes human remains, presumably of sacrificial victims.

According to Kent Flannery and Joyce Marcus, Period II temple rituals were similar to those practised in the area during the sixteenth century, and so the nature of earlier rituals could be inferred from these later better-documented examples. With this idea they examined Period II temples at San José Mogote in an attempt to throw light on Zapotec beliefs concerning temple sanctification, sacrificial offerings of animals and humans, and the transformation of high-ranking ancestors into supernatural beings identified with clouds and lightning.

Investigating three superimposed twin-roomed temples they found the remains of quail, a favourite sacrificial bird of the Zapotec, obsidian knives and blades used for heart sacrifice and bloodletting, and even the smoky stains of incense burners. Several offertory boxes were uncovered, one containing jade figurines and beads, the other a remarkable ritual scene composed as a miniature tomb. Here a kneeling ceramic figure had been placed inside a bowl alongside a sacrificed quail; on the roof of the miniature tomb was a 'Flying Figure' wearing a lightning mask, two deer-antler drumsticks and four ceramic female effigies wearing masks of the lightning god Cocijo. Flannery and Marcus believe this unique ensemble could represent the transformation of a Zapotec lord into an ancestral 'Cloud Person' associated with lightning.

During Period II also, Monte Albán's first ballcourts were built in a characteristically standardised 'I' shape. The most famous of these lies on the eastern side of the main plaza and is 41m in length and flanked by steep-sloping walls, possibly used by the spectators. Investigations have revealed little information concerning Monte Albán's rubber ball-game, though a fragment of a ball-player's mask was found. The game may have had political and cosmological significance as in later Mesoamerican times. Far more insight has been provided by the site of Dainzú which has preserved forty-seven carved stone slabs depicting ball-players wearing protective masks and clothing and handling small solid-rubber balls. Later ethnohistorical evidence indicates that the Zapotecs called their ball-game *queye*, and the ballcourt *lachi*.

An indication that Zapotec society was becoming ever more hierarchical at this time is the increasing size and sophistication of the palaces and their accompanying tombs. Elite burials such as Tomb 118 are large and elaborate – reached by a steep stairway and opening out into a main chamber some 3m long and over 1.5m high.

Another unusual Period II construction is the so-called Building J, an arrowhead-shaped structure in the great plaza. Still adorning its walls are some of the forty original carved-stone images – in fact Zapotec glyphs which record the names of Monte Albán's provinces. These are called the 'conquest slabs', and typically consist of three elements: a central part depicting a 'hill' indicating 'place of', on top of which is the specific name element, such as the head of a jackrabbit – the two elements combined yielding 'Hill of/place of the Jackrabbit'. Below is sometimes an upturned human head, usually with closed eyes, which is thought to represent the dead ruler of the named place. When considered together, each tripartite glyph may represent the name of a conquered community.

In later colonial times, local Zapotec lords identified their territory by using glyphs showing hills rather than towns, as the former were eternal, the latter ephemeral. This continuity of style in representing places can sometimes also be correlated with much later Aztec tribute lists which use similar glyphic designs to identify the towns they had conquered in this region. By the end of Period II, *c.* AD 100, the Zapotecs probably had a small empire, controlling a strategic area from the Tehuacán Valley in the north to the Pacific Coast area beyond the settlement of Ocelotepec in the south.

The succeeding period, known as Monte Albán III, is divided into two parts, Period IIIa (AD 200–500) and Period IIIb (AD 500–750), and it was during this time that Zapotec civilisation reached its height. Generally speaking, Period III saw the extremes of social differentiation, with Zapotec hereditary rulers (called *coqui*) living in sophisticated palaces whose sixteenth-century counterparts were called *yòho quèhi* or 'royal houses'. As with other Mesoamerican elites, Zapotec rulers wore elaborate costumes and seemed particularly fond of dramatic masks and headdresses. Ceramic representations of these powerful men are found on the so-designated funerary urns which accompanied the deceased's body into the tomb, itself often built beneath the palace, its walls covered with colourful murals depicting supernatural beings. The urns may have been unique masterworks designed to be the physical home of the ruler's vital life force or *pèe*. Typically, these urn figures would be sitting cross-legged, wearing a fantastical mask, adorned with heavy jade and shell jewellery, and sometimes grasping a decapitated trophy head. Such images were once thought to represent gods, but are now considered more likely to have been powerful ancestor figures.

Elite Zapotec burials at this time were often made beneath the floors of the palaces, many in the northern part of the city. They differ in design from what are considered the more official, perhaps administrative, palace buildings ranged around the great plaza. Typical of these high-class burials is Tomb 104, above whose entrance is a clay sculpture depicting an elaborately dressed figure holding a bag of incense, wearing jade ear flares and sporting a headdress composed of several feline heads. The single body inside was accompanied by a typically elaborate funerary urn and four simpler ones. Dazzling murals showing gods or ancestor beings covered the walls within which niches had been cut to take some of the pottery vessels. The murals themselves are thought to represent ancestor figures, their elite status indicated by the presence of the royal glyph known as the Jaws of the Sky. Glyphs depicting 5-Turquoise and 1-Lightning appear several times in the tomb and probably represent especially important ancestral figures.

If elaborate funerary rituals eased the passage of Zapotec royalty into the afterlife, they were matched by spectacular ceremonies which saw their coronation in life. The inauguration of a new ruler was a long-drawn out affair in Mesoamerica, replete with pomp and splendour, and the Zapotecs were no different than the Maya or Aztecs in this respect.

One well-documented example of such a ceremony is that of a Monte Albán ruler known as 12-Jaguar, who commemorated the event and its associated activities in a series of specially commissioned carved stone monuments. These monuments show captives he had taken in battle, high-ranking ambassadors from the great metropolis of Teotihuacán, and the ruler himself seated on a jaguar-cushion throne. Around this inaugural scene are glyphs telling of his divine ancestry and the various ritual activities he had undertaken to prepare for his assumption of power. While such propaganda imagery is the norm in Mesoamerica, there is a sense that 12-Jaguar was overly concerned with establishing and justifying his new position, giving us the merest glimpse perhaps of the power politics of the time.

Undoubtedly one of the most intriguing aspects of Zapotec power politics was the superpower relationship they had with Teotihuacán to the north. There are several carved stone slabs depicting Teotihuacán imagery at Monte Albán. The most politically significant appears to be one which shows four high-ranking Teotihuacán ambassadors who attended 12-Jaguar's inauguration. Richly garbed in typical Teotihuacán dress they ceremonially approach a Zapotec lord. Significantly, they carry small incense bags, not weapons. They have been identified by their accompanying glyphs as 9-Monkey, 1-Owl, 13-Knot, and Sacrificed Heart. It may be that this is a show of Teotihuacán support for 12-Jaguar, or at least an acknowledgement of his new position. Further evidence for this little-understood relationship comes from Teotihuacán itself. Here archaeologists have discovered a Zapotec enclave on the outskirts of the metropolis, where locally made Zapotec style pottery has been found.

As Period III progressed, Monte Albán's population continued to grow, from perhaps 16,000 during Period IIIa to as much as 25,000 by around AD 600 in Period IIIb. The city was now spread over an area of 22sq. km, and such was the explosion of population that smaller, quite separate hilltops were also built upon, such as Cerro Atzompa and El Plumaje. At Monte Albán itself, and most of the other major towns, defensive walls were built, suggesting serious unrest, though whether the threat was from within or without the Oaxaca area is unclear. One possibile explanation for increasing hostilities and defences may have been the spectacular rise of the city of Jalieza only one day's walk from Monte Albán, while another may have been the expansion of the Mixtec peoples to the northwest.

THE ZAPOTEC HERITAGE

By AD 900, in the middle of the period designated Monte Albán IV (AD 750–1000), the Zapotec state had collapsed and the city, while not deserted, was no longer the great urban phenomenon it had once been. The provinces once held by Monte Albán's power separated off and became independent political entities centred on towns such as Lambityeco, Mitla, Zaachila and Cuilapan. The monopoly on monumental glyphic texts which Monte Albán had enjoyed at its apogee was now broken, and once junior centres like Zaachila invented their own smaller version – the so-called genealogical registers – that emphasised their rulers' preoccupation with establishing their legitimacy.

In the period that followed (Monte Albán V, AD 1000–1521), it seems the whole Oaxaca Valley area underwent a process of balkanisation. Some archaeologists refer to this period as the City State Stage. It appears that the Mixtec peoples from the rugged mountainous region to the north had become the area's dominant cultural force, conquering some towns, expelling local Zapotec lords and establishing a political presence at Cuilapan. The Mixtecs, living in their major towns of Yanhuitlán, Tilantongo and Coixtlahuaca, were also concerned to record their genealogies, wars and marriage alliances, but unlike the Zapotecs they preferred painting them on deer-hide books known as codices rather than carving them in stone. Against all odds, some of these codices have survived in European museums, such as the Codex Bodley, the Codex Zouche-Nuttall and the Codex Vindobonensis.

Several of these codices record the military exploits of the great Mixtec warrior-lord known as 8-Deer 'Tiger Claw', who had conquered perhaps a hundred communities during the eleventh century AD and who is depicted in the Codex Bodley sitting on a great jaguar-skin throne. In the Codex Zouche-Nuttall he is shown having his nose pierced to receive a nose ornament as a sign of elite status. Born in the Mixtec town of Tilantongo, this ruler temporarily welded together a large area from the Mixtec homeland to the Pacific coast before being captured and sacrificed by his enemies.

The Mixtecs clearly held Monte Albán as a special place, perhaps a revered centre for ancestor worship. Mixtec-style tombs are found in the city, the most famous of which is known as Tomb 7. The original tomb was Classic Zapotec in design, but it had been reopened and reused during Mixtec times and yielded an astonishing quantity of luxury items including a skull with turquoise-mosaic inlays, silver and gold objects, quartz crystal gems, wafer-thin obsidian ear plugs, and necklaces of jade, pearl, amber, coral and jet, as well as beautiful and typically Mixtec polychrome pottery. Delicately carved jaguar bones depict mythic images of how Mixtec nobles were born from trees, a theme graphically portrayed also in the Codex Vindobonensis.

During the late fifteenth century, the Mixtec allied themselves with their Zapotec neighbours in order to fight off the encroaching Aztecs who sought a strategic route south to the Pacific coast from their home in the valley of Mexico. Despite several notable victories and stand-offs, such as that at the hilltop fortress of Guiengola in 1497, the Aztecs kept coming, deals were negotiated, and the Mixtec and Zapotec region eventually became the richest tribute area of the whole Aztec empire. Local rulers were allowed to keep their thrones by the Aztecs, but there was now no doubt as to who was in charge.

After Cortés finally defeated the Aztecs in 1521, the Spanish entered the Oaxaca Valley along with Aztec interpreters. At this time it was the royal dynasty of Zaachila which produced the most powerful Zapotec kings. The Aztecs told their new Spanish masters that the area had two main cultural groups whom they called the Zapotecatl and Mixtecatl, although in the mutually unintelligible languages of the natives themselves they were the 'People of the Clouds' and the 'People of the Rain' respectively. The Aztec names stuck, however, and changed easily into the modern ones we now use.

During these momentous early decades of the sixteenth century, local reaction to the Spanish presence was volatile. Some Zapotec peoples befriended the Spanish, hoping to benefit, while others isolated themselves for decades. It was not until the 1530s, and in some areas the 1560s, that Spanish rule was finally consolidated.

The Spanish made detailed written records of their dealings with the indigenous Zapotec lords of the time that have added immeasurably to our knowledge of Oaxacan culture, some aspects of which, as we have seen, can be extended by analogy into the pre-Columbian past. This ethnohistoric record comprises Spanish accounts of native religious practices, interviews with native leaders, hybrid Zapotec/Spanish maps and *lienzos* (i.e., maps painted on linen) of the region, and dictionaries of the local languages, such as the Dominican Friar Juan de Córdoba's study of the Zapotec language published in the sixteenth century. All these sources embody insights into indigenous Oaxacan philosophies – ideas of the world and of life and death that probably emerged from the earliest times at San José Mogote over two millennia earlier.

As with other Mesoamerican cultures that were subjugated by the Spanish, the new religion of Christianity was interpreted in the Oaxaca region in terms of older pre-Columbian beliefs. The Christian San Pedro was identified with the Zapotec deity Cocijo, and the natives, although claiming to be Christians, often either continued worshipping the old gods in secret, or quickly reverted back to them even under the eyes of the Spanish priests in the numerous churches that were constructed.

The Zapotec masons who, under Spanish pressure and super-vision, built the seventeenth-century church at Teotitlán del Valle, incorporated fragments of ancient Zapotec art into the church walls – a practice that reportedly continues to the present. This was a sign of continuity, and of their age-old identity and beliefs. In different places, and in many ways, Zapotec culture has adapted and remains vibrantly alive despite five hundred years of European influence and control.

FOUR

Teotihuacán

Teotihuacán, whose Aztec name means 'place of the gods', was Mesoamerica's greatest metropolis. A pre-industrial city with a population of perhaps as many as two hundred thousand spread over some 20sq. km, Teotihuacán was dominated by 600 pyramids, of which two – the Pyramids of the Sun and the Moon – were among Mesoamerica's largest single constructions. Ruled by a secretive and corporate elite, with its control based on a heady mix of ideological and religious prestige, economic and military power, and sheer size, Teotihuacán exercised a still little understood religious and political influence across Mesoamerica during the Classic Period, between AD 250 and 750. This chapter describes and assesses the city's unique contribution to Mesoamerican civilisation.

THE EARLY CITY

Between 500 and 150 BC, the valley of Mexico was dominated by the great centre of Cuicuilco, whose ceremonial centre was an impressive circular pyramid some 27m high and with eleven other monumental buildings nearby. With a population of some twenty thousand spread over an area of perhaps 400ha, Cuicuilco was by far the largest settlement at a time when Teotihuacán was just a medium-sized agricultural community.

Nevertheless, by *c.* 100 BC, Teotihuacán had grown to rival Cuicuilco in size, and when the latter was seriously damaged by an explosion of the volcano Xitle around 50 BC, the former's growth accelerated again to encompass perhaps 90 per cent of the whole of the valley of Mexico's inhabitants. The tectonic forces unleashed by nature in the south played a vital role in the north with the early expansion of Teotihuacán – a fact probably interpreted symbolically by the early population, as similar events were to be with other, later Mesoamerican civilisations.

This earliest era of Teotihuacán, between 150 BC and AD 150, encompasses two phases, the Patlachique and Tzacualli periods. It was at the beginning of this era that a settlement of the local Cuanalan culture had moved from its location at the modern town of San Juan Teotihuacán to a position just 1km away from where the Pyramid of the Moon would be built. This so-called 'Old City' saw the explosion of population referred to above. The presence of fresh water sources had clearly been a major factor in the location of the Cuanalan settlement, and the modest eastward movement would not have prejudiced access to these supplies. However, other more spiritual and ideological imperatives may have prompted the move.

Symbolic thinking and religious ideas probably played an equally vital role in the relocation and subsequent architectural development of Teotihuacán. Such ideas are often seamlessly woven into physical realities in ways not always immediately obvious. First was the sheer physical presence of the mountain in whose shadow the new settlement was built. In pre-Columbian times it was known as Tenan, i.e. Mother of Stone or Mother of Waters, though today more prosaically it is called in Spanish Cerro Gordo (Fat Mountain). Mountains were sacred places in Mesoamerica and often regarded as the source of water and fertility. Equally part of this metaphysical way of looking at the world was the incorporation of the geological nature of Teotihuacán's landscape into its subsequent layout.

The dried lava that formed the land was, by virtue of its cooling process, characterised by natural spaces or caves beneath the surface. One of these caves is located beneath where the Pyramid of the Sun now stands – one of the largest structures ever built in the Americas. It was in 1971 that this 'cave' was discovered at the bottom of a 7m stairway leading down from the surface. Originally thought to have been a natural formation altered by human action, recent investigations suggest it may have been completely artificial. Whatever the truth, it takes the form of a tunnel which snakes its way about 100m to a petal-shaped central chamber which lies almost at the central point of the pyramid above. The remains of stone drains and the lack of a natural spring indicate that water was brought in as part of rituals based on flowing water – a ceremonial practice heavily emphasised in Mesoamerican conceptions of caves as sacred places and sources of water and fertility.

Mud was still in place on the cave walls and there was evidence that artificial walls had once been built across the tunnel making a series of chambers. Fragments of pottery and fish bones combined with this architectural arrangement suggest this was a sacred ritual place – perhaps the *axis mundi* of Teotihuacán. At the time this 'cave' was being carved out of the subsoil (or having its natural shape extended and altered), it also had a small shrine built at ground level over the central chamber, though this appears soon to have been covered by the Pyramid of the Sun.

This huge structure, larger in prehistory than today thanks to faulty reconstruction work, was probably originally girded with a hallmark of Teotihuacán architecture known as *talud-tablero*. The *tablero* is a rectangular segment with recessed inset and which rests on the *talud*, an outward-sloping base. This feature appears throughout the city and in other parts of Mesoamerica where it was either willingly adopted, or perhaps forcibly imposed through Teotihuacán military presence. It is thought that originally the pyramid was faced with a blinding white layer of lime plaster – a truly sacred place dedicated by the sacrifice of children whose remains have been found at its four corners.

Although dating is often problematic with monumental architecture, it is thought that the Pyramid of the Sun was built during the Tzacualli phase of this early period of the city. In the plaza in front of it was originally a platform decorated with carved stone representations of human skulls, some of which have been found during archaeological excavations, as have sculptures of jaguars or pumas. The Pyramid of the Sun itself may yet conceal a major tomb, though whether it was dedicated to the deity referred to as Teotihuacán's Great Goddess (see below) is still debated.

Those who conceived the new city clearly wanted to materialise their cosmological ideas and beliefs in architectural form, and to this end they surveyed then built the great ceremonial avenue of Teotihuacán known today by the much later Aztec name 'The Street of the Dead'. This became the central axis of the city, flanked along its 1.5km length by many temples and palaces in what must be one of Mesoamerica's single most impressive sights, at the time as well as today. The position of Tenan was crucial, as The Street of the Dead was aligned to its summit where a shrine was built, despite the fact that this meant it was oriented at an unusual angle, some 15.5 degrees east of north. This apparent anomaly was in all probability the result of precise mathematical calculation, perhaps tied to alignments between architecture, the Tenan mountain and the movements of celestial bodies.

At the northern end of The Street of the Dead, also in the shadow of Tenan, was the Pyramid of the Moon, its great ceremonial plaza surrounded by a suite of smaller temples. Recent excavations have revealed several extraordinary tombs and a building sequence of seven stages for the pyramid's construction. In 1998, a bound and evidently sacrificed male was found in a burial chamber (designated Burial 2) along with pyrite mirrors, greenstone figurines, obsidian blades, nine eagles, one wolf, three rattlesnakes and two felines (probably pumas). The presence of excrement and soil marks indicating decayed wooden bars suggests that the wolf and the felines were buried alive.

By the end of this period, *c.* AD 150, the city had grown to spread over 20sq. km, and its inhabitants may have numbered as many as eighty thousand people – a population explosion caused by inward migration from many parts of the valley of Mexico.

THE CLASSIC CITY

Teotihuacán's succeeding period, between AD 150 and 300, spans the phases known as Miccaotli and Early Tlamimilolpa. It was now that the city was at its largest, sprawling across some 22.5sq. km of the valley floor. It was also now that the great rectangular enclosure known as the Ciudadela was built about 1 km south of the Pyramid of the Moon set back from The Street of the Dead. At its centre is the so-called Temple of Quetzalcoatl, at the time the third largest of the city's temple-pyramids.

The name Quetzalcoatl has led to many arguments about the identification and meaning of the carved stone images that adorn the temple façades. The presence of stunning feathered rattlesnake images has been interpreted in the light of much later Aztec ideas and beliefs about their feathered-serpent god called Quetzalcoatl, although there is no connection between these two civilisations which are separated in time by at least 600 years.

A second image, appearing in the middle of the feathered-snake body, depicts a strange creature with two goggles or circles placed between the eyes and two large but blunt canines and an elaborate headdress. This figure has been identified as the Teotihuacán version of the later Aztec rain deity known as Tlaloc. Interpreting this image has also been problematical – perhaps it is another masked manifestation of the feathered-serpent creature or maybe a quite different snake-being associated with war. What is striking, however, is the wavy and flowing image of the feathered-serpent body, the goggles worn by the second creature, and the various seashells that appear in the background. All these, in their various ways, are known to be associated with ideas of running water, fertility and the sea in later Mesoamerican civilisations.

Set around this ceremonial heart of the Ciudadela's ambiguous temple-pyramid are large buildings known as apartment compounds where the city's ruling elite may have lived. The distinctive nature of the Ciudadela complex suggests that perhaps the Temple of Quetzalcoatl may have served as the cosmic focus of the ancient city. Such a view may be reinforced by the dramatic discovery of 130 people buried within and nearby the Quetzalcoatl temple and that seem to have been dedicatory sacrifices made at the time of the temple's construction in time-honoured Mesoamerican fashion. From the ritual regalia with which they were found, it is probable that they were high-status individuals – perhaps war captives, or even members of Teotihuacán society. All were bound, though this may be part of the ritual of humiliation and does not necessarily mean they were either unwilling victims, or only enemies of the state.

Painstaking excavation revealed three main kinds of sacrificial victims: teenage women buried with a few obsidian blades, beads and shell ear-spools; young men (presumably warriors) in their twenties interred with many more obsidian blades, slate discs (usually a backing for ritual mirrors made of pyrite mosaic), and collars made of imitation and sometimes real human jaws and teeth; and a group who were buried accompanied mainly by greenstone jewellery and figurines, seashells and long obsidian blades. These three groups, together with several other individuals buried with distinctive grave goods, indicate a high level of social stratification in Teotihuacán society.

Contemporary with the Ciudadela on the other side of The Street of the Dead is the so-called Great Compound which has been interpreted as a large marketplace that may have incorporated a mix of craft activities, storage and possibly also aspects of the city's bureaucratic functions.

The ethnic identity of the Teotihuacanos is unknown, as is their language, though there is evidence in some of the city's art of contact with the Totonac peoples from the eastern Gulf Coast region. It may be that the main language of Teotihuacán was Totonac, though some experts champion an early form of Nahuatl, the language of the later Aztecs. If, as some believe, Teotihuacán's society was multi-ethnic, then it would be reasonable to expect a multilingual population, with Totonac perhaps as a lingua franca.

The nature of Teotihuacán influence beyond the central valley of Mexico, whose small-scale societies it so dramatically rearranged during its height, is ambiguous. So far, it seems unlikely that there was ever a true empire based on military control and bureaucratic integration. For the Maya region, it may be more likely that local leaders and dynasties allied themselves with Teotihuacán for propaganda purposes rather than being under direct control of the great city's rulers.

Life in the city

The latter part of Teotihuacán's golden age was between AD 300 and 750, during the Late Tlamimilolpa, Xolalpan and Metepec phases. It was at this time that the city's population may have grown to a maximum of two hundred thousand. No new large-scale architectural projects were undertaken and it seems as if this era was characterised by renovation and enlargement, processes that suggest a large degree of social stability.

This stability manifested itself symbolically in art and iconography in terms quite different from other contemporary Mesoamerican societies, notably the Zapotec and Classic Maya, where self-aggrandisement in large propagandist monuments and glyphic inscriptions was the norm. At Teotihuacán there is none of this but rather a sense of an apparently anonymous collective who took great pains not to display themselves as individuals. Status was displayed, but by means of impersonal, stylised and elaborate ritual costumes rather than with individually identifiable regalia. There is little doubt that this was a deliberate policy on the part of Teotihuacán's rulers, though its internal significance and the cultural and psychological effects it had on contemporary non-Teotihuacán peoples can only be guessed at.

This period saw the appearance of a distinctive, if standardised kind of dwelling known as the apartment compound. Perhaps prompted by overcrowding in the rapidly expanding city, the previous, presumably randomly spaced dwellings were pulled down to make room for a more structured and ordered kind of life. Built of stone and adobe brick, apartment compounds had high windowless walls surrounding an open central patio with plastered floors and an obviously preplanned underground drainage system. Built in a variety of sizes across the city, some two thousand of these compounds were eventually built and almost all Teotihuacán's inhabitants ended up living in them, either by choice, or perhaps – given the scale of the presumably state-sponsored investment – by coercion.

It is thought that those who lived in these compounds were kin groups, though a wider kind of inclusion perhaps based on occupation may also have been operating. The larger units could have housed as many as a hundred individuals, an intermediate size perhaps fifty people, and the smaller ones perhaps only several extended families comprising about twenty individuals. Judging by the effort expended in this vast process of urban renewal it seems reasonable to suggest that whatever else they were meant to achieve, the new apartment compounds could have served to organise Teotihuacán society into basic administrative units, and thereby facilitate social and economic control.

This control did not manifest itself in location, however, as, apart from the immediate vicinity of The Street of the Dead, high-class and low-class compounds could occur next to each other. Yet, while there appears to have been no definitive high-class or slum areas, the quality of apartment compounds varied greatly. Some were well built and decorated with colourful murals, while others were poorly constructed and left undecorated – here life must have been unpleasant and short, as in the Tlajinga compound. Clusters of compounds could form neighbourhoods or *barrios*, and some of these seem to have specialised in various economic activities such as the making of obsidian tools, pottery production and the fashioning of mineral jewellery.

At the city's height there were some four hundred obsidian workshops in operation, some serving local *barrio* needs, others located near the Pyramid of the Moon and the Ciudadela and possibly making obsidian items for export. Excavation has provided some insights into everyday life in some of these compounds. While areas for cooking, sleeping, storage and even burial are found as basic divisions of a compound, some have yielded more meaningful clues as to their inhabitants' lives.

At the compound at Oztoyahualco it would seem that the inhabitants were specialist stucco workers, at the Xolalpan compound that they were mural and pottery painters, and at the compound of Tlamimilolpa that they engaged in the production of textiles. To the west of The Street of the Dead a cluster of compounds were excavated which were decorated with stunning polychrome murals, suggesting habitation by a relatively well-to-do segment of the city's population. These now famous compounds include Tetitla, Atetelco and Zacuala Palace.

Careful study of these compounds reveals the processes and nature of mural painting at Teotihuacán. First a thin layer of clay was applied to the wall and this was then followed by a layer of lime mixed with quartz sand. A coating of red was then applied and on to this the figures were outlined in black, and detail filled in with green and blue. The finished piece was then burnished with a rubbing stone to give a final lustre. The appearance of the city's murals is decidely two-dimensional, with no attempt to show the depth of the images being painted. The art historian Arthur Miller considers this a deliberate practice intended to show the entirety of an image unobscured by such artistic devices as overlapping figures or perspective. An imperative for clarity of expression seems to have outweighed any desire to convey the illusion of space in these artworks.

Many murals depict regularised scenes of gods and/or priests dressed in elaborate plumed regalia, such as the image of the so-called Maguey Priest located in a room east of the Pyramid of the Moon. This shows a flat-profile human figure apparently walking, wearing a monstrous feline-like helmet from which rich plumes of quetzal feathers spring. An elaborate speech-scroll seems to emerge from his mouth, and his right hand is making the typical 'casting gesture' and from it a stream of water or blood falls to the ground. Six thorny maguey plant motifs give the mural its modern name.

Similar priestly figures appear in other murals, notably the spectacular set of three elaborately garbed individuals seen advancing in profile within a framework of interlaced feathered-rattle-snakes at the Tepantitla compound behind the Pyramid of the Sun. Other animals appear frequently in Teotihuacán mural art, such as various birds and especially the owl. However, it is the feline which takes pride of place, either as a tawny-coloured puma or as the so-called netted-jaguar – a representation in which the jaguar's body is covered with net-like designs, as on Mural 2 in the Palace of the Jaguars near the Pyramid of the Moon.

It seems likely that with the felines at least, we see at Teotihuacán an age-old metaphorical identification of these fierce predators with warriors – a symbolic association well documented for later Aztec times. On Mural 1 in the building known as the Zacuala Palace on the western side of The Street of the Dead there is a brilliantly coloured 'jaguar warrior' shown in typically Teotihuacán profile pose, wearing a fierce jaguar helmet and carrying a feather-fringed shield.

Virtually all of the city's mural art is religious in nature, but what gods did they worship? After AD 250, some experts believe the most visible deity was that identified as the Great Goddess, most vividly portrayed in a stunning polychrome mural in the Tepantitla compound, dated to the Metepec phase, between AD 600 and 750. Wearing an elaborate quetzal-plumed headdress, she emerges from the watery depths, a tree behind her heavy with dripping moisture and flowers. A womb-like space in her abdomen appears full of seeds, and from her outstretched hands water flows. On either side she is flanked by priests making offerings in the typical 'hand scattering' gesture. Perhaps the Great Goddess was an abstraction, an embodiment and personification of the natural world, and whose disembodied eyes so frequently depicted in her murals represent her all-seeing, ever-present nature.

Nevertheless, however closely associated Mesoamerican deities were with fertility and abundance, the relationship was usually framed by ritual events that included blood sacrifice. The Great Goddess was probably no different, as indicated perhaps by the structure called the Venus Enclosure which can be seen on various murals in different compounds. This enclosure has been interpreted as the site for bloody rituals of heart sacrifice carried out by the elaborately costumed priests in honour of the Great Goddess.

While such elaborately costumed and stylised kinds of image are typical of the iconography of Teotihuacán's murals, among the masterpieces at the compound of Tepantitla there is one which is radically different. It depicts a scene in which many miniature human figures are apparently dancing and singing, while a river flows along the bottom after having emerged from a hill. Bordering the river are designs which have been interpreted as representing fields under cultivation. Many of the figures have speech glyphs coming from their mouths, and there are flowers, butterflies and fish interspersed throughout. Perhaps most interesting is the fact that a rubber ball-game is also shown being played, although no ballcourt

– so typical among other contemporary Mesoamerican civilisations – has ever been found at the city. The whole scene has a paradisiacal feel about it, hence its modern name – the Tlalocan Mural – referring to the shimmering and fertile realm of the later Aztec rain god Tlaloc.

While all compounds differed from each other, each tailored to the needs and status of the group who occupied it, it is clear that there was also a strong ritual dimension to their construction. Whether in the densely packed central area or the suburbs, compound walls were built following the distinctive orientation of the city itself, signalling perhaps a replication in miniature of the city's grander cosmological orientation.

Everyday life was the backdrop to these events. It may have been the case that many of those who lived in the apartment compounds spent at least some of their time growing maize (corn), beans, squash, tomatoes and chillis, with the balance of their lives engaged in specialist activities. Some food plants, such as amaranth, maize and various beans, have been found by archaeologists, while others such as tamales (made from maize kernels) and squash are depicted on murals. Supplementing these domesticated plants were rabbits, deer, ducks and dogs, all of whose remains have been discovered. Whatever trade and exchange system the Classic Teotihuacanos employed, it brought in exotic species like seashells, cacao beans, avocado and cotton, the last used to make clothing.

At the city developed, there were also changes in the kinds of material culture which were used, especially in pottery. Small and rather basic incense burners called *candeleros* appear, as does a far more elaborate composite variety known as the 'theatre type'. These are a hallmark of the later period and incorporate removable mould-made elements of typical Teotihuacán motifs such as miniature feathered headdresses and plumes, and the diagnostic and stylised Teotihuacán human face with nose ornament and ear-flares. An incense burner workshop was discovered just to the north of the Ciudadela and yielded defective items, tools and what may have been a kiln.

Foreign relations

During this latter part of the city's life, its relationships with greater Mesoamerica appears significant but tantalisingly ambiguous. They were perhaps associated in some way with calendrical reforms instituted by Teotihuacán and which incorporated sacred warfare and human sacrifice. At the Classic Maya city of Tikal in present-day lowland Guatemala, it seems that an earlier and purely Maya ruling dynasty had been ousted in January AD 378 by an armed incursion of Teotihuacanos under the leadership of a lord called Siyaj K'ak ('Fire Born'), who proceeds to destroy the old order's monuments and impose his political will on large swathes of the region. One consequence of this was the installation of new rulers in many centres, either Teotihuacanos or local Mayas controlled by Teotihuacán. One indisputable sign of central Mexican influence at this time is the appearance of the typically Teotihuacán architectural feature of *talud-tablero* in buildings and residential areas.

At Tikal in AD 379, Siyaj K'ak appears to have installed a ruler of his choice, traditionally known as Curl Nose but now called Yax Nuun Ayiin. On his inaugural stela, he is shown wearing a Teotihuacán headdress and on a later commemorative monument erected by his son 'Stormy Sky' he was portrayed twice, adorned in a complete Teotihuacán costume with a feather-fringed shield decorated with goggle-eyed god motif. His tomb has yielded a beautiful ceramic vessel whose decoration is a hybrid of Classic Maya style and Teotihuacán imagery.

The highland Maya city of Kaminaljuyú may have been controlled directly by Teotihuacán for several generations, perhaps as a way of accessing such valuable exotic items as quetzal feathers, greenstones and cacao. *Talud-tablero* architecture is again present, as are burials which have preserved Teotihuacán-style mirrors and shell headdresses. There is also Teotihuacán imagery present at the great Maya city of Copán associated with its king Yax Kuk Mo, who became ruler in AD 426 and may well have been an outsider from central Mexico.

There is little doubt that the sources of certain kinds of obsidian were controlled by Teotihuacán, and that there was a thriving industry in making obsidian blades and perhaps exporting them to other parts of Mesoamerica. Green obsidian is an example of this and appears at Tikal in due course. Nevertheless, there is little convincing evidence for a Teotihuacán trade empire. As with many prehistoric (and modern) civilisations, ideology, prestige and religious ideas travel with and within objects. In areas beyond the immediate valley of Mexico, Teotihuacán's influence must have been a mix of all these elements.

More or less contemporary with developments in the Maya region is the appearance of at least two special building complexes or *barrios* at Teotihuacán itself and that provide further insights into the city's foreign relations.

One *barrio* shows evidence of having been inhabited by Zapotec people from Monte Albán, the other, the so-called Merchants' Enclave, has yielded pottery from the Gulf Coast. While it is tempting to interpret these in a modern light, perhaps as embassies of contemporary foreign powers, the evidence indicates otherwise. The Oaxaca *barrio*, located on Teotihuacán's western edge, had Zapotec-style burials but was otherwise a group of typical Teotihuacán apartment compounds. Also, its Zapotec-style pottery was made from local clays, and one *barrio* temple at least was built in the *talud-tablero* style. There seems little to suggest that these were high-ranking foreigners, though their exact status is a mystery.

The Merchants' *barrio* on the eastern side of the city is equally intriguing. Instead of apartment compounds it is a grouping of typically Gulf Coast round buildings, yet despite this, they appear to be arranged in north–south rows which follow the Teotihuacán orientation. Excavation has revealed pottery from the Gulf Coast region, some from the Maya area, and evidence for the processing of cinnabar used in mortuary rituals and pottery decoration.

END OF AN ERA

Somewhere between AD 650 and 750, there is evidence for major, if selective, burning and destruction of the city's main temples, compounds and sculptures. While it is impossible to know whether these events were perpetrated by outsiders or Teotihuacán's own population, it is probably true that only some breakdown in the political system would have allowed such previously sacreligious acts to have been committed. A valuable insight into who the perpetrators might have been is gained by looking at the pattern of destruction.

This was not a wholesale sacking of a city as might be expected if it had been carried out by an invading army. In fact, it has all the hallmarks of an inside job. Temple after temple of The Street of the Dead was not only burnt but smashed into rubble and the Ciudadela treated similarly. Given the nature of Mesoamerican temples, which saw them as the physical embodiment of sacred power, there is a sense that they had become so identified with the presumably increasingly malfunctioning city administration that only their total destruction would achieve change. What was being destroyed was not the city as a physical place, but the emblems and structures of its divine ruling dynasty, however corporate they may have been. Across the city, civic and religious buildings went up in smoke. This was the end of a Mesoamerican era.

In the wake of this seismic upheaval, it may be that the city was totally or mainly abandoned, perhaps for a generation or two. However, people soon returned, and during the so-called Xometla phase, as many as forty thousand people may have inhabited parts of the old city. It is possible that in the fall and rise of Teotihuacán there was also a population transfusion inasmuch as the partly reoccupied city was initially repopulated by between 10,000 and 20,000 people belonging to a different (perhaps Nahuatl-speaking) ethnic group. This view is supported by the changing nature of material culture which saw typically Classic-period Teotihuacán features such as architecture and pottery disappear along with figurines and even cooking utensils. The new repertoire of everyday objects was a feature of the following Mazapan phase during which the undamaged apartment compounds were never re-used, and smaller new kinds of house were built.

As the political and economic force of Classic-period Teotihuacán failed, other regional cities arose to take its place. To the south, centres like Xochicalco and Cacaxtla rose to prominence, the latter featuring spectacular polychrome murals in typical Maya style and depicting bloody human sacrifice and the Maya God L dressed as a merchant. Although currently difficult to date or accurately interpret, Cacaxtla seems to be an example of a post-Teotihuacán balkanised political landscape in which trade and warfare are both equally prominent. The city of Cholula is also problematical in terms of its exact role in the post-Teotihuacán world, though may well span the period of the great city's demise.

The main beneficiary of Teotihuacán's collapse is the postclassic city of Tula, dealt with in more detail in Chapter Six. While different in size, layout and material culture such as pottery types to Teotihuacán, Tula nevertheless does preserve some similar features in its artistic portrayals of felines and coyotes. It is still a moot point to what extent the rise of Tula was due to the fall of Teotihuacán, either built directly by refugees (or their descendants) who left the former city, or perhaps by those who had moved into the Tula area once the political control exercised by Teotihuacán on local peoples had faded.

The final act for Teotihuacán in pre-Columbian times was its role as a cosmic stage for the creation of the Aztec universe. While the Aztecs had no knowledge of what Teotihuacán was, or who had built it and when, they nevertheless had to account for its physical presence on the landscape – an immense backdrop to scenes of cosmogonic splendour.

Aztec views of Teotihuacán have shaped our appreciation of the site today. Their erroneous belief that the two largest pyramids were dedicated to the sun and moon have led to the popular names we now use for these impressive structures. Similarly, The Street of the Dead is so-called because the Aztecs considered this ceremonial avenue to be a huge necropolis in which the great lords of Teotihuacán were buried.

These Aztec identifications served to integrate the ruins of Teotihuacán into the Aztec worldview or cosmovision as a sacred place, and the ritual focus of cult and pilgrimage in the years leading up to the arrival of the Spanish in 1519. Such was the power of Teotihuacán in the Aztec imagination that they dug up its objects and placed them in the offerings of their own Great Temple in their island capital of Tenochtitlán (now Mexico City). Aztec artisans were clearly inspired by Teotihuacán forms in mural painting, carved-stone sculpture, and even aspects of the distinctive *talud-tablero* architectural style.

This was not simply copying or imitating in the modern sense, but rather recycling the sacredness of objects emanating from this mythical city. Even fragments of Teotihuacán objects were infused with magical force and thus ritually buried in the Aztec capital. Hundred of years after Teotihuacán's final demise, and in typical Mesoamerican fashion, the Aztecs were symbolically acquiring their own imagined past and recycling it for their greater imperial and cosmic glory.

FIVE

Maya

The Classic Maya were arguably Mesoamerica's most sophisticated civilisation. Between AD 250 and 900, they created a
society with complex mathematics, hieroglyphics and dozens of city-
states whose imposing pyramid-temples rose majestically out of the
tropical rainforests. Living under god-like dynastic rulers, they
possessed peerless architectural skills, and a rich and elaborate
artistic and ceremonial life which focused on bloody rituals of
sacrifice. This chapter charts the high points of Maya culture and
explains how their civilisation was based on a sophisticated
manipulation of landscape and natural resources, and cast their
politics in a cosmological setting.

ORIGIN MYTHS

Maya myths of origin, like most Mesoamerican accounts of cos-
mogony, were concerned mainly with sacrifice, fertility and the
establishment of a sacred charter for a hierarchical social system
dominated by the ruling elite. Yet, our knowledge of these epochal
events comes less from direct investigations of the Classic Maya, and
more from written evidence of much later Maya cultures. Usually, it
is filtered through the Spanish colonial period during which hybrid –
part Maya, part Spanish – documents were produced. A careful
reading of these accounts has allowed some of the events described
to be identified in earlier Maya civilisation, especially in scenes
depicted in Classic Maya art on beautifully painted pottery.

Without doubt, the single most important and influential of these
hybrid written sources for Maya origins is the Popol Vuh, or council
book, a unique masterpiece of Maya literature in its own right. It was
discovered during the eighteenth century among the Quiché Maya of
highland Guatemala and translated into Spanish. It is considered by
experts to be a colonial-period copy of a now lost hieroglyphic

original. Its three main themes are the world's creation, the epic tale of the Hero Twins, and the origins of the Quiché dynasties.

The Popol Vuh tells of previous unsuccessful creations – in this case three, involving animals, people of mud, and people of wood – all of which ended in destruction. It then relates the adventures of the Hero Twins called Hunaphu and Xbalanque. These are trickster figures who defeat the underworld Lords of Xibalba in a cosmic ball-game and rise to become the sun and moon. This in turn leads to the fourth and final creation, where the gods fashion humans from maize – these are the four founders of the Quiché lineages.

To begin at the beginning, the Quiché Maya account of the world's first dawn describes the appearance of the sun, moon and stars in terms of mythology and astronomy. In their view, the first-made people were the founders of the four Quiché lineages. They were overjoyed when they observed the planet Venus rise before the sun in the eastern sky. They unwrapped three kinds of precious copal incense which they had brought, and burned it towards the east. As the smoke curled into the sky they wept with joy and anticipation at the imminent dawn. As the sun climbed, all the animals of the world gathered on the mountain peaks and fixed their stare to the east.

All were happy as the sun rose into the sky. The first to cry out was the parrot, then the eagle, the vulture, the jaguar and the puma. As the sun's heat grew, it dried the surface of the earth and turned the original animals to stone. It is said that if the first jaguar, puma and rattlesnake had not been baked hard by the sun, humans would have no relief from these dangerous beasts today. The sun left only his cosmic reflection after the first dawn, and so today's visible sun is but this shiny disc – a remembrance of that glorious first dawn.

Although much of the Popol Vuh is concerned with telling the details of various attempts at world creation, it also recounts the adventures of two sets of twins. It is these twins, and their cosmic adventures that seem to be represented on so many Classic Maya artworks. The story begins when twins named Hun Hunahpu ('1-Hunter') and Vucub Hunahpu ('7-Hunter'), are summoned to the underworld of Xibalba – 'the place of fear' – by its gruesome rulers with such suitably blood-chilling names as '1-Death', 'Pus Master', 'Bone Sceptre' and 'Bloody Claws'. On arrival, the brothers fail one tortuous test after another until finally they are defeated in a ball-game by the underworld gods, and are decapitated. Their remains are buried in the ballcourt, with the exception of Hun Hunahpu's head, which is suspended from a calabash tree.

A young underworld goddess named Xquic visits the tree and its strange fruit, whereupon the head spits into her hand and she becomes pregnant with the Hero Twins, Hunahpu ('Hunter') and Xbalanque ('Jaguar Deer'). Her father is outraged and attempts to sacrifice her, whereupon she escapes to the upper world of the earth's surface and lives with Hun Hunahpu's mother until she finally gives birth. Throughout childhood, the twins exhibit great wit and cleverness, finally becoming skilful ballplayers, blowgunners and tricksters. They confront and defeat not only the terrible anthropomorphic macaw Vucub Caquix, whose jewelled teeth shone so brightly that he considered himself the sun, but also two half-brothers whom they turn into monkeys.

Their constant ball-playing, however, disturbs the lords of the underworld and, as their fathers before them, Hunahpu and Xbalanque are commanded to journey to Xibalba. Their mother and grandmother are worried that the same fate will befall them as did their father and uncle. In a typically Mesoamerican gesture, full of symbolic resonances, the twins plant maize seeds in the earthen floor of their house, telling their worried relatives that if they survive the maize will flourish, if they perish it will die.

The twins arrive in Xibalba where every night they play the ball-game with the lords of the underworld, and after which the gods try unsuccessfully to sacrifice the two boys but are constantly outwitted. Each night, the Hero Twins are set a new task which they complete against all odds. When told to keep their cigars alight all night they attach fireflies to the ends; in the Jaguar House they avoid being eaten when they offer the jaguars the flesh of other animals; and in the Cold House they keep themselves warm by shutting out the wind and rain. However, one night, in the Bat House, Hunahpu has his head sliced off by a vampire bat, and although Xbalanque replaces it with a realistically painted pumpkin, the gods use the decapitated head as a substitute for the rubber ball in the next ball-game. Xbalanque concocts a ruse whereby a rabbit impersonates the ball and bounds away, leading the gods astray long enough for him to retrieve his brother's head and restore him to life.

Eventually, the twins permit themselves to be killed by jumping into a great fire, and reappear in Xibalba disguised as sorcerers. They hoodwink the gods with feats of magic, by killing then restoring to life a dog, a human, then Hunahpu himself. The underworld gods 1-Death and 7-Death are so impressed they demand to be sacrificed themselves. The Hero Twins oblige but do not revive the hated deities, and punish the surviving Death Gods by telling them that from now on they can only devour guilty and violent humans. The twins return to the ballcourt and partly re-assemble their father, promising he will be remembered and con-sulted in religious rituals, before they ascend to the sky as the sun and moon.

Although the Popol Vuh is an early colonial-period document, most experts consider that it embodies far older Maya beliefs, per-haps going back as far as the Early Classic Period. The events surrounding the Hero Twins' encounters with the lords of the under-world have been interpreted as representing the search for maize at

Bowl from the Maya city of Altar de Sacrificios, showing Maya burial ritual. (© *Pauline Stringfellow, after J. Henderson,* The World of the Ancient Maya. *Orbis, London, 1981, Fig. 50)*

the beginning of mythic time – maize being the plant from which humanity is finally created. On Late Classic Maya painted ceramics, there are beautifully rendered scenes that have been interpreted as portraying Hun Hunahpu as the Maize God rising out of the earth, resurrected by his Hero Twin sons after their cosmic defeat of the underworld lords – a ritual image symbolising the annual appearance of the maize crop growing up from the earth's interior.

Pottery and incised bones buried in high-status tombs also depict scenes which appear to show the journey of the deceased's soul after death. The burial of the Tikal king Hasaw Ka'an K'awil included bones carved with images of the dead ruler being paddled to the underworld in a canoe, recalling the underworld journeys of the Hero Twins. Stunningly painted funerary ceramics portray episodes which seem to come from the Popol Vuh, and include scenes showing Hun Hunaphu's severed head coming to life, the impending decapitation of Hunahpu by the killer-bat monster Camazotz, and meetings between the Hero Twins and Itzamná – an episode lost, or at least not transmitted in the later Popol Vuh.

RELIGION AND WORLDVIEW

Mythology was brought into everyday Maya life as part of world-view and religion. Perhaps more than any other Mesoamerican civilisation, the sheer number and sophistication of temple-pyramid buildings, and the art and glyphic inscriptions which decorated them, were religious in nature. Maya religion was not imperialistic as was, in part, that of the later Aztecs or the Inka of South America. Rather, it served the royal dynasties that controlled the numerous Maya city-states that flourished during the Classic Period.

The Mesoamerican dual-calendar system which the Maya developed to its most sophisticated form, and the many gods who were deemed to control time and the universe, lay at the heart of Maya religion. The Maya may have acquired the dual-calendar system from the Zapotec where it makes its earliest appearance. (It comprised two separate but interlocking calendars which expressed a uniquely cyclical view of time, integrating the parallel spheres of everyday and sacred life.)

The solar calendar was the Haab, which had 18 months each of 20 days which gave a total of 360 days, known as a *tun*. To this were added 5 unlucky days, the *uayeb*, to make a total of 365.

Running in parallel, and intercalated with the solar year, was the sacred calendar, or Tzolkin, made up of 260 days divided into 20 'weeks' of 13 days. Each of these 'weeks' was presided over by a particular deity or deities, and every day also had its own god or goddess. For the Maya, the intermeshing of the two calendars produced a 'Calendar Round' of 52 years. Thus time and the fate of individuals and society were conceived as cyclical – a continuum along which events of myth and reality were fused together.

Associated with the calendar was the mathematical system which made it work. This is known as the bar-and-dot notation system, and probably also first appears among the Zapotec of Oaxaca. Unlike our modern base-10 (decimal) system, the Maya used a base-20 (vigesimal) system, in which a dot = 1, a bar = 5, and a stylised shell = 0. The stroke of genius was to make a number's value dependent on its position, not as elsewhere by having to invent ever larger ways of writing numbers, such 100, 1,000 or 1,000,000. In the Maya positional-notation system, an infinite number of values could be expressed merely by combining dots, bars and shells in different positions.

Whereas the modern Western mathematical system increases in value from left to right by a factor of 10, in the Maya system, values increase from the bottom to the top by a factor of 20, beginning with the lowest level with a value of 1, the next level a value of 20, then 400, 8,000 and so on. In this way, a single dot placed at each of the first three levels would signify 421, and a single bar placed at each of the first three levels would represent 2,105.

Despite this sophistication, the Maya shared with all other Mesoamerican peoples a worldview that saw spiritual force and the power of ancestors in every feature of the natural world, from trees to water, clouds to caves, to the sinuous slithering of serpents and the dappled body of the jaguar as it moved stealthily through the jungle. This worldview was but one (albeit distinctively Mayan) variation of pan-Amerindian philosophies of life, death and the natural world.

For the Maya, as for all Mesoamerica's peoples, geographical landscapes were sacred places, with natural features interpreted as culturally significant locations. As at Teotihuacán, caves were especially sacred, regarded as entrances to the underworld, dangerous thresholds between the physical and spiritual, and thus prime locations for rituals concerned with death, the afterlife and fertility. These ideas persist today among modern Maya communities, albeit shorn of the baroque splendour of the Classic Period. The most famous ancient Maya cave site is Naj Tunich in the Petén region of Guatemala, and has pottery and burials from late Preclassic to late Classic times. It has also preserved glyphic inscriptions and scenes from the eighth century AD that include depictions of the ball-game, Maya gods and the ever-popular Hero Twins Hunahpu and Xbalanque.

Equally eloquent of Maya conceptions of the world is their spiritual view of water and its dazzling reflections, perhaps the place beneath its shiny surface being seen as a symbolic entrance to the spirit world. It may be that the common practice of building great reservoirs in the centre of Maya cities was associated with such beliefs. While Maya rulers would have emphasised their control of water for such practical life-giving purposes as drinking and irrigation, it seems they were also concerned to control its metaphysical dimensions. Water's magical qualities were accessed by ritual bathing and the placing of reservoirs near to temple-pyramids in order to reflect these grand buildings and the ancestral royal burials they often contained.

Access to the supernatural was restricted to the Maya elite in rituals that stressed the multi-sensual experience of the world. Smoking cigars rolled from powerfully narcotic wild tobacco was one way of accessing the numinous, and is shown in Classic Maya art. Another was the ritual ingestion of hallucinogenic plants and intoxicating drinks. These included *balche*, an alcoholic beverage made from honey and tree bark, various kinds of hallucinogenic mushrooms such as the one called *xibalbaj okox* or 'underworld mushroom', and perhaps also secretions of the poisonous *Bufo marinus* toad. The use of enemas to insert powerful narcotic substances into the body and thereby induce trance is found across Mesoamerica and South America. The Classic Maya seem to have shared this practice, as bone tubes interpreted as the remains of enema syringes have been discovered in royal tombs.

This visionary aspect of Maya religion was embodied in later Maya times in the figure of the shaman-priest known as Chilam, who interpreted the words of the spirits and presented them as prophecies to his colleagues and rulers. Late Postclassic Maya examples of these sayings have survived, translated into Spanish, then English, as *The Book of Chilam Balam of Chumayel*, and *The Book of Chilam Balam of Maní*, where Chilam Balam means

'Jaguar Priest'. For the Classic Maya, however, nothing was as potent as human blood in binding humans to the supernatural realm (see below).

Using insights from the Popol Vuh, other fragmentary Maya codices, recent studies in iconography, and the advances in deciphering hieroglyphs, our understanding of Maya worldview and religion has been transformed over the past twenty years. The Maya evidently conceived the earth as flat, with four sacred directions each associated with a colour: white for north, yellow for south, red for east, and black for west. In characteristic Mesoamerican fashion, the centre was also a sacred direction and was coloured green. In one tradition, the sky was supported by four supernaturals known as Bacabs, and in another, different kinds of trees supported the corners with a great cosmic Ceiba tree holding up the centre. Moving upwards, there were thirteen levels to the sky, each having its own deity, while moving downwards, the underworld had nine levels controlled by nine gods of darkness. Trees in general, and the Ceiba in particular, were seen as penetrating all three cosmic levels – with roots in the underworld, trunk in the earthly world, and topmost branches scraping the sky.

In Maya art, parts of the world, and multi-layered philosophical ideas about them, were often represented as animals, with the sky appearing as a double-headed serpent decorated with motifs signifiying the heavenly bodies, and the earth depicted as a huge crocodile floating in water surrounded by water lilies. In the Classic Maya mind, complex ideas of genealogy, astronomy, rulership and the natural world were combined to produce monstrous supernatural creatures, symbols that spoke to the educated elite of their royal lineage and otherworldy powers.

The Celestial Monster was one such composite being, with two heads and a crocodile body. The front head featured a long nose, prominent fangs and a beard, and bore a glyph of the planet Venus. The rear head had fleshy eyes and a skeletal lower jaw, and was decorated with the kin glyph signifying the Sun. This fantastical being has been interpreted as a zoomorphic representation of Venus and the sun, with the planet announcing sunrise in its heliacal rising at dawn, and signalling the descent of the sun as it followed it below the horizon at sunset.

Equally grotesque in its appearance is the so-called Cauac Monster, seen by Maya specialists Linda Schele and Mary Ellen

Miller as representing the essence of stone, associated with rock-built structures, boulders and natural rock fissures. It, too, is zoomorphic, with half-closed eyes and a cleft forehead out of which maize sometimes emerges. It seems to be connected with lightning, its chthonic associations reinforced by the Maya belief that flint and obsidian are created when lightning strikes the earth. Also typically Mayan are the 'Water-Lily Monster', symbol of watery places such as lakes and swamps, and the 'Vision Serpent', a snake-like personification of hallucinatory visions, and closely associated with blood (see below).

The gods

In this grand cosmic scheme, the Maya placed a seemingly endless number of gods, though as with the later Aztec, it is probable that a smaller number of core deities had an almost infinite number of different guises and manifestations. As the Maya scholar Michael Coe has noted, some deities had four versions according to colour, others appeared in old and young forms, some had a male and female essence and many incorporated different aspects of animal appearance in a kaleidoscope of fantastical and sometimes monstrous images. Western ideas of straightforward gods, each with but one set of qualities and responsibilities, do not fit the Maya pattern.

Apart from painted ceramics and carved stone sculptures, the most important images of Maya deities come from three Postclassic-period, but nevertheless still pre-conquest codices that have survived: the Codex Dresden, Codex Paris and Codex Madrid. All are painted on bark paper, with the Dresden codex presenting precise information on deity names and attributes, the Paris seemingly associated with the late Maya city of Mayapán, and the Madrid being the largest survivor, extending over fifty-six leaves, and concerned with the gods of northern Yucatan. Such are the complexities of identifying gods and their variable attributes that differences between Maya scholars as to subtleties of interpretation certainly exist. Nevertheless, a general appreciation of the Maya pantheon is as follows.

The two main Maya gods were a cosmic pair, from whom all other deities were descended. The most important (male) god was Itzamná ('Lizard House'), shown in art as an old man and described as the patron deity of writing and learning. During the Classic

Period, he is shown on painted ceramics as a scribe with the glyphic title *ah dzib* ('He of the Writing'). He commonly wears a beaded disc on his forehead which is thought to denote blackness and may represent an obsidian mirror, a magical divinatory device across Mesoamerica.

In his role as creator of the world, Itzamná was called Hunab Ku, but this was a vague and remote aspect of his being, and no images of the god in this guise are known. Nevertheless, this creator role, together with the reptilian nature of earth and sky in Maya cosmology, combined to make Itzamná associated with the Milky Way which was understood and represented artistically as a double-headed serpent. Itzamná appears also to have been a patron of Maya royalty, especially in another of his guises, that of Kinich *Ahau*, the Sun God.

In some interpretations, Itzamná's consort was Ix Chel ('Lady Rainbow'). During Classic Maya times, she was associated with the moon, and sometimes also with destruction through her connections to God L, the deity of war. At this time, she is shown as an old woman with snakes for hair and adept at sorcery. However, in later, Postclassic times, she presided over weaving and medicine and was responsible for pregnancy and childbirth. In this more benevolent guise she became the focus of pilgrimage and a ritual cult at her island sanctuaries on Cozumel and Isla Mujeres off the east coast of Yucatan.

Kinich Ahau, the Sun God, was either a deity in his own right or perhaps one of Itzamná's many guises. He is often identified by wearing the Maya kin (sun) glyph on his body. As such, he seems have enjoyed a close relationship with Classic Maya rulers who identify with him. The Maya (and wider Amerindian) passion for transformation is revealed by Kinich Ahau's shapeshifting into the Jaguar God of the underworld when he disappeared from view in the west and travelled through the nether regions to rise again in the east at dawn.

The important rain god was known as Chac, and he also may have been a distinct deity or perhaps a manifestation of Itzamná, whose reptilian nature and appearance identified him with water. Known as Chac throughout the Classic and Postclassic Periods, he himself had four transformational aspects, each of whom was associated with a different colour and appeared to humans as thunder and lightning. During the Classic Period, Chac is sometimes shown fishing, and wears catfish whiskers and body scales as identifiers of his watery nature. He may also carry an axe or lightning bolt as his supernatural weapons.

Another important deity is Bolon Tza'cab, also known as God K. He shares with Itzamná a reptilian aspect, and has an axe or smoking cigar attached to his forehead. He first appears associated with the manikin sceptre (an instrument associated with the inauguration of a ruler) at Tikal in the wake of Teotihuacán influence at the site. It may be that the manikin sceptre itself evolved from the Central Mexican weapon called the *atl-atl* (spear-thrower).

There are a host of other lesser gods that were prominent in Maya religious thought and manifested various qualities that, while characteristically Maya, were nevertheless also typically Mesoamerican. Ek Chuah, whose name means Black Scorpion, was the black-faced god of traders and cacao growers; Ah Chicum Ek or 'Guiding Star' has a glyph which denotes 'North' and has been identified as a consequence with the North Star. Yum Kaax is a maize god and appears as a virile youth associated with agricultural fertility.

In the underworld, there appear three main deities: 'God L' is represented smoking a large cigar and wearing an owl headdress, and is associated with death and war; 'God N' presided over the year's ending and is associated with the four supernaturals who support the world; and 'God D' is identified as Itzamná in another of his guises, here associated with the earth. The Jaguar god of the underworld is also present, as is the deity labelled 'G1' identified as the Rain God and here, in the nether regions, associated with ritual decapitation.

EARLY MAYA CULTURE

The earliest era of Maya civilisation is known as the Preclassic and dates to between 2000 BC and AD 250. One of the earliest examples of settled village life in the Maya tradition comes from the site of Cuello in Belize whose Swasey phase has been dated to 1200–900 BC. Several typical Maya cultural features were in place here by the end of the period: houses clustered around a central patio; the dead buried beneath the floors of houses; maize a staple food; chert used to make stone tools; and distinctive red pottery, usually in the form of dishes and bowls. From now on, other features that characterised later Maya civilisation also begin appearing, such as obsidian and jade – both brought to the area by long-distance traders.

Major changes in the Maya region took place between about 600 and 400 BC during the so-called Mamom phase. It is at this point that from the northern Yucatan to the southern Petén region, pottery types assume a uniformity in their raw material and shapes, indicating a degree of common culture throughout the region, regardless of diverse local geography. At this time, unlike elsewhere in Mesoamerica, there were no large public buildings. However, between the end of the Mamom phase in *c.* 400 BC and the beginning of the Classic Maya era in *c.* AD 250, the Maya world was transformed.

A pan-Maya approach to art and iconography based on widely shared religious ideas lies at the metaphysical heart of what happened during this era, called by archaeologists the Late Preclassic Period. The distinctive traits of the subsequent Classic Maya civilisation are evident for the first time: huge public architecture; ceremonial precincts adorned with symbols of divine rulership; glyphic writing; bar-and-dot notation system; and carved stone stelae as royal propaganda monuments. Many of these developments required intellectual skills and practical organisational abilities, not least in the expansion of hydraulic agriculture that was to be the economic base of expanding Maya cities. For example, between 200 BC and AD 100, inhabitants of the Maya city of Edzna built a 12km long canal, associated with seven smaller canals and several reservoirs. Altogether it may have taken 1.7 million workdays to create.

The sheer scale of Maya imagination, and its subsequent realisation in large and small material culture, is astonishing. The large cities drew in population from surrounding areas, attracted partly by the prospect of work, food and protection offered by the emerging elite who employed them to construct the monumental pyramid-temples and associated buildings at the ceremonial heart of the new communities. These massive new undertakings are typified by such sites as Seibal, Nohmul, Calakmul and Tikal. By far the largest Preclassic city, however, was El Mirador whose huge pyramids of Monos and El Tigre were raised around 150 BC to a height of 55m, and the Danta pyramid which may be the tallest-ever Maya construction. These and other contemporary buildings were adorned with great stucco masks of supernatural beings flanked by jaguar imagery, and oriented so as to take advantage of the movements of celestial bodies and thereby appear to link the heavens with the earth in rituals designed to extol the divine nature of their rulers.

The political dimension of this emerging Maya ideology and worldview also manifests itself at this time, visible on large stone slabs (called stelae) carved with representations of rulers and accompanied by glyphic inscriptions and calendrical calculations in the typically Mesoamerican bar-and-dot mathematical system. Stela 2 at El Mirador, and Stelae 2 and 5 at Abaj Takalik, are early examples of what would soon become a common practice. It now seems clear that throughout the Maya region many Preclassic Maya centres continued into the Early Classic Period without any dramatic social or political changes.

CLASSIC MAYA CIVILISATION

AD 250 is the commonly accepted starting date for the Classic Period and it is at this time that Maya civilisation, building on its Preclassic developments, accelerates ever faster. There is now an explosion of dated stelae especially in the area around the city of Tikal in the central Maya lowland region of the Petén. Several hundred inscribed stelae now appear, the majority bearing dates in the so-called Initial Series system and which equate with the period between AD 238 and 593. So-called Emblem Glyphs are also evident, which are believed to identify the rapidly rising number of autonomous city-states, the average size of which, according to some calculations, may have been some 2,000sq. km.

Archaeologists often face serious problems in attempting to identify and investigate Early Classic Maya buildings as many were subsequently demolished or built over in later times as the cities became ever larger and temple-pyramids grander in design and size. Illustrating this process is the Mundo Perdido ('Lost World') group of buildings at Tikal, where the Preclassic pyramid designated 5C–54 was constantly enlarged and the whole area finally re-modelled *c.* AD 250. Royal burials were then inserted into these structures and, in the opinion of some experts, may belong to the dynasty known as 'Jaguar Paw'. Not long after, in AD 378–9, a new cultural force can be identified at Tikal, bringing with it architectural forms from central Mexico. This political, and presumably also military, incursion seems to have been from the great metropolis of Teotihuacán (see Chapter Four).

The influence of a new Teotihuacán-backed regime at Tikal also manifests itself in other parts of the central Maya region with new rulers coming to power, probably in alliance with the Tikal dynasty headed by the king traditionally called 'Curl Nose' but now called Yax Nuun Ayiin. There are images of this ruler in which he is shown wearing typically Teotihuacán regalia, and in his tomb hybrid Teotihuacán-Maya iconography adorns the ceramics which accompanied the deceased ruler into the afterlife.

Only 60km away from Tikal, the Maya city of Rio Azul became a dominant force between AD 400 and 550, and evidence points to its rulers being imposed by, or allied to, Teotihiuacán or its Tikal satellite. At the beginning of this period a number of painted tombs were constructed, one of which – Tomb 19 – has yielded dramatic insights into high-ranking Maya burials by virtue of being unlooted when archaeologists discovered it. In this tomb and others nearby there is evidence of Teotihuacán influence in iconography and pottery although these are accompanied by typically Maya glyphic inscriptions telling of the royal identity of the deceased. Some pottery was in Teotihuacán style but made on the spot of local materials, a practice also found in other contemporary sites such as Nohmul.

There was evidently a cultural break in this heartland of Classic Maya civilisation between AD 534 and 593. Called by archaeologists the Hiatus, it was clearly a period of political intrigue and manoeuvrings, most probably dominated by the attempts of the city of Calakmul to forge a series of alliances and thereby surround and subdue Tikal. For the next two hundred years, from *c.* AD 600 until AD 800, a resurgence of Maya culture takes place leading most experts to agree that this so-called Late Classic Period represented the apogee of Maya civilisation. It was during these years that some of the greatest architecture was raised and population density reached, and probably exceeded, the capacity of the land to support it. At this time, the great Maya cities took their final form – vast and imposing ceremonial centres surrounded by densely packed suburbs of craftsmen and farmers.

Ceremonial roads, called *sacbé* (plural, *sacbeob*), linked the different temple-pyramid neighbourhoods of cities and also stretched out beyond the suburbs to link with other cities. Smaller Maya settlements appear dotted throughout the region as miniature versions of the great cities, with perhaps a simple central patio, or in some cases small pyramids. Feeding this burgeoning population was probably accomplished by a variety of agricultural measures, including draining some swampy areas, building reservoirs and canal systems, implementing localised slash-and-burn practices, and trading in quantities of foodstuffs from outside the city areas – all supplemented by fishing and hunting, particularly of deer.

War, blood, politics and sacrifice

All Mesoamerican civilisations waged war and celebrated victory with public ceremonial incorporating rituals of human sacrifice. The Classic Maya were no different in this respect. They undoubtedly undertook military campaigns against neighbouring cities in order to expand their territory, to impose political control (and possibly exact tribute), and gain prestige for their royal dynasties. One of the most successful of Maya conquerors was the king known as Ruler 3 of the Maya city of Dos Pilas, who expanded his control over many lesser cities and created a short-lived superstate until he in turn was captured by one of the rebellious cities.

Nevertheless, during the Classic Period at least, artistic and hieroglyphic evidence suggest that Maya raiding and warfare were undertaken primarily to capture high-ranking warriors, preferably of royal blood, and ideally (if rarely), the enemy ruler himself. These individuals would then be sacrificed, their blood offered to the gods in acts of worship made possible by the valour and strategic competence of the victor. For this reason, Maya warfare, unlike its Old World counterpart, was not designed to kill men on the battlefield, but rather to defeat them in hand-to-hand combat and capture them alive – in many ways a far more difficult undertaking.

One interpretation of this kind of warfare is that, for the Maya, blood was the mortar that cemented the universe together, keeping its innumerable parts from falling away into cosmic, political and social chaos. The gods desired blood, and it was the duty of Maya dynasties to supply it in a number of highly ritualised ways. Most of all perhaps, the symbolic power of blood sanctified and legitimated the byzantine complexities of Classic Maya power politics. As a sacred liquid, the blood of high-ranking individuals was spilt on special occasions – to dedicate a new temple-pyramid, to designate a new heir, and to inaugurate a new king.

The Classic Maya imagination, or at least that of their constantly bickering and competing royal families, knew no bounds when it came to inventing ways of humiliating, torturing and finally despatching their victims. A special fate awaited a ruler should he be captured. In AD 738, just such an event occurred when K'ak Tiliw (also known as 'Cauac Sky'), the ruler of the small centre of Quirigua, ambushed the mighty Waxaklajun Ub'ah K'awil (also called '18-Rabbit') of Copán. Amid what must have been ecstatic scenes, the unfortunate captive was decapitated as the finale to a ball-game which celebrated the military victory and set the whole event in a mythic and cosmological framework by re-enacting the ball-game defeat of the underworld gods by the Hero Twins.

How this unlikely event happened we will never know, though it seems that despite its small size Quirigua had the shadowy backing of the large and powerful city of Calakmul. What followed this victory, however, was typical of Maya warfare and politics. To celebrate his sacrificing of Waxaklajun Ub'ah K'awil, K'ak Tiliw commissioned a stunning range of propaganda monuments at Quirigua and in its surrounding territory. Extraordinary sculptures were carved with consummate skill and covered with eloquent glyphic texts extolling the cosmic virtues of Quirigua's king.

After the state execution, and throughout his life, K'ak Tiliw erected tall stone stelae and great boulders carved with strange zoomorphic beings such as the monument known as Zoomorph B, dedicated on 2 December AD 780, some forty-two years after the event. This represents K'ak Tiliw emerging from the mouth of a great crocodilian who carries the sun and floats in the watery underworld. The whole elaborate scene has been interpreted as representing a doorway connecting the living world to the spirit realm, and thereby associating the ruler with ideas of transform-ation, death and rebirth. For the Maya, such monuments were images of the numinous accessed through art and ritual.

Such commemorative monuments, at Quirigua and elsewhere, give us insights into the bizarre world of Maya politics, where warfare, sacrifice, blood, urban renewal and elaborate art forms were intertwined with mythology and religion. Myth and history were seen as one, and thus quite different from the way we regard them today.

A different, and so far uniquely intimate and detailed view of the causes, course and aftermath of Classic Maya warfare has been preserved in a set of colourful murals at the city of Bonampak. On a terrace in the central acropolis of the site is a three-roomed building on whose walls is set out a sequence of rituals celebrating the

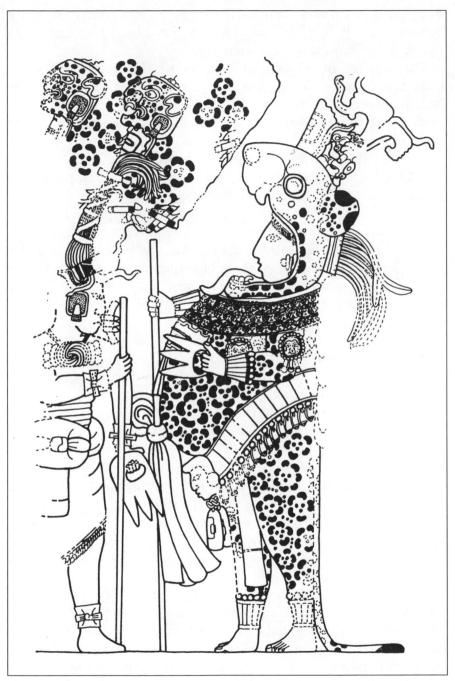

Classic Maya ruler known as Dark Sun at Tikal wearing an elaborate jaguar costume. (© *Pauline Stringfellow, after R.J. Sharer, S.G. Morley and G.W. Brainerd, The Ancient Maya (5th edition), Standford University Press, Stanford, Fig. 11, 20)*

designation of a new heir to the city's throne that took place between AD 790 and 792, and seems to have been associated with Venus as the Maya symbol of sacred war.

The sequence of events begins in Room 1 in AD 790. This first scene takes place in an unidentified palace, with the parents of the heir apparent, King Chaan Muan and his wife, watching events from a great throne. The scene then shifts to almost a year later to show Chaan Muan and two companions getting ready for the ceremony, and the final image depicts a procession of richly attired lords, the three previous figures now dancing, and all accompanied by musicians playing percussion instruments.

In Room 2, a dramatic battle scene is masterfully painted, giving a unique insight into the fury and savagery of Maya warfare. Warriors grapple with each other, spears are thrown, and prisoners are pulled by the hair. At the centre of these bloody events stand two figures dressed in the jaguar pelts worn by royalty, and which identify them as Chaan Muan and probably his ally, King Shield Jaguar II from the city of Yaxchilan.

The second scene in this room focuses on the presentation of the war captives. Chaan Muan is once again the central figure, wearing a plumed headdress and carrying his jaguar-pelted war-spear. Behind him are his similarly jaguar-pelted allies, while sprawling at his feet are his prisoners, stripped of clothing, bleeding from the fingernails, with one already decapitated. These are the presumably royal captives whose ritual death will purify and sanctify the official naming of Chaan Muan's son as his heir.

Although heavily damaged, Room 3 appears to show the culmination of events, with richly attired members of the royal family accompanied by musicians and dancers, and what appears to be a view of Chaan Muan and his followers standing above his seated family, members of whom are practising autosacrificial bloodletting rites. From the evidence of the associated glyphs, it seems that while the battle and its bloody aftermath were necessary to legitimise Chaan Muan's son as named heir, timing was also crucial, to tie in earthly events with celestial and supernatural influences. The battle took place on 2 August AD 792 when Venus, the planet of war and destruction, passed in front of the sun and disappeared from the sky; the scene displaying the humiliation of the captives and their imminent sacrifice took place several days later on the day when Venus first reappeared and rose before the sun at dawn.

This association of Venus with warfare appears widespread, and is indicated by what Maya scholars have called the shell/star glyph. Apart from Bonampak, another famous example of shell/star, or Venus-regulated warfare, was the two-day battle between the cities of Seibal and Dos Pilas in December AD 735. On the commemorative Stela 16 at Dos Pilas, Ruler 3, the victor, had recorded how he led Jaguar Paw, the captured king of Seibal, back to his city where he was stripped of his finery, tortured and bound. The stela depicts Ruler 3 in profile to show off every symbolic detail of his finery; in his clawed-jaguar boots, he stands over the squashed image of Jaguar Paw.

The sacred nature of war and blood sacrifice led to their being a constant theme in all kinds of Maya art, though monumental sculpture, originally brightly painted, takes precedence. Examples of this elaborate kind of conflict are endless, though the city of Yaxchilan may have produced the most richly informative Classic Period art to commemorate such events. Two of the city's rulers, 'Shield Jaguar' and his son 'Bird Jaguar', built temples and had glyphic inscriptions carved on lintels which portrayed the various stages of Maya warfare, including bloodletting, the vision quest and prisoner capture. One of the most famous of all Maya images is that carved on to Yaxchilan's Lintel 26. Dated to 12 February AD 724, it shows Shield Jaguar receiving his water-lily jaguar war helmet from his wife; around her mouth are traces of blood which may indicate that she has recently completed the painful autosacrificial bloodletting rites that are shown on another masterpiece of Maya sculpture known as Lintel 24.

What is clear is that for the Preclassic, Classic and Postclassic Maya, bloodletting rituals were linked to rites of passage and royal accession, as well as to the humiliation of high-ranking war captives. For the Maya, blood was identity and legitimacy, and was associated with fertility as shown by depictions of high-ranking men piercing their penis. Human blood was a precious liquid that bound the universe together and linked living kings with the cosmos.

THE LATER MAYA

Classic Maya civilisation began to collapse in the early ninth century AD, during the period called by archaeologists the Terminal Classic. A late flourish came at Seibal in *c.* AD 830, but ten years later the ruler known as Aj B'olon Haabtal erected five stelae on which he is portrayed in typical Classic Maya style, but so are others with characteristically central Mexican features. The end of the Classic Period was clearly a complex and confused affair, perhaps a combination of overpopulation and malnutrition, drought, disease and outside interference. Whatever the exact cause or causes, the last dated Maya stela was erected on 15 January AD 909, at the city of Toniná; thereafter the finely crafted ritual speech of once divine Classic Maya kings was never heard again.

What followed was an era during which the great cities were abandoned, or had little more than squatter populations sheltering in them. There was a population collapse in the central Petén region; the millions who had lived there a century earlier now abandoned their homes. Some moved to the highlands of Guatemala, while others, identified today as the Putún Maya (and who called themselves the Itzá), moved down from the north and inland from their coastal homelands of Campeche and Tabasco, to form independent political groups and settle around lakes in the heart of the Petén, most notably at the island town of Tayasal. One consequence of the movements into highland Guatemala was that the Quiché Maya became the pre-eminent group, dominating their contemporaries the Tzutujil, Kekchi and Cakchiquel, from their capital at Gumarcaaj (usually known by its Aztec name, Utatlán).

In the northern Yucatan, the most famous yet mysterious event of the late Terminal Classic and early Postclassic Periods was the apparent revitalisation and redevelopment of the city of Chichén Itzá, whose name means 'at the mouth of the well of the Itzá'. The site itself is an enigma as parts of it seem typically to belong to the Postclassic Toltec culture of Central Mexico (see Chapter Six). The Chac Mool sculptures, the presence of a carved *tzompantli* (skull-rack), feathered-serpent imagery, and the great four-sided pyramid known as El Castillo are all Central Mexican rather than Mayan, yet their masterful workmanship and visual flourish speak of Maya craftsmen working for outsiders.

Nevertheless, there is also evidence in some parts of the city of the earlier Terminal Classic architectural style known as Puuc. Archaeologists disagree on how to interpret this hybrid site. Traditionally, it has been thought that there was a Toltec invasion of the Yucatan that brought with it the cult of heart sacrifice and the

Toltec-Maya carving from Chichén-Itzá showing a jaguar eating a human heart.
(© *Pauline Stringfellow*)

imagery of Quetzalcoatl – the feathered-serpent – called *Kukulkán*
by the local Maya. Golden discs retrieved from the great natural
well known as the 'Cenote of Sacrifice' portray typically Toltec
warriors cutting out a victim's heart. Recent thinking, however, has
suggested that the Putún (Itzá) Maya , perhaps with central Mexican
and possibly Toltec groups, built Chichén Itzá completely as one city
in a deliberately hybrid style.

Whatever the true nature of Chichén Itzá, it collapsed around AD
1221, after several hundred years of dominating the northern
Yucatan. In its wake, the fortified city of Mayapán became the
dominant force under the Kokoom lineage, from whose ranks the
ruler was chosen. However, much of the city's architecture seems

just a pale imitation of its more sophisticated predecessor. The Kokoom kept control until about AD 1441 when they were massacred by the rival lineage known as Xiu. Mayapán collapsed as did its wide tribute-based network of towns, and before long the whole region had become balkanised, with an endless array of towns and small cities vying for power and influence – a process still under way when Europeans arrived.

During the late Postclassic Period, there was a move towards sea-borne trading, probably at the behest of the Putún. Extensive trade networks were interlaced around the Yucatan coast, north to eastern Mexico, and south to Honduras and beyond. The greatest settlement at this time was Tulum on the east coast of the Yucatan, which flourished as a trading port and cult centre between AD 1200 and 1519. Although a shadow of the great Classic Maya cities, both temple and town were strategically located for maritime trade and the pilgrimage cult of the Maya moon goddess Ix Chel.

Nearby was another trading port called Tancah, famous now for its pre-Columbian murals depicting maritime warfare. It is possible that the whole eastern coast of the Yucatan had come under the control of the sea-trading Putún. Tancah and Tulum appear to have been at the heart of this phenomenon, perhaps associated with the religious and astronomical beliefs concerning the planet Venus, whose glyph has been found carved on the wall of Tancah's cenote.

The island of Cozumel, some 16km off Yucatan's north-eastern coast, also seems to have been an important trading and ritual centre, probably part of the commercial network that included Tulum, Tancah and the Isla de Mujeres. It was on Cozumel that the Putún Maya blended spiritual, commercial and defensive issues in the small coastal shrines that may also have served as watchtowers. The Spanish priest Fray Diego de Landa later commented that the Maya regarded Cozumel as a centre of pilgrimage akin to Christian Jerusalem.

The trading Maya of the Postclassic Period entered European history during Christopher Columbus's fourth voyage between AD 1502 and 1504. Offshore of Honduras, near the Bay Islands, Columbus's expedition encountered a large sea-going Maya trading canoe. From its size, its thirty passengers, and its cargo of cacao, copper bells, axes and metalworking equipment, it was obvious to the Spanish that these were by far the most sophisticated people they had hitherto encountered in the Americas.

SPANISH CONQUEST

In AD 1511, a shipwrecked crew of Europeans were cast ashore in eastern Yucatan. Only two Spaniards survived their ensuing capture by Maya lords – Gerónimo de Aguilar ended up serving a local Maya ruler, and Gonzalo de Guerrero married a local ruler's daughter. In 1517, another expedition led by Francisco Hernández de Córdoba landed at Isla de Mujeres and later at Champoton, where he died of wounds fighting the local Maya. The next year, Juan de Grijalva's expedition landed on Cozumel island, from where he travelled south and saw first-hand the coastal trading centre of Tulum.

Grijalva retraced his route, and sailed around the Yucatan peninsula and up the eastern coast of Mexico where he was the first European to hear of the great Aztec civilisation. In the wake of the stories told by Grijalva back in Cuba, Hernán Cortés was put in charge of a further expedition in 1519. Cortés's first port of call was Cozumel where he spent several days destroying the pagan idols of Ix Chel and replacing them with Christian crosses. Cortés then marched into history with his subsequent conquest of the Aztec empire, leaving behind the Yucatan and gold-poor Maya culture.

In the year's following the Spanish conquest of central Mexico, the Yucatan Maya were subdued by Francisco de Montejo who had been a member of the Grijalva and Cortés expeditions. In 1526, Montejo was given royal permission to conquer and colonise the Yucatan, a process that was not completed until 1546. The initial invasion made good progress, encountering little resistance until in 1528 at Chauaca the Spanish killed over one thousand Maya warriors, the resulting psychological effect being so traumatic that all Maya resistance in the area collapsed.

The second phase of conquest lasted from 1531 until 1535, during which time Montejo was based at Champoton. In 1531, the Maya ruler Ah Canul surrendered, and Montejo sent his son (Montejo the Younger) to the old Maya centre of Chichén Itzá where he established a 'royal city' but was forced to abandon it when the local Maya rose against him. Father and son were reunited at Dzibikal but soon afterwards news arrived of Francisco Pizarro's conquest of the fabulously wealthy Inka empire in Peru. In seven years of fighting, Yucatan had yielded little gold and many soldiers now left for South America. With the army depleted, the conquest was put on hold.

In 1541, Montejo the Elder formally handed over the pursuit of conquest to his son who promptly established his base of operations at Campeche. The powerful Xiu Maya submitted, but those of Ah Canul refused. In a campaign conducted against them, Montejo's cousin established the city of Mérida in central northern Yucatan where he received the submission of Tutul Xiu, the ruler of Maní, the most powerful independent Maya kingdom. The conversion of Tutul Xiu to Christianity led to further submissions in western Yucatan but in the east, Maya towns either held out, or submitted then rebelled. The largest of these rebellions came in 1546 and involved an alliance of many different Maya groups, and was only supressed by an expedition led by Montejo himself.

After twenty years, the Spanish had finally ended over two millennia of Maya civilisation in the Yucatan. Further south, however, events took a different turn. In 1524/5, Hernán Cortés himself had led an expedition, called an *entrada*, into the central Maya lowlands where he finally met the Itzá ruler Canek and was invited to visit the capital of Tayasal. Canek announced that he would consider becoming a Christian, and it was his guides who enabled the Spanish expedition to soldier on and avoid disaster in the jungle. Meanwhile, further south in the highlands, the Quiché and Cakchiquel Maya were raiding towns that had declared themselves allies to the Spanish despite having sent official word that they too would submit to the Spanish. Cortés responded by sending his trusted lieutenant Pedro de Alvarado to conquer these southern Maya whose territory lay in what is today Guatemala.

Alvarado's campaign swept into the Maya domain, defeating a Quiché force in battle then terrorising the area. The shock value of his cavalry was used to good effect against another Quiché attack after which the Spanish and their central Mexican Indian allies entered the abandoned town of Xelahu (now called Quetzaltenango). After a third cataclysmic defeat a few days later, during which many leading Quiché were killed, the Maya sued for peace, and invited the Spanish to their capital Utatlán. Alvarado captured and killed many of the Quiché leaders and burnt the town, then turned his attention to the Cakchiquel Maya at their capital of Iximche.

Initially, the Cakchiquel became allies of the Spanish, sending some four thousand warriors to help Alavarado finish off the remains of Quiché resistance. They also persuaded the Spanish to help them defeat their other traditional enemies the Tzutujil.

The alliance worked well, and soon the Tzutujil had offered their allegiance to the Spanish Crown. However, Alvarado's demands for gold soon alienated the Cakchiquel and they rebelled. A bitter and cruel war followed until finally the Cakchiquel admitted defeat.

The end of any truly independent Maya nation came with the Spanish defeat of the Itzá, whose base was on their island capital of Tayasal in Lake Petén Itzá. In 1618, Spanish missionaries spent time at Tayasal, during which they smashed an idol called Tzimin Chac – a stone sculpture of a horse left there by Cortés almost a century before. Subsequently, a Spanish force sent against the Itzá was caught by surprise and massacred, and for almost a century the Itzá were left to their own devices, with nearby Maya villages renouncing their previous conversion and returning to the old gods. In 1696, a small group of Franciscan missionaries arrived at Tayasal to convert the Itzá, only to be told that according to their sacred books the time was not quite right, but if they returned several months later the Maya would indeed convert.

When finally a Spanish force was despatched to take over the Itzá it was attacked and defeated once again, and it became apparent that only a crushing military defeat would subjugate this last Maya kingdom. By early 1697, a Spanish army was at the shore of Lake Petén Itzá, and having built a galley to navigate the lake, attacked Tayasal on the morning of 13 March. The Spanish fired their arquebus whereupon panic set in among the defenders, who took to the lake in their efforts to swim away from danger. The town was stormed and soon the Spanish flag stood on Tayasal's highest temple. It was here that over two thousand years of independent pre-Columbian Maya civilisation came to an end.

LEGACY

Despite the end of their political sovereignty, Maya peoples did not disappear from history, and their ethnic and linguistic diversity survive to the present. In the Yucatan, during the years and centuries following their pacification, Maya slaves escaped their masters and took refuge in the countryside. Uprisings were inspired by shaman-priests who claimed to have received divine revelations from the gods, some of which were written down in hybrid Maya-Spanish documents known as the The Books of Chilam Balam. Throughout the colonial period, the Yucatan Maya resisted their Spanish masters, making idols of their gods to be distributed throughout the region, creating underground religious movements, talking of prophecies of the end of Spanish rule, and sometimes killing Spaniards and their supporters.

As late as 1848, the so-called Maya Caste War saw thousands of Mayas and Whites perish in fighting provoked by agrarian reform. Yet there was also a strong religious dimension to this conflict which did not formally end until 1901. In 1850, a Maya cult of the Talking Cross emerged in which the Maya peoples were exhorted to liberate their lands from the Spanish. Perhaps using native ventriloquists, those Maya who sponsored the Talking Cross would make it appear to decide on military strategy as well as religious affairs. The Talking Cross gave a voice to the emotions and desires of its Maya followers, the Cruzob, speaking and even writing letters through the agency of the individual known as the scribe or Secretary to the Cross. The position of the scribe seems to have continued down to at least 1957.

Today, in various parts of the Maya realm, native festivals outwardly shaped by Christianity but with an ancient pre-Columbian philosophy at their heart continue to be celebrated. One such event is a pre-Lent carnival at the highland Maya town of Chamula, where the sponsor of the celebrations is called a 'Passion' and is a Maya impersonator of Christ through whom God returns to walk the earth during Easter. Here, and elsewhere, the Christian Passion has been Indianised, made relevant to the people, and thus has become a part of their own history.

SIX

Aztec

The Aztec (AD 1350–1521) were Mesoamerica's last great pre-Columbian culture – seen, confronted and described by their Spanish conquerors from 1519, and ultimately destroyed in 1521. For this reason, we have more information of more varied kinds on Aztec civilisation than on any of its predecessors.

The Aztecs belong to the so-called Postclassic Period of Meso-america, an era which begins between AD 900 and 1000, lasts until the arrival of the Spanish in 1519, and was a time of unprecedented political and cultural upheaval. With the demise of Teotihuacán, the Zapotecs and the Classic Maya, Mesoamerica experienced profound changes that reconfigured the cultural map of the region. Maya peoples, having left their great dynastic cities, forged new trading routes around the Yucatan's Caribbean coast and moved up into the Maya highlands of Guatemala. At the same time, groups from central Mexico evidently moved into the Yucatan, where the old Maya city of Chichén Itzá was rebuilt and extended by Maya work-men but in central Mexican style between *c.* AD 900 and 1200.

In central Mexico there was a similar mixing of cultures and styles at places such as Xochicalco and Cacaxtla, the latter of whose extra-ordinary polychrome murals invoke typically central Mexican themes but are executed in peerless Maya style. Of all the pre-Aztec cultures to flourish during the Postclassic Period, it was the Toltecs at their capital of Tula who appear to have been most influential.

The are two versions of Toltec history – that which has been inter-preted from the archaeological excavations at the site of Tula, and another which comes mainly from central Mexican mythology and oral tradition. In the former, archaeological sense, Toltec culture at Tula lasted between *c.* AD 900 and 1200; in the latter, the Aztecs and their contemporaries viewed the Toltecs as revered warrior ancestors who created a golden age of civilisation to which they attached themselves through a mix of real and spurious genealogical connections. During Aztec times, Toltec heritage was the much sought after gold standard of cultural and political legitimacy.

One problem with discerning an accurate picture of who the Toltecs really were lies in the fact that the name Tula – more accurately Tollan – refers to 'a place of reeds', the name given to any large civilised community. Similarly, the term Toltec was applied to anyone who lived in such a sophisticated cosmopolitan city. Thus, at the time of the Spanish arrival, the Aztec capital of Tenochtitlán was one of several places to which the term Tollan could be applied.

Archaeologically, Tula was a major city during its brief life, covering some 14sq. km and lying about 70km north of modern Mexico City. At its height, it may have controlled an area whose population reached three hundred thousand. At the city itself, there may have been as many as forty thousand people living in single-storey houses in a densely packed residential area surrounding the ceremonial centre known today at Tula Grande. The main architectural features here were large open plazas, ball-courts, temple-pyramids and palaces. The most famous and best-preserved temple is Pyramid B, which has impressive (if reconstructed) cyclindrical statues of so-called Atlantean Warriors on its summit. Around the base of the pyramid are the remains of once more extensive decorative panels depicting felines (possibly pumas), coyotes and eagles; some of these are shown in what has been taken to be the act of devouring hearts, and it is thought they may in fact be symbolic representations of elite Toltec warriors engaged in human sacrifice – an early forerunner of later Aztec Jaguar and Eagle Warrior societies.

Historically, the picture is more complex, a result of the often contradictory and semi-mythologised accounts that have come down to us from Aztec times. According to these accounts, a leader of the Tolteca-Chichimeca peoples known as Mixcoatl ('Cloud Serpent') led his people to the valley of Mexico in AD 908 where they settled at Culhuacan. Mixcoatl's son, Topiltzin Quetzalcoatl, moved the Toltec capital north to Tula, where he reigned as a benign king. Internal political strife was stirred up by the followers of the god Tezcatlipoca, perhaps a more militant faction within Toltec society. Eventually, Topiltzin Quetzalcoatl and his followers left Tula and made their arduous way to the Gulf of Mexico. For what now transpired, two different versions are given.

One is that he set himself aflame, dressed in a magnificent regalia of bird plumes and became transformed into a god of the Morning

Star. The other account says he set off on a great raft made of serpents, heading east, and with a prediction that one day he would return. Perhaps significantly, there are Maya accounts of a highland Mexican conqueror who arrived in the Yucatan in about AD 987 whose name in the Maya language was Kukulkan or Feathered Serpent. Back at Tula, Toltec civilisation reached its height, and generated all kinds of fabulous stories about its inhabitants: they caused giant maize to grow, cotton to appear already coloured, and built palaces of jade, gold and quetzal feathers. This was clearly a place of legend, the manifestation of a golden age at which all who came later looked back with envy and longing.

Riven by factionalism and perhaps affected by droughts, Tula was abandoned in AD 1156 or 1168 (sources differ) during the reign of the ruler Huemac. The Toltec population dispersed across Mesoamerica, some ending up in the various city-states of the valley of Mexico, where their Toltec heritage stood them in good stead with local peoples.

The aura surrounding Tula and the Toltecs was such that not only did many ruling families in highland Mexico claim Toltec descent, but the later Aztecs appear to have looted the site. They dug up sculptures, friezes and semi-precious offerings and took them back to their own city of Tenochtitlán, where they were re-used and presumably drew attention to the Aztecs as in some senses the new Toltecs.

ORIGIN MYTHS

For the Aztecs, as for all pre-Columbian peoples of the Americas, mythology was an alternative reality, a way of making sense of the world as they saw it. In Mesoamerica, mythology would seem to have been concerned mainly with cosmology and creation, and sacrifice and fertility, albeit in many different guises. The relationships between deities, rulers, and ruled, were enshrined in myths that told of great cosmic battles between gods, and epic sacrifices in supernatural landscapes.

In the beginning there was one god, Ometeotl, the self-created Lord of Duality. In characteristic Mesoamerican fashion, he had a male and female aspect, Ometecuhtli ('Two Lord'), and Omecihuatl ('Two Lady'). Born of these two cosmic figures were the great gods of the Aztecs, often called the four Tezcatlipocas: the Red Tezcatlipoca known as Xipe Totec, the Blue Tezcatlipoca called

Huitzilopochtli, the White Tezcatlipoca identified as Quetzalcoatl, and the Black Tezcatlipoca known simply as Tezcatlipoca, the supreme Aztec god. It was the duty of these four deities to create and manage the world, and it was disagreements and confrontations between them that led to a never-ending cycle of creation and destruction epic accounts of which are the basis of Aztec myths concerning the origins of the universe. These myths take many forms and appear in alternative versions. As with all mythology, there is no single true account; each version reflects the circumstances at the time it was created, and later written down by the Spanish who, of course, had their own agenda. The cosmic struggle for supremacy between these major gods led to the five successive world eras or 'suns', each identified by the cataclysm which engulfed it.

On the great circular slab of stone known as the Sun Stone, discovered in downtown Mexico City in 1790, are carved images of Aztec cosmology, including the five eras. In the centre is the face of either the Sun God Tonatiuh, or the earth monster Tlaltecuhtli, with a sacrificial flint knife for a tongue. This central image represents the fifth and current era of creation and is known as 4-Movement. Around this four boxes appear, each containing the glyphic date of the destruction of the previous four eras. These are 4-Jaguar, presided over by Tezcatlipoca and destroyed by jaguars; 4-Wind, controlled by Quetzalcoatl and brought to an end by hurricanes; 4-Rain, dominated by Tlaloc and destroyed by fiery rain; and 4-Water ruled by Chalchiuhtlicue and destroyed by floods. According to Aztec calculations, the fifth era, our own, will end in 2027.

Apart from this elaborate cosmic scheme, other myths recount the creation of gods, people and the earth. One of these tells how the gods gathered at the ancient city of Teotihuacán in order to set the world in motion by creating the sun. Two gods, Nanahuatzin and Tecciztecatl, accompanied by the jaguar and the eagle threw themselves into a huge fire and were consumed by the flames. Tecciztecatl became the moon when the gods threw a rabbit at him, and Nanahuatzin turned into the sun (Tonatiuh), but failed to advance across the sky. When asked why he refused to move, Nanahuatzin replied that he was waiting for divine nourishment in the form of blood, whereupon Quetzalcoatl cut out and offered up the hearts of the assembled deities. This act of self-sacrifice by the gods to create the world was a sacred charter and mythic justification for Aztec human sacrifice which was regarded both as repaying the debt to the gods, and as a way of strengthening the sun in his daily journey through the underworld.

As for the origins of the Aztecs themselves, this was accounted for in several overlapping ways, and tied them closely to their tribal war god Huitzilopochtli. One myth recounts how the Aztecs left the mythical land of Aztlán in northwest Mexico, probably during the early twelfth century AD. They were guided on their wanderings by a speaking idol of Huitzilopochtli, who persuaded them to change their name to Mexica and predicted their future greatness. They arrived first at the Seven Caves known as Chicomoztoc, a traditional place of departure for many Mexican peoples. When they reached the Serpent Mountain known as Coatepec, Huitzilopochtli was symbolically reborn after a cosmic battle with his sister the moon goddess Coyolxauhqui and her brothers the 400 stars, known as the Centzon Huitznahua.

This battle came about because the earth goddess Coatlicue, Coyolxauhqui's mother, had become pregnant with Huitzilopochtli through the intervention of magical feathers. Coatlicue's jealous children planned to kill her before the powerful Huitzilopochtli could be born, but in a pre-emptive strike he emerged fully formed and wielding his flaming fire-serpent or *xiuhcoatl*. Huitzilopochtli cut off Coyolxauhqui's head and threw her dismembered body to the base of Coatepec before routing his brothers. Now established as the most powerful of all gods, he eventually led his people to the old Toltec city of Tula, and from there to the valley of Mexico where they founded their island capital of Tenochtitlán in the middle of Lake Texcoco.

Aztec creation myths established the nature of the universe, justified royal prerogatives and the social order, and sanctified the age-old Mesoamerican practice of human sacrifice, but on a grander scale. Ancestor worship, fertility rites and sacred warfare were all part of the mythology which gave structure and meaning to Aztec civilisation.

RELIGION AND WORLDVIEW

It was religion which brought the meanings of mythology into everyday life, and fleshed out its ideological framework in rituals and ceremonies. Aztec religion became suitably imperial in its aims, and featured a sophisticated calendar of ritual festivals during which the powerful and complex gods were venerated alongside the reigning emperor.

In Aztec belief, the land was full of spiritual force and animated by the power of ancestors. This was the concept known in Nahuatl, the Aztec language, as *teotl*. This wide-ranging and nebulous idea of sacred power characterises Aztec gods and flows between them, their ritual costumes, those who impersonated them during sacrifices and rituals, and their statues and images. It was also a feature of the natural world, resident in mountains, lakes, clouds and the animals and plants of the Aztec world. From the smallest mineral fragment to the largest snow-capped volcano and the most dangerous animal predators, such as the jaguar, crocodile, eagle and serpent, the mysterious power of *teotl* was ever present. Jade was seen as a glistening precious stone whose greenness engendered growth in nearby plants; turquoise was equally precious and beloved of the gods to whom it belonged, while the milkiness of quartz crystal made it the ideal tool for sorcerers who could see the past and divine the future in its lucid depths.

The same power manifested itself in the jaguar which was considered noble, wise and proud and the lord of the animal kingdom. Those born under the calendrical sign of the jaguar shared this power and thus the animal's characteristics. *Teotl* was thus the Aztec term given to a spiritually animated universe which was a fundamental quality of the indigenous worldview throughout the Americas. The pervasiveness of *teotl* linked the physical world with the sacred, endowing geographical places with numinous power. This was particularly evident in Aztec views of the celestial sphere. In Aztec worldview (sometimes called cosmovision), celestial phenomena were seen as inseparable from earthly events, the two being expressed through the ceremonies of the Aztec calendar.

As with all Mesoamerican societies, Aztec astronomers were also priests. They saw the sun, moon, planets and stars as divine and as exercising power over human lives on earth. They measured the movements of the celestial bodies to maintain the accuracy of their two calendars, one secular, the other sacred. Their interest in astronomy was essentially astrological, using their knowledge to predict the future and discover the will of the gods. They observed the Milky Way, invented their own constellations, and tracked the movements of the planet Venus. They measured the rising and setting of sun, moon and stars on the horizon and calculated their positions in relation to nearby mountains. They also predicted eclipses, and feared the unexpected and unpredictable arrival of comets and meteors.

The purpose of Aztec astronomy was to regulate their version of the ancient Mesoamerican two-calendar system. The everyday calendar (*xiuhpohualli*) had 365 days, and was divided into 18 months of 20 days each, the extra 5 days, known as the *nemonteni*, being regarded as particularly unlucky. The smaller religious calendar (*tonalpohualli*) had 260 days, and was divided into 13 months of 20 days each. The two calendars fitted together like cogwheels, and produced a different date every day for 52 years before starting again – the so-called 'calendar round'.

The end of a 52-year calendar period was a time of danger and uncertainty. People kept silent, refused to eat and extinguished their fires. The new 52-year period was celebrated by the New Fire ceremony, whose timing was calculated by the astronomer-priests. As the star group known as the Pleiades passed overhead, the sun rose, and fire was sparked in the chest of a sacrificial victim. Warriors lit their torches in the fire and carried them to Tenochtitlán to rekindle the temple fires, and begin the world anew.

Time itself was sacred. It was divided into hours, days, weeks, months and ultimately the 52-year calendar round. Each unit of time had a patron deity whose influence determined whether it was good or bad for different kinds of activity. Some dates were good for childbirth, others for planting and harvesting, while other times were avoided in trade and warfare. In the religious calendar (*tonalpohualli*), Aztec 'weeks' lasted 13 days, with each week controlled by a different god. Each of the 20 days that made up a month was also identified with a god. Days named after the rabbit (*tochtli*) were controlled by Mayahuel the goddess of the alcoholic drink made from the maguey plant. Those born on Rabbit days were doomed to live a miserable drunken life.

Astronomical knowledge and mythological beliefs determined the shape, size and artistic decoration of Aztec material culture. Temples were built to align with prominent mountains, and positioned to take advantage of sunrise and sunset. Tenochtitlán's Great Temple was designed so that on the spring equinox (21 March) the sun could be seen to rise between the two shrines of Huitzilopochtli and Tlaloc. In this way, the celestial bodies in the sky merged with earthly landscapes and architecture through ritual and ceremony to produce an integrated and holistic view of life and death. Perhaps nowhere is Aztec cosmovision seen to better effect than in the Great Temple at Tenochtitlán.

Discovered in 1978 in downtown Mexico City, a great stone disc carved came to light. Its decoration portrayed an image of the Aztec moon goddess Coyolxauhqui. Subsequent archaeological excavations discovered the remains of seven Great Temples, whose imposing stairways were stacked one inside the other. The earliest temple had two shrines, one to Tlaloc the other to Huitzilopochtli, and a painted sculpture of a reclining figure (Chac Mool) holding a dish for sacrificed hearts. Altogether, the temple precinct had seventy-eight buildings, including a skull-rack (*tzompantli*), a temple of the Eagle Warriors, and almost a hundred burials of human skulls, animal bones, sculptures and pottery effigies sacrificed to the gods, especially Tlaloc.

The Great Temple was a stepped pyramid, known as a *teocalli* (god house) to the Aztecs. It was begun in AD 1325, was aligned with two sacred volcanoes nearby, and regarded as the great cosmic water-mountain (*altepetl*) at the centre of the universe. On its summit, as we have seen, were shrines to the rain god Tlaloc and the war god Huitzilopochtli. It was here that human sacrifices took place, re-enacting the epic events of the Aztec myth of the birth of Huitzilophochtli at the Serpent Mountain of Coatepec.

The Gods

The Aztec pantheon was full of dazzling gods, both male and female, some of whom appeared as supernatural characters in the creation myths. Although it can look as though the Aztecs have an endless number of deities, each with different costumes and powers, in fact they are closely related. Aztec gods wore many disguises but shared a common divinity through *teotl*. They were concerned with different aspects of life, though the main gods represented the powerful forces of nature. There were gods of wind, fire and water, of childbirth, disease and misfortune, as well as of the sun, moon and stars. There were, however, four main deities, Huitzilopochtli, Tlaloc, Quetzalcoatl and Tezcatlipoca.

Huitzilopochtli and Tlaloc were special gods for the Aztecs, and each was worshipped in his own shrine on the summit of the Great Temple. Huitzilopochtli's shrine was painted blood red, Tlaloc's green – the two cosmic colours that represented the symbolic connections between blood and water in Mesoamerica.

Huitzilopochtli was the Aztec tribal war god, a cosmic warrior armed with his magical 'fire serpent' (*xiuhcoatl*). It was he who had guided the Aztecs to Lake Texcoco in the valley of Mexico, where they founded their city of Tenochtitlán, and honoured him as the sun through war and human sacrifice. Huitzilopochtli's name means Hummingbird of the South and refers to the souls of fallen warriors that were transformed into hummingbirds. A uniquely Aztec god, in the codices he is seen wearing the hummingbird's feathers on his left leg. He was identified with sacred warfare and death, and as a hero figure reborn as a god during the migrations to the valley of Mexico.

Alongside Huitzilopochtli on the summit of the Great Temple was Tlaloc, an ancient Mesoamerican deity who represented water and fertility. Tlaloc sent the rains that made the crops and flowers grow. His cosmic dwelling place was Tlalocan, conceived by the Aztecs as a paradise which shimmered with sunlight, jewels and rich vegetation, and which was the final resting place of the disabled, those killed by lightning and those who had drowned. In his rain-bringing activities, Tlaloc was aided by his supernatural assistants, the *tlaloques*.

Quetzalcoatl, whose name means the Feathered Serpent, was also an ancient deity, assimilated and reinvigorated by the Aztecs. He was a benevolent god of learning, the patron of twins and the priesthood, and inventor of the calendar. He often appears disguised as Ehecatl the wind god.

Tezcatlipoca, Lord of the Smoking Mirror, was the most powerful Aztec god. He was the Master of Sorcerers, patron of Aztec royalty and inventor of human sacrifice. An omnipotent deity, he saw everything that happened in the world by wielding his magic obsidian mirror. Invisible but ever-present, he inspired such fear that the Aztecs described themselves as his slaves.

Other Aztec gods were more directly associated with specific aspects of sacrifice and agricultural fertility. Xipe Totec, Our Lord the Flayed One, was the god of springtime, who wore the skin of a victim sacrificed in his honour. As the skin dried and fell away, the Aztecs believed it encouraged the newborn maize cob to burst forth from its crinkled leaves. The urge to grow was itself characterised as the goddess Chicomecoatl, who is shown wearing maize cobs, and the youngest sweetest corn was represented by Xilonen, a young and tender woman. Also associated with growth and regeneration was Xochipilli (Prince of Flowers) and Xochiquetzal (Flower Quetzal), the eternally young and desirable goddess of pregnancy and motherhood and of weaving. Chalchiuhtlicue (She of the Jade Skirt) was the consort of Tlaloc, a female deity of lakes and streams and, by analogy, the goddess of human fertility and the breaking waters of childbirth.

SOCIETY

Aztec society was class-based and characterised by the rights, privileges, costumes and insignia of each class. At the top was the sacred emperor, known as the Huey Tlatoani, or First Speaker. The most powerful person in Aztec society, he ruled as the divine representative of the supreme god Tezcatlipoca. In customary Aztec fashion, the emperor's position was not inherited but achieved through election by a council of nobles from the most able men in the royal family.

Once chosen, each new emperor underwent a long series of colourful rituals which included a Coronation War to prove his military abilities, and a final confirmation ceremony. The Florentine Codex describes these events, especially the emperor making ritualised speeches to Tezcatlipoca in which he asked for strength and guidance. Once crowned, the new emperor was carried on the jaguar-and-eagle throne to the Great Temple where he pierced his body with a jaguar claw in a blood offering that tied him forever to the gods.

Aztec rulers had an intimate if ambiguous relationship with their patron deity Tezcatlipoca who was also the inventor of human blood sacrifice. Emperors, like nobles and commoners, were expected to shed their blood in honour of the gods. The famous stone monument known as the Dedication Stone, dating to AD 1487, shows the emperor Ahuitzotl and his predecessor, the emperor Tizoc, bleeding from their legs and piercing their ears with spikes that sends blood flowing into the earth. This scene appears to be one way in which Ahuitzotl's ascension to the throne was legitimated. Although emperors lived in great luxury in palaces that resembled small towns, they had to prove themselves on the battlefield to protect and extend the empire. The emperor was, ultimately, the commander-in-chief of the Aztec armies, and the most successful rulers were all great military leaders, such as Itzcoatl, Moctezuma I (Ilhuicamina), and Ahuitzotl.

Beneath the emperor came the nobility, who constituted the top 10 per cent of Aztec society. Their position was acquired less through inheritance than by achieving high status through individual actions. Aztec lords were known as *tecuhtli* and included the empire's pre-eminent administrators and the royal families of conquered cities. They are often shown, as in the Codex Mendoza, wearing their distinctive cloaks and seated on reed thrones, the traditional seat of authority in ancient Mesoamerica.

The nobility were given official residences from whose lands they drew their livelihood. The sons of Aztec lords were born into a junior class of nobles known as the *pipiltin*, from the ranks of which the emperor selected many of his high officials. Belonging to the *pipiltin* class was no guarantee of achieving wealth or honour, however. The children of nobles attended exclusive schools known as *calmecac*. The aim was to educate the next generation of leaders in government, the priesthood and the army. It was in the *calmecac* that the Aztec virtues of self-discipline and obedience were instilled. Students learnt about the gods, ceremonial life, astronomy and warfare. By the time they left they had become fully trained warriors.

Beneath the nobility were the commoners, or *macehualtin*, who made up the majority of society. They could achieve noble status if they acted with distinction, especially by performing acts of bravery in war. The *macehualtin* were divided into hereditary clans known as *calpulli* which themselves were organised into units of 20 families arranged in groups of 100 households. Each *calpulli* had its own school and temple and was controlled by a leader elected for life. The children of the *macehualtin* attended schools called *telpochcalli*, where girls and boys were taught separately and discipline was strict. They learnt how to dance, sing and play music for the many religious rituals in which they would participate as adults. Boys learned how to build roads and repair temples but mainly were instructed in the skills of war. A special and perhaps distinctively Aztec class were the long distance merchants known as *Pochteca*. They undertook trade beyond the empire's borders and also served as government spies. They were organised into guilds, lived communally and worshipped their own god called Yacatecuhtli. Their trading caravans travelled widely across Mesoamerica, exchanging gold, obsidian and crystal for exotic local items such as jaguar skins, seashells, bird plumage and cacao beans. Sometimes, a *pochteca* trading venture was a prelude to war, and because of this it was a dangerous occupation.

At the bottom of society were the slaves, or *tlacotin*, though Aztec civilisation was not based on their labour. Nobody was born into slavery, and estimates derived from historical sources suggest they comprised perhaps only 2 per cent of the population. Their work was unpaid, but they enjoyed free food and shelter. The main slave market was at the old Tepanec capital of Azcapotzalco, and here men and women from all over Mexico could be bought and sold. While some slaves were convicted criminals, others sold themselves into slavery for limited periods to clear their debts. There was no stigma attached to being a slave and some were able to achieve high status, own land and even acquire slaves of their own. It was even possible for a male slave to marry his master's wife if she became widowed. The mother of the great emperor Itzcoatl was a slave.

Everyday life in Aztec society is best described in the hybrid Aztec-Spanish book known as the Codex Mendoza which was written some twenty years after the Spanish conquest. Its vivid paintings in Aztec style have accompanying Spanish captions and take us on an intimate journey through life in Tenochtitlán.

Childbirth was a time of joy and danger, both physically and spiritually. Babies were delivered by professional midwives who prayed to Chalchiuhtlicue, the goddess of fertility and motherhood. If the baby was a boy, the umbilical cord was given to warriors to bury on a battlefield, and if a girl, it was placed beneath the hearth in the parents' home, symbolising her future domestic duties. A newborn baby's name was chosen after parental consultation with priests who determined the supernatural influences associated with the time and date of birth. If the birthdate was judged lucky, the baby was named the following day, if unlucky, another, more auspicious date was chosen. Soon after birth, babies were given miniature symbols of their future adult life. Some boys were presented with a warrior's shield, others a goldsmith's tool, while girls had a broom or a spindle full of cotton thread. Boys and girls were welcomed equally into Aztec families and were described in loving terms as 'precious necklaces' or 'beautiful feathers'.

Children stayed at home until they started school at fifteen. Parents taught sons to ferry canoes full of reeds around the capital's canals, while girls learned to spin cotton and prepare meals. Family discipline was harsh. If caught lying, boys could be beaten or have their bodies pierced by thorns, while girls were forced to inhale chilli smoke.

Most Aztec men were married by their early twenties, though girls usually before they were fifteen. Long negotiations with a prospective partner's parents and priests were carried on by elderly women serving as matchmakers. Once a favourable date had been calculated, the marriage ceremony began with feasting in the bride's house, after which the bride was carried in a torch-lit procession to her husband's house, where she sat on a reed mat with her husband and they tied their robes together.

Aztec men could have more than one wife, though they had to be able to support them. Commoners could usually only afford one wife, but nobles often had more. Nevertheless, there could only ever be one principal wife who controlled all the others. Political marriages between the emperor and the ruling families of other cities were one way of forging strategic diplomatic alliances. Adultery was punished with death by stoning or strangulation, though divorce was possible for men and women if the marriage failed.

Aztec society was primarily agricultural, though many people also engaged in informal exchange of goods and services and in making pottery, textiles and sometimes paper from tree bark. The basis of much agriculture in the valley of Mexico was the *chinampa* system, often erroneously called 'floating gardens'. This ancient method of hydraulic agriculture produced fertile garden plots by dredging up mud and plants from the lake floor to create artificial islands separated by canals. Kept in place by willow trees, the rich soil that developed was used to grow flowers, chillis, tomatoes, maize and many other plants. All agricultural activity was done by hand as there were neither horses nor cattle in Mesoamerica until the Spanish arrived.

The staple food was maize (*Zea mays*), ground into flour and baked as the flat bread known as tortillas, or steamed then stuffed with vegetables and meat, and known as *tamales*. Tomatoes, chillis, rabbit, deer and turkey were eaten, as was a hairless breed of dog. Insect eggs and water fly larvae were considered delicacies, and chocolate was drunk by the higher classes. The main alcoholic drink was *pulque* made from the ubiquitous maguey plant. Although most of our information comes from the great urban metropolis of Tenochtitlán and its lake environment, recent investigations have shed light on life in rural areas.

Examination of the sites of the two small farming villages of Capilco and Cuexcomate indicate that in late Aztec times population was increasing and more land was being irrigated to grow more food. Surplus food was traded for salt, obsidian and expensive, beautifully painted pottery. Somewhat larger was the local city of Yautepec which grew to around 2.1sq. km in the years before the Spanish arrival. Although individual houses were not much larger than those at Cuexcomate, arts and crafts were more developed. Yautepec's population included specialist obsidian workers making blades and tools, potters making clay figurines and others manufacturing cotton textiles and jewellery.

WAR AND EMPIRE

Warfare

Ancient Mexican warfare was different in several fundamental respects from its European equivalent. The Aztecs, like their contemporaries in Mesoamerica, did not wage war primarily to conquer and integrate territory, or convert the defeated to their own religion. Their motivation was rather to defeat their enemies then impose tribute on them, and to capture prisoners for later sacrifice to the gods. Administering conquered areas was expensive and impractical so the Aztecs ruled indirectly through local chiefs and by political marriage alliances. The reward for this approach was the fabulous wealth which poured into Tenochtitlán. Battlefield killing, laying waste to the land, and destroying towns was self-defeating to this end. Exceptions occurred, however. Death in war was frequent and towns were sometimes destroyed and their populations slaughtered to serve as a warning to others.

The common motif for victory was a glyph which showed a temple with its straw roof tilted upward and burning – symbolising Aztec conquest. This was also a visual statement of the superiority of Aztec gods over those of the conquered, the statues and images of which were taken to Tenochtitlán and kept as symbolic hostages.

Dressed in elaborate and often impractical costumes and headdresses, Aztec warriors fought vicious hand-to-hand battles, with superior numbers often deciding the outcome. Brave and esteemed warriors were those who captured rather than killed the most opponents. For those who did die in battle, the Aztecs believed that their souls transformed into shimmering butterflies and hummingbirds. Aztec warriors had no advantage in weapons or tactics over their enemies. The nobility wore body armour of quilted cotton and carried round shields decorated with feather mosaic or inlaid with gold and turquoise. Weapons were basic but effective and included the javelin, bow, sling, and a 1m long wooden sword inset with sharp obsidian barbs known as *maquahuitl*.

Aztec warfare was a sacred act, halfway between combat and sacrifice. Always at the forefront of battle were the elite cadres known as the Jaguar Warriors and the Eagle Warriors. They wore costumes designed to mimic their animal patrons and to intimidate their enemies. The hearts and bodies of their victims were offered up to the war god Huitzilopochtli. These warriors also played an important role in sacrifical rituals, some of which took the form of gladiatorial combat. Here, a fully armed Jaguar Warrior fought a captive bound to a great stone and armed with a sword decorated with feathers. The role of the Jaguar and Eagle Warriors is commemorated at the rock-cut temple of Malinalco high in the mountains southwest of Tenochtitlán. The shrine's entrance is carved in the shape of a giant serpent, and at the base of the stairway stand two stone jaguar statues. Inside, there is a semi-circular stone bench from which emerges the sculpted head of a jaguar, its paws flanked by two eagles with a third eagle sculpture in the centre of the floor.

War was a defining reality to the Aztecs. As we have seen, Aztec boys were trained in the martial arts from the age of fifteen, and dedicated themselves to the god Tezcatlipoca, the master of a warrior's fate. The symbolism of war pervaded many aspects of Aztec society: the rubber-ball game mixed symbols of war and death with cosmic themes, indicating that even this public game could end in death as a kind of ritual warfare. Carved stone monuments, such as the Stone of Tizoc, also commemorated warfare. This example records the emperor Tizoc's imperial victories and shows him taking captive the rulers of fifteen regions whose names are engraved in glyphs. In typical Aztec fashion, Tizoc grasps the hair of his opponents as a sign of victory.

The distinctiveness of Aztec warfare is illustrated by the special kind of conflict known as the 'War of Flowers' or *xochiyaoyotl*. This name refers to the colourful costumes of the warriors, and is a metaphorical analogy for their fall in battle – like a shower of blossoms. These battles took place not for conquest but in order to capture prisoners for sacrifice to the gods. Flower wars were regularly fought with the cities of Tlaxcala and Cholula, as their inhabitants spoke the Aztec language Nahuatl, and consequently their war captives were considered especially valuable as sacrifices. Priests watched these battles, and once they decided enough prisoners had been taken hostilities were ended.

Empire

When the Aztecs arrived in the valley of Mexico during the thirteenth century AD they were only one of several migrant groups. They had left their homeland of Aztlán during the early years of the twelfth century and arrived on the western shores of Lake Texcoco at the place known then, and today, as Chapultepec, famed for its fresh-water springs. After a confused period, for which our sources are a mix of myth, history and propaganda, the Aztecs confronted an alliance of Tepanecs led by the cities of Azcapotzalco and Culhuacan. Although they suffered a disastrous defeat, some survivors eventually asked for help from the ruler at Culhuacan and were granted inhospitable volcanic land at nearby Tizaapan. The Aztecs served their Culhua masters well in a war against the people of Xochimilco and began calling themselves Culhua-Mexica as they became acculturated to the sophisticated city-dwelling lifestyle of the area, and the ancestral prestige of the Toltec civilisation began to attach itself to them.

Despite the apparent success of the Culhua-Mexica integration, the Aztec priests of Huitzilopochtli then caused a sensation. They prompted their leaders to ask Achitometl, one of the Culhua leaders, for his daughter to be the ritual 'wife of Huitzilopochtli'. Unware of the nature of the honour, Achitometl granted the request whereupon his daughter was sacrificed to the god and her skin worn by one of his priests. Achitometl was outraged and the Aztecs banished once again, making their way by canoe to a group of small islands in Lake Texcoco. In all probability this event is a stylised account of Aztec beliefs concerning ceremonial marriages with female earth deities as a way of becoming a settled agricultural people.

One of Huitzilopochtli's priests then had a vision in which he saw an eagle perched on a nopal cactus and which he interpreted as a divine sign from the god that this would be the place where the Aztecs should build their city. Perhaps not surprisingly, the eagle was soon spotted, and the Aztecs built a simple reed temple, the first of the many Great Temples. In this way, in the Aztec year 2-House (either AD 1325 or 1345 in the Western calendar), Tenochtitlán was founded. This event is graphically commemorated on the carved stone monument known as the Teocalli Stone.

The Aztecs set about establishing their position in the valley of Mexico, especially through trading relationships with their neighbours. They approached the rulers of Culhuacan and, in AD 1375, the mixed-blood Mexica/Culhua lord Acamapichtli was invited and became the new Aztec ruler. In the years that followed, the Aztec leaders intermarried with the nobility of neighbouring cities, and forged increasingly close ties with the Tepanec city of Azcapotzalco, especially during the fifty-year rule of the great Tepanec ruler Tezozomoc.

Although the Aztecs paid tribute to the Tepanecs, they also learned much that would help them in their own rise to power. Tezozomoc allowed the Aztecs to participate in military conquests as a form of tribute payment and later also to make conquests in their own right. Alone, or with the Tepanecs, the Aztecs conquered the rich agricultural *chinampa*-based towns in the south-eastern part of the valley of Mexico, as well as Xaltocan, and the valley of Puebla. In AD 1417, the newly installed Aztec ruler Chimalpopoca remained loyal to the Tepanecs when they were attacked by Ixtlilxochitl, the new ruler of the city of Texcoco, despite being his father in law. In a series of hard-fought battles the Aztec-Tepanec coalition prevailed, Ixtlilxochitl was killed, and the Aztecs received Texcoco as a tribute city. In just a few years, the Aztecs had transformed themselves from tribute-payers to the Tepanecs to equal partners, and tribute collectors in their own right.

Tezozomoc died soon after, and was succeeded by his less astute son Maxtla. Political intrigues followed, during which Chimalpopoca was killed, and a new *tlatoani* elected. Yet this was no ordinary change of ruler. While Itzcoatl became the new Aztec *tlatoani*, he was but part of a powerful triumvirate which included the future emperor Moctezuma I (Ihuilcamina) and his brother the extraordinary Tlacaelel who would serve as *cihuacoatl* ('Snake Woman') for sixty years as advisor to five successive emperors. Between them, these three devised a strategy to break free of their Tepanec masters, though struggled to convince Tenochtitlán's commoners that they could win a battle with their powerful overlords.

It was Tlacaelel who precipitated events by declaring war during a diplomatic embassy to Maxtla. In Tenochtitlán, it seems that the three leaders made a bargain with the still understandably edgy population. If the war was won, the people would serve their leaders in every conceivable way, but if lost then the leaders would offer themselves up for retribution. As this bargain was being struck, Nezahualcoyotl, the son of the murdered Ixtlilxochitl of Texcoco, and Itzcoatl's nephew, appeared. He had fled Texcoco and taken refuge in the city of Huexotzingo after Maxtla had unsuccessfully tried to have him killed. Itzcoatl meanwhile had sent an embassy to Huexotzingo asking for military help against Maxtla.

Nezahualcoyotl saw his chance. Together with the Aztecs and the former Tepanec town of Tlacopan/Tacuba, he led a mixed force of his own Texcocan warriors and Huexotzingan allies in an attack on the Tepanec capital of Azcapotzalco. After a long siege, the armies of the newly formed Triple Alliance of Tenochtitlán, Texcoco and Tlacopan broke through the city's defences and Maxtla was captured by Nezahualcoyotl. In typical Mexican fashion, Maxtla was sacrificed in front of the richly arrayed allied armies by having his heart cut out by Nezahualcoyotl, the blood scattered to the four cardinal points, and then the body treated to the funeral rites due to a ruler.

Maxtla's ritual sacrifice achieved many ends: it signalled the collapse of Tepanec rule over central Mexico; claimed Tepanec lands for the Triple Alliance; and symbolically fertilised the earth and regenerated society through the shedding of royal blood. Tenochtitlán and Texcoco became autonomous city-states, dominating the junior ally of Tlacopan in the Triple Alliance. It was, however, the redistribution of formerly Tepanec lands among the allies and within Aztec society that brought the greatest changes. At this critical juncture, social hierarchy was embodied in the differential ownership of land, with the *tlatoani* and nobility owning the largest share, and the smallest portions being awarded to the *calplulli* and which were in turn worked by individual families. Land could be given to warriors as a reward for outstanding service, and royal palaces and temples also owned their own lands.

The defeat of Azcapotzalco was thus a turning point for the Aztecs, politically, economically and also symbolically. Tenochtitlán was the dominant member of the Triple Alliance, and soon their ideas of conquest and tribute spread out beyond the valley of Mexico. As the Aztecs became more overtly imperial, they developed an accompanying ideology which saw an explosion of spectacular public ceremonies, systems of alliance, tribute, grand mythologies, and sophisticated art and architecture welded together.

The Triple Alliance's first major conquest beyond the valley of Mexico was the agriculturally rich lowland area controlled by the town of Cuahnahuac (modern Cuernavaca) to the south. After this successful venture, a complex tribute system was devised whereby participating allies could receive tribute from towns located within another ruler's area. When Moctezuma Ilhuicamina succeeded Itzcoatl in 1440, a period of political consolidation began before new military conquests were undertaken. When military action was resumed, it was against the people of Chalco and then, in 1458, against the Mixtecs and their town of Coixtlahuaca which barred the way to the rich lands of Oaxaca further south. The Codex Mendoza records the tribute imposed on Coixtlahuaca after the Aztec victory – it includes greenstone jewellery, gold dust, cochineal dye, green feathers and woven blankets. This practice was followed in subsequent conquests by Moctezuma in the humid tropics of eastern Mexico and by 1469, when Moctezuma died, vast quantities of tribute wealth were pouring into the Aztec capital.

Moctezuma was succeeded by Axayacatl. During his thirteen-year reign, Tenochtitlán's sister city of Tlatelolco rebelled but was mercilessly defeated, its lands taken and tribute levied. Axayacatl led victorious campaigns to the west of the valley of Mexico between 1475 and 1478, but then suffered a disastrous defeat at the hands of the Tarascans whose lands lay further west in what today is the state of Michoacan. Of an invasion force of some thirty-two thousand Triple Alliance warriors only about two thousand returned home.

Axayacatl died in 1481 and was replaced by his brother Tizoc who proved to be a less than successful military commander. After an inconclusive battle against the town of Metztitlan and the putting down of rebellions, there was a sense that the empire and the tribute upon which it depended were at a critical impasse. In 1486, Tizoc was assassinated and replaced by his brother Ahuitzotl, a fearless and brilliant warrior who soon stamped his authority on the army and empire, ruthlessly suppressing rebellious towns and reimposing tribute. In 1487, after a punitive expedition against the towns of Mexico's Gulf Coast, Ahuitzotl devised a propaganda coup to coincide with the rededication of the Great Temple in Tenochtitlán.

Tens of thousands of prisoners of war lined the streets of the capital and in front of an invited audience of foreign rulers and ambassadors they were sacrificed one by one in a bloody ceremony that lasted four days. Heart sacrifice had become a political tool for intimidation and control, and Ahuitzotl identified himself ever more closely with Huitzilopochtli the Aztec tribal war god seen as a cosmic warrior. In the wake of this defining event, the empire expanded at an increasing pace, with civic and religious architecture now built in newly conquered areas, such as Malinalco to the west and Tepoztlan to the south. Such buildings were a statement of Aztec imperial presence. However, unlike the Inkas in Peru, the Aztecs' lack of a sophisticated and specialist bureaucracy meant that stable political integration of conquered regions into a true state-level empire never really occurred.

In 1502, the last true Aztec emperor came to power. Moctezuma II (Xocoyotzin) was clearly not the inspirational and ferocious military figure that his predecessor had been, though he was a highly accomplished warrior-leader. He made sweeping reforms to keep the support of the nobility – an indication perhaps of his less than sure grip on political power within Tenochtitlán. Sumptuary laws were instituted that marked out the nobles by virtue of the costumes and jewellery only they were allowed to wear. Elaborate ritual behaviour in court ceremonial was enforced, and he replaced Ahuitzotl's faction with his own. Under this second Moctezuma, the empire was consolidated and expanded, though bitter conflicts with the cities of Tlaxcala and Huexotzingo were a military stalemate and led to deep-rooted rivalries that saw these two communities flock to the Spanish banner when Cortés invaded.

THE SPANISH CONQUEST

The Spanish conquistador Hernán Cortés arrived on Mexico's eastern shore on Good Friday 1519. He had sailed from Cuba with 500 soldiers and headed first for the Maya island of Cozumel off the Yucatan peninsula. Here he had rescued Gerónimo de Aguilar, a Spaniard who had been stranded several years before and who now spoke fluent Yucatec Maya. This providential event was reinforced a little later when local leaders at Potonchan gave him a noblewoman called Malintzin (known to history as Malinche), who spoke Maya and the Aztec language Nahuatl. Malintzin subsequently became Cortés's mistress and had a son by him.

When the Spanish landed near to modern-day Veracruz they were met by ambassadors sent by the Aztec emperor Moctezuma II who presented Cortés with gifts of gold, feathers and semi-precious minerals such as greenstones. The ambassadors were forced to witness what to them must have appeared the magical effects of

Spanish arquebus and cannon before being allowed to report back to Moctezuma.

Over the coming months, which he spent exploring the region and impressing the local Totonac peoples, Cortés gathered intelligence about the Aztecs and their imperial capital of Tenochtitlán. He quickly realised that Aztec demands for tribute made their subject peoples bitterly resentful, and that here was a ready-made army of Indian allies. The Spanish set off for the Aztec realm, picking up several thousand more supporters from the city of Tlaxcala, a traditional enemy of the Aztecs. From here he went to the sacred city of Cholula and, despite receiving more gift-bearing embassies from Moctezuma en route, pressed on toward Tenochtitlán.

When this impressive force of Europeans and Indians finally crossed over into the valley of Mexico, the Spanish were astonished by what they saw. Hardly able to believe they were not dreaming, they gazed with incredulity at a vast lake system around whose shores were dotted many large towns, and in whose centre lay the great island metropolis of Tenochtitlán connected to the mainland by great causeways. The lake was full of canoes and Tenochtitlán's temples shimmered in the sunlight. Moctezuma welcomed Cortés on the great southern causeway and placed a glittering necklace of gold and semi-precious stones around the Spaniard's neck. He led the Spanish back into the city whose streets and roofs were crowded with people eager for a view of these strangers and their even stranger animals. Moctezuma housed Cortés and his men in the palace of his father Axayacatl surrounded by the shrines and statues of his gods.

Although both men were initially polite and reverential to each other they were clearly testing each other's nature and resolve. Cortés acted first, taking Moctezuma prisoner, but giving the impression to the populace that the emperor still ruled the city. In April 1520, news arrived that a new Spanish fleet now lay off the coast with orders from Cuba's governor Diego de Velásquez to arrest Cortés for disobeying an earlier order to return and not invade Mexico. Cortés wasted no time, and took half his force back to the coast where he defeated the newcomers and persuaded the soldiers to join his cause.

While Cortés was thus engaged, his lieutenant Pedro de Alvardo who had been left in charge of Tenochtitlán, had provoked an Aztec rebellion by massacring those who were preparing human sacrifices in honour of their god Huitzilopochtli. Events moved quickly.

Cortés was able to fight his way back into the palace where his comrades were beseiged, but Moctezuma had by now lost the trust of his people. He was replaced as emperor by his brother Cuitlahuac and soon afterwards killed, though by whom is not known.

Cortés organised his men for a breakout, and on the night of 30 June 1520 the Spanish made their move. Many were laden down with stolen treasure and perished, and much gold was lost to the lake as they retreated along the causeway – harried mercilessly by Aztec warriors. This disastrous escape was called the *noche triste* ('night of sorrows') by the Spanish.

After reorganising his troops at the friendly city of Tlaxcala, Cortés and some seventy thousand Indian allies attacked Tenochtitlán again in 1521. Disease carried by their European enemy had meanwhile broken out in the city and, combined with famine, served to undermine the strength of the Aztecs. After several months of seige, during which Cuitlahuac died of smallpox and a new emperor Cuauhtemoc was appointed, the Aztec capital fell, its inhabitants slaughtered by Cortés's Tlaxcallan allies. The effects of European disease, against which native Mexicans had no immunity, together with the desire of other Indian nations to throw off the shackles of Aztec tribute combined to make the ultimate fate of the Aztecs all but inevitable. This was reinforced by Cortés's political astuteness in taking advantage of disaffected Indian peoples, and by Moctezuma's hesitation at confronting the Spanish before they had advanced into the valley of Mexico.

This strategic mistake by Moctezuma was subsequently explained in post-conquest accounts that sought to justify his otherwise inexplicable actions. In versions written down by the Spanish during interviews with the surviving nobility and priests, it was said that Moctezuma believed Cortés to be the returning god Quetzalcoatl in their year called 1-Reed (i.e. 1519). A series of prophecies was also elaborated after the event, explaining how strange portents such as temples burning and the finding of a bird in Lake Texcoco with a mirror inset into its head all predicted the end of the Aztec era.

LEGACY OF CONQUEST

The Aztec capital of Tenochtitlán and its sprawling tribute-empire collapsed in 1521. However, the Aztecs themselves and the other indigenous peoples of Mesoamerica did not just fade from history.

The Aztec state may have collapsed, but indigenous ideas and beliefs continued to flourish in a bewildering mosaic of native accommodations to the new economic and religious order imposed by the Spanish during the colonial period.

In the years following 1521, the Spanish conversion of Mesoamerica's native peoples proceeded apace, but was often more apparent than real. Trial records for 1536 to 1540 reveal that such pre-Columbian customs as concubinage, idolatry and human sacrifice were still being practised. In 1565, the Spanish bishops of Mexico City were complaining how easily the natives reverted back to their pre-conquest rituals, hiding idols behind altars in newly built churches, partaking of hallucinogens, and invoking ancient colour symbolism. Franciscan fathers regarded Tezcatlipoca not only as the chief Aztec deity, but also as Lucifer whose malign influence they saw everywhere at work among the indigenous peoples.

During the post-conquest years, native Mesoamerican and Christian ideas mingled, producing a syncretic worldview that borrowed equally from both. Christianity was being changed – reconfigured, revitalised and re-presented by indigenous peoples. These complex developments were often invisible to contemporary Spanish eyes, at least in the subtleties of their symbolism. The unusually perceptive priest Diego Durán was an exception, admitting that the Spanish understood nothing of what was going on all around them, not even when the Indians worshipped idols in their presence.

Between 1526 and 1600, over four hundred *conventos* (monasteries) were built and decorated by native artisans in styles which drew equally on pre-Columbian and European ideas. Were these natives forced to adopt the styles of the European Renaissance, or did they incorporate pre-Columbian motifs and meanings into otherwise Christian murals and sculpture as a form of native resistance to Spanish conversion strategies?

A fascinating but complex example illustrating these cultural cross-currents are the dazzling murals at the Augustinian *convento* church of San Miguel at Ixmiquilpan north of Mexico City. Built in the 1550s, its nave was decorated with life-sized images of battling human warriors and mythical centaur-like creatures. Although rendered in an awkward European style, the protagonists are wearing only pre-Columbian dress, notably jaguar and coyote costumes that recall the elite Aztec warrior societies. Not only is there a complete absence of Christian symbolism, but severed heads, streams of blue-coloured blood and speech scrolls are all present. Many different explanations have been offered for these enigmatic murals which were whitewashed and forgotten for four hundred years before being accidentally rediscovered in 1960.

Spanish friars travelled the countryside destroying pre-Christian shrines and temples, and then erected large crosses in the centre of what would become the church forecourt. But these crosses were carved, decorated and put up by the natives under Spanish direction. Their size and vivid sculptural style were proof that ancient traditions and beliefs were thriving. On carved stone crosses, Christ became the cosmic tree of life, spilling his fertilising blood on to the sacred earth in the same way as the Aztecs and their predecessors had done. His wounds were represented by the Aztec sign for *chalchihuitl*, the precious liquid which can be both water and blood.

Magical powers were attributed to crosses placed where idols had previously stood. More overt, but apparently still not recognised by the Spanish, was the incorporation of obsidian discs at the inter-section of these large crosses, such as the one at the Franciscan convent at Taximaroa (modern Ciudad Hidalgo). While the Spanish priests admired the beauty of this decorative black stone, they appear to have been unaware that obsidian was the sacred substance of Tezcatlipoca – the very Satan they so feared.

Today, similarly, although five hundred years have passed, there are many cultural traditions and religious rituals which seem to speak in two tongues – that of Roman Catholicism, and that of ancient pre-Columbian ideas. High in the mountains of south-west Mexico is the remote village of Acatlán, founded in Aztec times, whose inhabitants still speak Nahuatl. Every year, a springtime ritual is enacted which echoes the bloody sacrifices by the Aztec Jaguar Warriors at Tenochtitlán. Young men of the village dress in jaguar costumes and fight each other in pairs on the summit of a local mountain. As the men prepare to fight, the women chant prayers to Catholic Santa Cruz, and light candles at the base of rocky shrines. The fiesta takes place in early May at the end of the dry season. The villagers believe that if they shed the potent blood of young men then the Jaguar God will be pleased and send the rains to fertilise the maize crop.

More openly syncretic and better known is Mexico's Day of the Dead or All Saints' Day celebrations that take place every year in early November. The frightening skulls and skeletons of Aztec sculpture are transformed today into miniatures made of sugar and chocolate as sweets for children. Across the country, from high sierra to tropical jungle, whole families spend the night at the graves of their loved ones which they adorn with brightly coloured flowers, a typically native gesture. Many modern Mexicans believe, as did their ancestors, that if the dead are not honoured in this way they will return to haunt the living.

The most famous and distinctive of all these hybrid Mexican-European cultural phenomena is undoubtedly the mix of Roman Catholicism and old Aztec religion in the cult of the Virgin of Guadeloupe at Tepeyac in Mexico City. This area was originally sacred to the Aztec goddess Tonantzin who was ritually addressed in prayers as Our Mother. Some believe that she was transformed into Our Lady of Guadeloupe when she appeared miraculously to a recently converted shepherd whom she asked to build her a church on that spot. Miracles followed, a chapel was built in 1555, and now hundreds of thousands make their own pilgrimages to the shrine.

South America

PART THREE

South America –
Kingdoms and Empires

SEVEN

Andean Origins and Chavín

The origins of civilisation in South America, especially in the Andean region of modern-day Peru, encompass three periods of prehistory which together span some three thousand years of cultural development. These are the Preceramic Period (3000–1800 BC), the Initial Period (1800–900 BC), and the Early Horizon (900–200 BC).

Early times: the Preceramic Period

During this comparatively short-lived period, the basic foundations of ancient Andean civilisation were laid. By this time most of the domesticated plants and animals that were to be so important to ancient Peruvian societies had appeared – the result of the long and developing relationships between people and environment during the preceding Lithic Period (12000–3000 BC). The Preceramic Period can be seen as giving rise to two kinds of cultural traditions, that of the Andean highlands and that which belonged to the desert coasts. Nevertheless, as has probably always been the case, objects, beliefs and religious and artistic influences always moved back and forth between the highlands and the coast.

The site of La Galgada is particularly significant in this respect, as it is strategically located mid-way between the coast and the tropical rainforest in the corridor route of the Tablachaca Valley in northern Peru. Here, by about 2300 BC, a ceremonial centre of two large platforms and associated smaller buildings had been constructed, and continued in use into the Early Ceramic Period c. 1200 BC. The ceremonial platforms were enlarged several times and their mud-and-stone summit temples were faced with white-painted plaster. One was clad in stone with a sunken circular court in front. A peculiar feature of both temple-sanctuaries was a central hearth fed by an underground ventilation shaft in which the burning of chillis appears to have been part of some religious ritual. The subsequent use of these chambers as crypts for the dead is an early manifestation of a later widespread practice – the dual function of such locations for ritual and as sacred tombs for the ancestors.

Archaeological investigations indicate that La Galgada depended partly on local irrigation agriculture – remains of domesticated chillis, cotton, beans and gourds have been found – and partly on exotic goods obtained through trade with peoples from other environmental areas. In several well-preserved human burials, these items included plumage of tropical forest birds, deer bone, turquoise, Spondylus shells and salt crystals. At this early time, the inhabitants of La Galgada appear not have used llama or alpaca either as pack animals or as a source of wool. The later period at the site crossed the boundary into the ceramic era and, together with pottery, the diagnostic feature of the incipient Initial Period is evident in the ceremonial U-shaped structures.

Although La Galgada was half-way between coast and mountains, it was part of the so-called Kotosh Religious Tradition which is best known from the highland sites of Shillacoto, Huaricoto, Waira-jirca and the type-site of Kotosh. These ceremonial centres are characterised by small private rooms, more suitable for limited numbers of devotees than for the large public ceremonies so typical of coastal sites. Built by local farming communities, these early centres would seem to have focused their ritual on what have been called 'fire pits' – centrally located stone-lined depressions where burnt offerings were made. These features were regularly and carefully 'buried', thereby raising the level of the new but identical structures built on top, and leading to mounds much like the tells of the Middle East.

At Kotosh, where religious activity can be detected from about 2800 BC, the most famous structure is the 'Temple of the Crossed Hands' which features two low-relief clay friezes of crossed hands belonging to the late preceramic era known as the Mito Phase. Offerings of guinea pigs and llamas have also been found in niches during excavations. Nearby is the site of Shillacoto, and further down towards the tropical rainforest is Waira-jirca which also seems to have Mito Phase buildings. Despite partaking of the same general cult beliefs and activities, the sites of the Kotosh Religious Tradition also show local variation. At Huaricoto, for example, building was not of stone and gives the impression of a less sophisticated version

Amerindian petroglyph from Trinidad. (© *Author's collection*)

Carib church at Salybia, Dominica, with mural depicting Columbus's arrival. (*Author's collection*)

Olmec crying baby ceramic figurine. *(Werner Forman and Dr Kurt Stavenhagen Collection, Mexico City)*

La Venta female figurine wearing polished iron ore mirror. (© *Werner Forman and National Museum of Anthropology, Mexico*).

Danzante figure at Monte Albán. (© *Author's collection*)

Teotihuacán funerary urn. *(© Author's collection)*

The ball court at Monte Albán. (© *Author's collection*)

Teotihuacán mural figure. (*Werner Forman and Private Collection, New York*)

Teotihuacán, Quetzalcoatl head at the Pyramid of Quetzalcoatl. *(© Author's collection)*

The Aztec Calendar Stone. *(Werner Forman and National Museum of Anthropology, Mexico City).*

Jade burial mask of Pacal from Palenque. *(Werner Forman and National Museum of Anthropology, Mexico City)*

Above: A carved-stone jaguar heart container. *(© Author's collection)*

Right: Statue of the god Xipe Totec, 'Our Lord the Flayed One'. *(Werner Forman and Museum für Völkerkunde, Basel)*

Above: Jaguar men fighting at Acatlán. *(© Author's collection)*

Left: Chavín-style pottery vessel with stirrup spout and profile face showing fangs and eye. *(© Author's collection)*

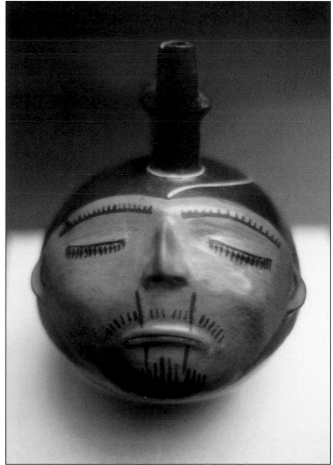

Above: Moche Sacrifice Scene depicted on a mural from Pañamarca, showing a priestess, helpers and victims. *(© Author's collection)*

Right: Nasca ceramic effigy of a trophy head. *(© Author's collection)*

Above: Nasca desert drawing of a hummingbird. *(© Author's collection)*

Left: Wari polychrome ceramic with modeled human head and feline decoration. *(© Author's collection)*

Gateway of the Sun at Tiwanaku. *(© Author's collection)*

General view of adobe-brick pyramid at El Purgatorio (Tucumé) (Sicán-Chimú-Inka; AD 1375–1533): *(© Author's collection)*

The Ponce Stela at Tiwanaku. *(© Author's collection)*

Adobe frieze at Huaca del Dragon in the Moche Valley, showing figures beneath a double-headed serpent. (© Author's collection)

The Coricancha temple to the Sun God Inti in Cuzco with the colonial monastery of Santo Domingo built on top. (© Author's collection)

Above: Inka agricultural terraces above the town of Pisac near Cuzco.
(© *Author's collection*)

Left: Inka effigy ceramic showing man carrying an aryballus on his back.
(©*Werner Forman and Museum fur Volkerkunde, Berlin*).

Fragment of a textile from Huaca Prieta (*c.* 2500–2000 BC) showing a condor with a serpent in its stomach. *(Roxanne Saunders, after M.E. Moseley,* The Maritime Foundations of Andean Civilization, *Menlo Park, 1975)*

of the other sites mentioned. Nevertheless, burnt offerings were made, including that of shells and quartz crystals.

Away from the mountains, down on the dry desert coast, an equally precocious preceramic site was that of Huaca Prieta, located at the mouth of the Chicama river. The inhabitants depended on a mix of locally grown domesticated food plants such as beans, squash and peppers, and also maritime resources obtained by collecting molluscs and fishing with nets. It was at Huaca Prieta that the tradition of incising gourds with artistic motifs first appears in Peru, though they had been made somewhat earlier in Ecuador by people of the Valdivia culture. Their decoration included abstract designs and anthropomorphic/zoomorphic faces and figures.

Huaca Prieta and La Galgada shared many aspects of material culture at this time – reed baskets and bags, gourd containers, and the basic but effective twining of cotton textiles. Here, the technical process of production highlighted geometrical shapes, and it is perhaps not surprising that abstract designs incorporating squares, straight lines, chevrons and diamonds were a characteristic of early textile art. Despite this, clearly representational designs were also made – Huaca Prieta textiles show condors, fish and double-headed serpents.

Apart from these developments, the Andean practice of constructing huge ceremonial architecture also began during the Preceramic Period. On the coast, the sites of Río Seco, Salinas de Chao, Bandurria and Aspero all belong to what archaeologists call the Aspero Tradition – ceremonial architecture that emphasises flat-topped mounds whose rituals could be observed by large numbers of people, and thus possessed a very public function. Archaeological evidence suggests that some of these sites were probably built by people from several valleys coming together to construct what in effect were corporate monuments.

Aspero itself is situated at the mouth of the Supe Valley on Peru's north coast and seems to have been thriving by about 3000 BC. Its 12ha area includes six major platforms and eleven smaller ones. Two of Aspero's monuments have been investigated archaeologically, those of Huaca de los Idolos and Huaca de los Sacrificios. Several burials have been excavated, but perhaps the most unusual discovery was a cache of thirteen figurines of unbaked clay found on the summit of Huaca de los Idolos (which takes its name from these 'idols'). All were broken, perhaps ritually smashed, and most represented women, several of whom may have been pregnant. Whether these symbolically

An early example of a Staff God with feline face engraved on a gourd from the Pativilca Valley around 2230 BC. (© *Rozanne Saunders, after J. Seagard, in J. Haas and W. Creamer 'Cultural Transformations in the Central Andean Late Archaic' in H. Silverman (ed.),* Andean Archaeology, *Blackwell, Oxford, 2004 pp. 35–50, Fig. 3.2)*

represented sacrifices, ancestors, or had been used in shamanic rituals (as is attested for later periods) is unknown.

The largest of these Preceramic Period monuments does not belong to the Aspero Cultural Tradition. El Paraiso, located just 2km from the ocean in the Chillon valley of central Peru, dates to about 2000 BC. As with other similar sites, El Paraiso extends into the early ceramic times of the Initial Period. The site covers some 58ha of the valley floor and is composed of nine main buildings all constructed of stone blocks, some 100,000 tons in total. The building technique employed collections of stones placed into fibre-net bags called *shicras* and used as fill. One estimate is that it took about 2 million labour days to erect all of El Paraiso's structures.

The U-shape appears in El Paraiso's monumental architecture. Inside some of the structures were found circular depressions whose concentration of charcoal has led to the interpretion that these were 'fire pits' used in some form of religious ritual. Other evidence includes the remains of domesticated plant foods and fish, though not in sufficient quantities to suggest that the builders were living on the site. The late preceramic date of El Paraiso – so close to the beginning of the Initial Period – suggests to some experts that it may be a site in transition, its U-shaped structures helping to usher in the new ceramic era.

By the late Preceramic Period, the coastal valleys of Peru had seen the development of large-scale architecture in huge centres with populations of between a thousand and three thousand people. These centres supported themselves on a mixed economy of agriculture and maritime resources, and clearly were co-operating across valley (and perhaps political and ethnic) boundaries in order to build such massive corporate structures as El Paraiso, as well as lesser known but equally monumental sites such as Caral in the Supe Valley.

Caral is a vast site covering 110ha of ceremonial and residential architecture and includes a nearby grouping of mounds and plazas known as Chupacigarro. It appears that the site was occupied by 2450 BC, at which time the earliest of the subsequently widespread sunken circular plazas was built. There are eight other large sites with monumental architecture in the Supe Valley (in addition to Aspero), and, together with similarly early sites from the adjacent valleys of Pativilica, Fortaleza and Huaura, are so precocious that they have been designated the Norte Chico ('Little Northern') group.

It is possible that when future investigations have cast more light on these monumental sites the early prehistory of Peru may have to be significantly reassessed. In the meantime, many experts believe that it is the high degree of social co-operation that marks out this period and that stamps itself firmly as a unique feature of early Andean civilisation that was further developed on a regional basis in later times down to the Inka period.

The Initial Period

Given a distinctive shape during the Preceramic Period, ancient Peruvian civilisation accelerated at an ever-increasing pace during the Initial Period (1800–900 BC). By just after 2000 BC, pottery appears for the first time in prehistoric Peru, though there is archaeological evidence that it had already been made for a thousand years further north in Ecuador.

Apart from the appearance of ceramics, the defining feature of the Initial Period was the erection of monumental buildings, usually of mud-brick (adobe) construction, on the Pacific coast of Peru, and clearly developing out of the tradition of huge architecture at the end of the preceding Preceramic Period. At La Florida in the Rimac Valley, a large U-shaped platform dates to *c.* 2000–1800 BC. Its construction took about 7 million labour days and clearly employed a workforce drawn from the nearby Chillón and Lurín Valleys as well as the Rimac Valley itself. There are many such monuments between the Lurín and Chancay Valleys, such as Mina Perdida and San Jacinto, with characteristically steep stairways leading up to the summit of pyramids from a central plaza.

Some 8km inland from the coast in the Rimac Valley, the site of Garagay seems first to have been inhabited after the demise of La Florida, perhaps in about 1500 BC, and survived until about 900 BC. It too was a U-shaped structure and was the largest site in the valley at the time. One unusual find suggests an overlap with the ritual centre of Chavín de Huántar in the highlands (see below); it is a piece of stone wrapped in cotton thread, covered with shiny hematite and then painted with a supernatural fanged deity similar to the one at the oldest part of Chavín. Where the Chavín deity holds a staff in each hand, this miniature has two cactus spines bound to its sides and also contains a bead made from the ritually important Spondylus shell which must originally have come from the warm waters of coastal

Ecuador. Suggestively, the spines come from the powerfully hallucino-genic San Pedro cactus (*Trichocereus pachanoi*), whose image also appears at Chavín, and which was (and still is) used by shamans during their curing seances. Inducing powerful visions, perhaps seen as making contact with the supernatural spirit realm, was clearly an age-old practice in Peru.

Garagay is famous for the colourful, sculpted and unbaked clay friezes which adorn the atrium of one of its temples. Originally painted in yellow, blue, red and white, this frieze is known especially for a profile monster-head shown with prominent fangs and associ-ated with spider imagery, suggesting perhaps a typically shamanic mixing of animal imagery. After careful excavation and restoration it was discovered that some of these images had been repainted up to ten times, preserving the original colour scheme. The temple area of the site was clearly a sacred place as votive offerings have been found – small clay figurines swaddled in textile and displaying a fanged and grimacing face. Contemporary with Garagay is the southernmost U-shaped site of Cardal, located in the Lurín Valley. Recently investigated by archaeologist Richard Burger during the 1980s, Cardal revealed sunken circular courts, the remains of friezes similar to those at Garagay, as well as evidence of burnt offerings around altar-like structures. It was clear also that the inhabitants of Cardal were growing cotton and making textiles. There is evidence of human burials, notably a male who was interred wearing a necklace of sea lion teeth and bone earrings.

Also built during this period was what is probably the single largest construction in the Americas at this time, the main U-shaped pyramid at Sechín Alto in the Casma Valley. Dated to c. 1700 BC, this building was twice the size of La Florida, its adobe core clad at a later stage by huge stones, some weighing over 2 tons. It is 40m high, and some fifteen times larger than the main temple at the more famous site of Chavín de Huántar. The platform was part of the so-called Sechín Alto Complex which sprawled over 10 sq. km – perhaps the accumulation of a thousand years of building activity.

Only a few kilometers away is Cerro Sechín with its famously gruesome display of some four hundred stone carvings dated to about 1500 BC. The carved stone images depict scenes of humans who have been mutilated, presumably either in warfare or sacrificial rites, their faces contorted in agony and their bowels spilling out on to the earth. Human heads, dismembered body parts, rows of eyes and vertebrae are everywhere, and seem to be the result of military action as there are also a number of stone images representing elaborately garbed (and presumably victorious) warriors. Whether these grisly scenes show war victims, sacrificed prisoners of war, or both, is not known. However, in typically Andean fashion, it may be that these images do not record a single historical event, but a mythological scene repeated over centuries and part of its society's claim to physical and spiritual ownership of the land.

Also situated in the Casma Valley is Moxeke, a huge sprawling site of some 220ha that dates to the early part of the Initial Period, between *c.* 1800 and 1400 BC. The architectural focus of the site is formed by two large pyramids that face each other across a great rectangular plaza. Early investigations of the largest structure brought to light stunning and colourful clay sculptures arranged either side of a monumental stairway. Originally some 3m tall, they depicted richly dressed human figures and serpent symbols. The other main structure, known as Huaca A, was divided into many small rooms and may have been used for storage, perhaps of food or tribute.

Only 20km away is yet another huge site, that of Las Haldas whose multi-stepped terraced platform has been dated to between 1600 and 1400 BC and is surrounded by seventeen smaller pyramids, rectangular plazas and sunken circular courts. The whole site extends over some 8ha, and archaeological evidence of subsistence illustrates that apart form the normal foods of potato, manioc and squash, maritime resources were also exploited – fishing weights, nets, and spine fish-hooks have all been found. However, there is little evidence for full-time craftwork here.

The Early Horizon and Chavín de Huántar

The period from 900 to 200 BC is called the Early Horizon and is known mainly from the highland site Chavín de Huántar and the influence its art had on far-flung parts of the Andes and adjacent coast.

Chavín de Huántar is located in the northern Peruvian Andes, at the confluence of two small rivers, the Mosna and the Huachecsa. It is strategically sited to receive and distribute cultural influences north–south along intermontane Valleys, and east–west between the humid rainforests of the Amazonian rainforest slopes of the Andes to the east and the desert valleys of the Pacific Coast to the west. Significantly, it is also situated only a few hours' walk away from three key environmental zones – irrigated valley floor, the potato fields of the upper valley slopes, and the high *puna* grassland used for grazing llamas and alpacas.

As with many other pre-Columbian culture sites, notably of the Olmec and Classic Maya of Mesoamerica, the early investigators of Chavín considered it a small ceremonial centre, mainly empty of permanent occupation, but the focus perhaps of religious pilgrimage. Today, the population evidence points in a different direction. The Mosna and Huachecsa rivers show evidence of having been canalised, there are traces of a Chavín-period stone bridge and also of large areas of contemporary terracing nearby, all suggestive of a larger site and a more permanent occupation of the area than hitherto realised.

To this can now be added the results of archaeological investigations at the site itself and beneath the colonial-period town which have revealed evidence of prehistoric houses and specialist craft production. It is now clear that while Chavín de Huántar was indeed an important religious centre with sophisticated monumental architecture decorated with startling imagery, it also had a sizeable resident population. These recent excavations have identified three main phases for the prehistory of Chavín, beginning in about 1000 BC and lasting until 200 BC.

The earliest period is called the Urabarriu Phase (1000–500 BC), and it was during this time that Chavín civilisation really took root. Chavín was a relatively small religious centre at this time, with perhaps a resident population of just a few hundred people. It may already have been divided into two parts – an upper sacred area which included the temple, and a lower secular part serving as a living area, and which also featured a massive wall, parts of which can still be seen today. It seems as if these two parts of the site were separated by about half a kilometre of (perhaps ritually) unoccupied land.

It may be, too, that the impressive wall of the lower area served partly to regulate access to the site from the lower Mosna river valley and the eastern jungles beyond. The everyday pottery, stone and bone tools found here indicate this was an occupation area, and suggest that its gallery-like buildings might have been used for storage of tribute or offerings brought to the site.

In the upper section of the site it was the religious architecture which dominated the view. The so-called 'Old Temple' is widely believed to be the oldest major construction here. It was clearly the focus of religious rituals and was built in a U shape enclosing a circular sunken court whose walls were adorned with a procession of Chavín-style jaguars and half-jaguar/half-human supernatural beings. The temple building itself was riddled with cleverly made galleries that may have been designed for their acoustic properties, and that focused on the great knife-like slab of stone called the Lanzón which seems to represent the great deity of Chavín (see below).

Despite the clear division of the site into two parts separated by the strip of unoccupied land, there is evidence of Chavín as a functioning pan-regional pilgrimage centre at this time. Discovered spread across both the upper and lower sections of the site are marine shells and pottery from outside the area, suggesting not only a close interaction between the two parts of the site, but also a widespread network of contacts throughout prehistoric Peru and perhaps beyond.

The following period is known as the Chakinani Phase (500–400 BC), and during this time people moved from the northernmost part of the site to gather around the temple area on both sides of the Huachecsa river. This area now grows to cover an estimated 15ha, and the site in general continues to suck in exotic goods from far-flung regions, including now the first appearance of the black volcaninc glass obsidian. During the short-lived Chakinani Period, Chavín's reputation as a pilgrimage centre continued to grow.

The final occupation period at Chavín is known as the Janabarriu Phase (400–200 BC), during which time the site grew at a phenomenal speed to cover more than 42ha. The main structure was the New Temple, built in two parts: first as an extension of the southern part of the Old Temple, then a platform mound with a rectangular sunken court immediately to the east. The entrance to the New Temple was via a megalithic stairway, one half of which was carved of white stone, the other half of black. At the top of the stairway was an impressive portico entrance flanked by one black and one white column carved with mythological creatures (see below).

In those areas given over to basic housing there is clear evidence for a cottage-industry arrangement of craft specialisation where jet mirrors and ear-spools were made and that are found alongside everyday cooking pottery. For this time also there is evidence that obsidian working was being carried on in specially designated areas of the site. Elsewhere, fossils, gold jewellery and several caches of the ritually important Spondylus shell were discovered.

Population expanded not only at the ceremonial centre itself but also on the surrounding valley slopes, and may have reached between two thousand and three thousand people. The local population were in all probablility joined by those of the surrounding region and together being organised to create large public works, such as valley-floor terracing and drainage, and the new religious buildings attached to the Old Temple. This wider support area included small villages such as Waman Wain and Pojoc that all have early Chavín levels and thus appear to have been part of the phenomenon from its inception. Artwork from these rural sites is also in the Chavín style but of a more rustic variety, such as the Chavín-style feline little more than etched on to a block of sandstone and found in the village of Waman Wain, and a more sophisticated image of a Chavín anthropomorphic supernatural carrying a trophy head from the small village of Yurayacu some 5km downstream of Chavín itself.

It seems that these agricultural hamlets contributed food, goods and labour to the elite who controlled the site of Chavín. This is clearly an ancient tradition in the Andes, and survived into the twentieth century when nearby villages sent labourers to the town of Chavín de Huántar to help build and maintain the church and town hall, the modern-day equivalent to the high-status temples of prehistoric times.

Chavín art and religion

Although Chavín de Huántar was a large and clearly prestigious ceremonial centre during Janabarriu times, it was the monumental architecture and art which have proved its most enduring legacy. It was in its art that Chavín most forcefully expressed its complex metaphorical messages and ideology that so influenced many other contemporary and later civilisations.

Undoubtedly, Chavín's strategic location was a key to its success. Intriguingly, its art reflects this, with a strong sense of the Amazon rainforest in its sophisticated iconography. The animals so masterfully depicted by Chavín artists are not the Andean puma, condor, or llama, but denizens of the jungle, such as the harpy eagle, jaguar and cayman. Even today, these are the classic animal familiars of powerful Amazonian shamans – creatures of sorcery and myth, whose cosmic identity associates them with shamans, priests and chiefs among the living, and the ancestors of the past. In prehistory, while Chavín was an Andean phenomenon, much of its spiritual inspiration appears to have come from the tropical rainforests.

More generally, from the archaeological standpoint the imagery of Chavín art provides one of the most insightful manifestations of shamanic worldview. Jungle animals (often dangerous predators), in their entirety and in isolated elements, are deconstructed and rebuilt, with different parts used to create supernatural beings. In South America, during prehistory and today, shamans often ritually consume powerful hallucinogens to connect with the spirit realm. Some of Chavín's imagery gives the impression of being drug-induced, but most convincing are the examples which depict supernatural beings holding the well-known hallucinogenic San Pedro cactus.

Jungle influences may have reached Chavín via the small site of Kotosh, the early cult centre on the eastern slopes of the Andes, and lying only 35km from the edge of the tropical rainforest. Although Kotosh and other contemporary sites long predate Chavín – with evidence of religious architecture, pottery and maize – the period after *c.* 890 BC yields only typically Chavín designs on pottery, gold and bone.

Most of Chavín's art focuses on realistic and fantastical represent-ations of felines, most likely the jaguar, though other smaller spotted cats such as the ocelot (*Felis pardalis*) may have been included. The feline image was not only important in its entirety, but also in its constituent parts, inasmuch as fangs, snouts, claws and the animal's rosette markings could stand alone, or be variously incorporated into anthropomorphic beings – perhaps as a symbol of supernatural status. For example, we see how the snarling cat-mouth with its prominent lips and bared fangs often replaces the normal mouth of humans or other animals and thus seems to be a transferable motif, either felinising another animal (or human) or lending itself to a totally fantastical supernatural being.

Closely associated with the feline element, and equally prominent in art, is the substitution of serpents for body hair – a typically Chavín metaphor first studied by the scholar John Rowe. Many of Chavín de Huántar's great art pieces have snakes instead of hair, suggesting a widely recognised and deepfelt symbolic connection. These artistic elements lay at the heart of the Chavín style, a style which appears to have embodied many concepts that were under-stood and attractive to people across ancient Peru at the time, and thus spread far and wide, either directly or indirectly by influencing local art styles.

Chavín's great artworks were produced throughout the lifespan of the site, from the Old Temple beginnings to the New Temple heyday. The focal point of the Old Temple and its honeycomb of interior galleries, passages and ventilation shafts was and remains the Lanzón, a lance-like shaft of white granite some 4.5m tall. The size and central position of this imposing sculpture suggest it may be the oldest item here. Perhaps the whole of the Old Temple was built around the sculpture, which functioned as a fearsome repre-sentation of a deified ancestor of the Chavín people. The Lanzón represents a striking anthropomorphic deity, variously referred to as the 'Smiling God' or the 'Snarling God'. It has an upturned cat-like mouth and projecting fangs, and hair on eyebrows and head have turned into long swirling serpents. A girdle and a long upward-projecting headdress are both made up of small feline heads with snarling mouths and crossed fangs. This fearsome supernatural being appears male, and its

The El Lanzón figure at Chavín de Huántar with protruding fangs and feline and serpent decoration. (© *Pauline Stringfellow, after J.H. Rowe, 'Form and Meaning in Chavin Art', in J.H. Rowe and D. Menzel (eds),* Peruvian Archaeology: Selected Readings, *Peek Publications, Palo Alto, pp. 72–103. Fig 5.)*

central location in dark echoing galleries would have made it an intimidating sight.

The fascination with feline imagery is also evident outside the Old Temple's galleries, where a spectacular procession of jaguars and half-human/half-feline supernatural beings adorns the circular sunken court which is part of the Old Temple layout. Only discovered in 1972 by the Peruvian archaeologist Luís Lumbreras, two parallel levels of beautifully rendered low-relief images show jaguars in profile and anthropomorphic creatures with clawed hands, serpent hair and snarling cat-mouths. Originally, carved stone anthropomorphic heads with feline features decorated the exterior walls of the Old Temple. With a single exception, these startling faces have long since disappeared, and now lay in museums, the temple's interior galleries, or private collections.

Perhaps the most intriguing supernatural creature from the Old Temple is that represented on the so-called 'Tello Obelisk', a rectangular granite shaft carved on all four sides. Its central mythical image, identified as being based on South America's black cayman (*Melanosuchus niger*), has been designated Cayman A and Cayman B, relating to the watery underworld and the sky respectively. This is a richly decorated piece of stone sculpture, heavy with motifs, symbols and allusions – with images of birds, plants, shells and fish – yet all, it seems, of a piece in the snarling cat-mouth motif that appears throughout, and which made the sculpture a coherent whole in the minds of those who created it.

During Janabarriu times at the New Temple, a granite slab known today as the Raimondi Stela was carved. It features the image of a standing human grasping a staff in each hand that has been subsequently referred to as the Staff God. The deity's hands and feet are clawed, it has a face (or wears a mask) with bared fangs, has prominent upward-staring eyes, and snakes emerge from its belt. The staffs themselves are decorated in characteristic Chavín style, with feline heads and cat-mouths. Only the lower third of the granite slab is taken up with this figure, the rest is filled with an elaborate headdress composed of fanged masks and serpents.

It is likely that the Staff God was not a new deity but a late-Chavín version of the earlier supreme being represented on the Lanzón, albeit in a more dazzlingly stylised (and human) form. Indeed, the Staff God itself seems to be much older than Chavín, with the earliest known examples coming from two incised gourds found in the Pativilca Valley on the coast and dated to 2230 BC. Other representations at Chavín show the Staff God holding the ritually important Spondylus and strombus shells, perhaps as symbols representing the female and male principles (values they certainly possessed in later times). Artistic themes found in the Old Temple continue into the new era – tenoned heads with their references to hallucinogenic religious rituals, and the imagery of felines, caymans, and raptorial birds. Arguably most famous of the New Temple constructions is the Black and White Portal referred to

Carving of shaman-priest wearing jaguar and serpent regalia at Chavín de Huántar. (© *Pauline Stringfellow, after P. Roe, 'Recent Discoveries in Chavín Art'. El Dorado 3 (1), 1978, pp. 1–41. Fig 1)*

above, whose two columns each carry intricate carvings of anthropomorphic raptorial birds. These creatures, perhaps the spirit-
helpers of the main deity, have grotesque upturned heads (or masks)
with snarling feline-mouths combined with a bird of prey beak, and
wings rendered in an ultra-stylised Chavín manner with cat-mouths
and bared fangs. Each grasps a staff and has clawed hands and feet
in precisely the same way as the Staff God of the Raimondi Stela.

It is the Janabarriu-phase Staff God who appears as a popular
motif in other parts of Peru during the Early Horizon, suggesting
perhaps that Chavín art (and maybe its ideology) was reinterpreted
by local cultures whose representatives had visited the site and
returned home with portable images of the main deity. Such local
variations of Chavín imagery are found throughout the Andes and
adjacent coastal regions.

In the northern Andes, the inhabitants of Pacopampa restructured
their temple to imitate the architecture of Chavín, and their pottery
and stone-carving were also influenced by its style. Similarly, Chavín
influence can be seen in the mud-brick (adobe) sculptures at Caballo
Muerto in the Moche Valley on the adjacent north coast. Elaborate
stirrup-spout ceramics bearing Chavín-related jaguar and bird
imagery have also been found on the north coast, as has an embossed golden crown decorated with the image of Chavín's main
deity and other similar items found at the site of Chongoyape.

On the south coast, spectacular tomb textiles from Karwa near
Paracas depict Staff God images painted on to cotton. At this time,
it seems, Chavín artistic influence was widespread, from rock
carvings to stone sculptures (including highly polished feline-shaped
stone mortars and pestles), to pottery, bone, shell and goldwork,
including crowns and miniature jaguar shapes presumably for
attachment to textiles.

The evidence of Chavín-influenced art among many different
prehistoric societies throughout Peru suggests that at least parts of
its religious worldview and ideology were attractive beyond its
Andean Valley homeland. It is also increasingly apparent that some
motifs and designs, previously thought to have originated at Chavín,
appear earlier elsewhere. In this case, pilgrims and visitors to Chavín
may have taken these images and ideas with them, and the master
craftsmen of Chavín then created bold new hybrid forms in new
media – from delicate goldwork to highly polished stonework and
sophisticated pottery. Nevertheless, as has long been thought,

Chavín de Huántar was an extraordinarily successful and influential ritual and pilgrimage centre which attracted devotees from all over ancient Peru and was itself a focus of economic interaction in terms of long-distance trade and perhaps llama herding activities.

It is possible, as some experts believe, that Chavín was an oracle, and that the many different examples of Chavín motifs from across the Andes indicate that part of the oracle's sacredness and power was transferred to other distant shrines, locally interpreted but ultimately deriving their spiritual efficacy from Chavín itself.

Chavín's legacy

Such had been the effect of Chavín's dominance as a cult centre and pilgrimage destination that long after the site itself had ceased to function, it retained its sacred aura. The dazzling artwork and memory of its heyday combined to make it a sacred place, a location where myth, art, a spiritual landscape and a shamanic view of the world came together. Chavín de Huántar slipped into what, to Western eyes would appear a curious but influential limbo – cut off from its historical past, yet living on in the spiritual present.

The tenacity of ancient Andean belief systems is evident at Chavín. During the seventeenth century, the Spanish chronicler Antonio Vasquez de Espinosa observed that at the time he was writing, Chavín was a religious centre comparable to Jerusalem or Rome. In other words, some two millennia after its heyday, and a century after the Spanish conquest, the site of Chavín de Huántar was still an important pilgrimage centre for indigenous Andean peoples.

EIGHT

Moche

The Moche civilisation (also called the Mochica), flourished on the north coast of Peru between AD 100 and 750. This fell mainly within the Early Intermediate Period of Peruvian prehistory (200 BC–AD 600), though continued on into the early part of the succeeding Middle Horizon (AD 600–1000). The Moche are justly famous for three cultural features – huge adobe (mud brick) structures, a richly expressive repertoire of modelled and painted ceramics, and a uniquely innovative tradition of sophisticated metalworking.

Moche civilisation was part of a North Coast cultural tradition and emerged between AD 100 and 200 from an earlier culture known as Gallinazo. The heartland seems to have been in the Moche and Chicama Valleys from where, in about AD 400, traditional thinking saw the Moche as extending their control through military conquest south and north along the coast. However, what was once considered to have been a straightforward process of conquest has now been revised to a more cautious approach. There were, it seems, differences between the process which brought the northern and southern valleys into the Moche sphere of influence, with different historical trajectories being experienced by individual valleys.

Many aspects of Moche civilisation had their origins in the preceding Gallinazo culture (which began *c.* 100 BC) to such an extent that recent interpretations suggest that Moche was merely a later phase of its predecessor. It seems as if many Gallinazo cultural features continued well into the Moche period. Certainly, there were shared aspects of cultural behaviour evident in elite burials, pottery forms and monumental adobe architecture. Sophisticated metalworking and pottery with the distinctive stirrup-spout handle were all to become diagnostic of Moche culture yet all were present during the Gallinazo period. Only in the ceramics belonging to the ruling elite were there significant differences. Here, high-quality

Moche pottery was decorated in a more sophisticated way than its plainer Gallinazo predecessors – an insight, perhaps, into changing ideas and practices surrounding the representation of political and ideological power.

Religion, power and pyramids

Embodying and representing the power and prestige of Moche civilisation are its two major constructions, the Huaca del Sol (Pyramid of the Sun) and Huaca de la Luna (Pyramid of the Moon), both located on the lower reaches of the Moche river valley.

The Huaca del Sol is thought to be a royal palace and mausoleum for the ruling dynasty, as shown by the discovery of elite burials beneath its various terraces. However, it was also a secular site where the everyday business of empire and administration took place, as evidenced by domestic refuse. It was constructed of an estimated 143 million adobes, the largest mud-brick building in the Americas. Today, about one third remains due to the destruction of the remainder by the Spanish who diverted the Moche river to cut into its flanks in their search for buried gold. Although there is tantalising evidence that gold artefacts were found, the Spanish looting did have one beneficial effect. By eroding through the Huaca del Sol the river effectively cut a cross-section through the structure and laid bare the construction techniques used by the Moche builders.

Given the scale of the building, its eight-stage construction probably took several generations, and employed many different labour gangs working simultaneously to a given plan. This became clear when it was discovered that each and every one of the millions of adobes used was stamped with one of about 100 makers' signs. While we can never be certain, it is likely that the bricks were made by individual communities whose workers were organised into groups who were responsible for building vertical sections of the structure with their own marked bricks and with both the adobes and the construction efforts being part of a labour tax (known as *mita* in later Inka times).

While probably contemporary with the Huaca del Sol, the smaller Huaca de la Luna seems to have had a different function, and certainly possessed aspects of construction and decoration that were not present in the larger pyramid. Built at the base of a (perhaps sacred) hill known as Cerro Blanco, the Huaca de la Luna was made up of three interconnected platforms surrounded by high walls, the two largest platforms showing evidence of having been enlarged or reconstructed on various occasions, whereas the smallest one, once finished, was never touched again.

An important feature is the presence of some of the most astonishing multi-coloured murals known from the Moche area; they depict typically supernatural creatures in human and animal form, as well as unusual animated items such as war clubs and shields. Some motifs show a snarling central face whose swirling hair and surrounding elements end in a bird-shaped head. Others depict grimacing anthropomorphic beings with upturned comma-shaped eyes, elaborate headdresses and arms that divide into looping designs and that end with zoomorphic heads shown in profile.

While the two principal constructions of the Huaca del Sol and Huaca de la Luna are the focal point of the settlement centred on Cerro Blanco, the area was also one of intense occupation and craft specialisation. Excavations have revealed the remains of metal-working, pottery production and the manufacture of elite jewellery made from lapis lazuli, and the ritually important Spondylus seashell. Investigations of the area between the two pyramids have revealed the houses where the Moche lived, apparently divided into three classes, with those of highest rank (and greatest material possessions) in the area nearest to the Huaca de la Luna.

Art and society

As the Huaca de la Luna's murals indicate, the Moche are famous for their outstanding artworks, achieved notably in precious metals and some of the most extraordinary pottery in the Americas. Moche pottery combined the symbolic with the realistic in ways which force us to question our own conceptions of the natural and supernatural worlds (and the boundaries between them) in our attempts to interpret them. Technically brilliant and beautifully decorated as Moche ceramics and metalwork are, they are nevertheless the product of a state system and official style, as well as embodiments of a worldview or natural philosophy very different from that of the modern West.

Moche ceramics come in a variety of forms, though the typically North Coast stirrup-spout handle is ubiquitous. Indeed, the different forms of the stirrup-spout have been divided into five types, each of which appears at a different time, but, confusingly, older forms continued to be made and used alongside new ones. Such has been the amount of attention given to the changing shape of stirrup-spout handles that the stages in their evolution have been taken to form the basis of Moche chronology: Moche Period 1 (AD 50–100), Moche Period 2 (AD 100–200), Moche Period 3 (AD 200–450), Moche Period 4 (AD 450–550), and Moche Period 5 (AD 550–800).

These ceramics were made to a standardised form in moulds and appear to have been used mainly for pouring libations during religious ceremonies. It is thought that those specialists who manufactured Moche ceramics developed a series of abstract picture signs which conveyed information to others within the tightly knit potter community. Although not an early writing system, such signs have been termed a kind of proto-writing.

Given the spiritual importance of sound, wind, music and human breath in South America, it is perhaps not surprising to find such accomplished potters as the Moche producing double-chambered stirrup-spout ceramics that whistle as the libation is poured out. Many of these, not surprisingly, are bird-shaped items. As we will shortly see, there may also have been a highly specific association of whistling with human sacrifice.

Stirrup-spout handles are found on the two main kinds of Moche pottery, those which were shaped as effigies of animals, mythological creatures and realistically portrayed human faces; and those whose flat surface was decorated with the superbly rendered fine-line paintings of ritual and mythological (and probably partly historical) scenes.

Effigy ceramics are of several different kinds, some realistically depicting real-life tasks, such as a bowl which shows four individuals engaged in metalworking. Most, however, are either the so-called portrait vessels of individual people, or beautifully modelled representations of half-human, half-animal beings, perhaps humans wearing animals masks, and, conceivably, animal images as metaphors for certain kinds of individuals such as war captives. Always richly dressed – they wear mantles and headdresses – these creatures sometimes look like deer. Situated within a wider study of Moche art, it seems likely that deer could represent an enemy warrior and perhaps also an enemy captive about to be sacrificed. There seems to be a conceptual equivalence in Moche art between warfare (i.e. the hunting of men), and deer-hunting perhaps as symbolic war.

It may be that in both cases humans and deer were captured only, or mainly, for sacrifice. Other, more clearly zoomorphic representations show llamas, jaguars and birds such as the macaw.

Some of the most intriguing of Moche effigy pots are those that represent what appear to be real people. These portrait vessels have become an international icon of Moche culture, exhibited in museums worldwide. Yet this ubiquity is misleading, for in Moche times such objects were limited in time and space. They were produced in only three of the fifteen valleys occupied by the Moche – the heartland of the Moche Valley, Chicama Valley, and Virú Valley – and produced almost entirely during the period AD 200–550 (i.e. Moche Periods 3 and 4). Before and after this time, human faces were rendered in a standardised generic fashion. While the realistic portrait vessels were made in large quantities, they clearly had a significance beyond that of simply being a more technically and artistically accomplished kind of pottery.

Christopher Donnan, the expert on Moche ceramics, has observed that the explosion of portrait vessels coincided with a wider trend in Moche art, away from representing supernatural beings and towards depicting elite individuals, and that the practice ended during the AD 560s as Moche culture underwent dramatic changes. It seems likely that as Moche culture reached its zenith, the military, political and ideological power of the ruling elite also climaxed, one consequence being the appearance of ceramic vessels that represented them in a highly personal and thus recognisable way. Whether this recognition factor was purely one of self-aggrandisement, or was perhaps aimed at the spirit world (or both) is not known.

On some occasions, multiple portrait vessels of the same individual were made from the same ceramic mould, although painted and adorned differently. Even more insightful are the forty-five portrait vessels apparently showing the scarred face of a single male at various ages, from around ten years old to maturity at thirty. On full-figure portrait vessels, it is sometimes possible to recognise an individual at various stages of adult life – as an elaborately-dressed warrior accompanied by full paraphernalia, to a naked and bound captive about to be sacrificed. It seems likely that, as with the Classic Maya in Mesoamerica, such combat-related scenes had a strong ceremonial nature that stressed the high status of those about to be ritually killed, and thus added to the prestige of the captor/ sacrificer in ways that were artistically framed in the medium of pottery. Scenes that depict such activities may not be straightforward records of war, but perhaps more sophisticated ideological manipulations of ceremonial events.

Fine-line ceramics were often painted with a background cream-coloured slip upon which delicately painted figures and scenes were rendered. For several decades, this kind of pottery has been the subject of painstaking investigations by Christopher Donnan and his colleagues. Their conclusions show how the Moche used a symbolic code and several major themes to illustrate the complex link between mythology, set scenes and a cast of natural and super-natural characters. These images depicted scenes and ceremonies associated with war, prisoner capture, human sacrifice and prob-ably also the acting out of important myths in grand events that combined all three elements. Among the major themes so far identi-fied are the so-called 'burial theme' and 'presentation theme' (now more usualy called the 'Sacrifice Ceremony'). In the latter, the main actor is an elaborately dressed individual called the 'Warrior Priest' who drinks the blood of sacrificed prisoners from a ceremonial goblet.

Apart from ceramics, the Moche also excelled at metalworking. Recent archaeological investigations and technical analyses have shown that Moche metalwork is arguably the finest technological achievement in ancient South America. During the Moche era, their master craftsmen innovated new ways of gilding, alloying and colouring metals to such a high degree of excellence that some experts regard Andean metallurgy as Moche metallurgy. The ways in which metalworking was integrated with, and representative of, Moche society are illustrated by the extraordinary discoveries made by the Peruvian archaeologist Walter Alva at the site of Sipán in Lambayeque Valley north of the Moche homeland.

Sipán itself consists of the eroded remains of two large adobe-brick pyramids and a burial platform built between AD 1 and 300. Here, since 1987, have been found twelve tombs of high-ranking Moche individuals, whose grave goods have allowed a social classification of those buried into rulers, priests, warrior-leaders, and assistants to these high-ranking individuals. Such were the quality and quantity of mortuary goods, that it has been possible to suggest interpretations concerning the complex symbolism of duality for Moche social identity as manifested by paired ornaments and items made of two precious metals, gold and silver.

Tomb 1 has been described as the richest unlooted tomb ever found in the Americas, and contained the remains of a royal personage called the 'Lord of Sipán'. He was accompanied into the Moche afterlife by eight retainers. The untouched burial chamber contained a wooden coffin within which were the remains of a male about forty years old. Surrounding him, in niches and cane coffins, were three adult men, three young women, one adult woman and a child.

Over four hundred and fifty further items were buried in the tomb, some of them masterpieces of the metalworker's art. These included metal banners composed of small metal squares sewn on to cloth, fringed with metal depictions of the *ulluchu* fruit and with a central image of an embossed anthropomorphic figure; pectorals made of thousands of shell beads; ear discs of gold and turquoise; a spectacular necklace of peanut-shaped pendants, made of gold on the right half and silver on the left; a gold and silver sceptre/knife decorated with scenes associated with prisoner-capture; the remains of a gold and feather headdress; and two ceremonial items called backflaps, one of gold, the other silver.

Tomb 2 contained the individual referred to as the 'Priest', and was probably contemporary with Tomb 1. This also contained an adult male around forty years old and who was accompanied by six retainers, one of whom had had his feet cut off. Although generally of less high quality than in Tomb 1, the objects found in Tomb 2 were also impressive. They included a great owl-shaped gilded-copper headdress with pendant metal squares, a bimetallic backflap, half gold, half silver, and a ceremonial goblet. The items buried here suggest that this individual could be identified as the so-called Bird Priest figure shown in sacrifice scenes of Moche pottery.

Tomb 3, the last of the major burials, yielded the remains of the individual dubbed the 'Old Lord of Sipán', so-called because this was a much earlier interment. The individual buried in this smaller and more basic tomb was around fifty years old, and had only one female retainer and a llama interred with him. Despite this, the metalwork was again of the highest quality and included an anthropomorphic crab-being made of gilded copper, two small sceptres (one of gold, the other silver), an elaborate copper burial mask with a necklace of owl heads, and a stunning necklace composed of ten discs each of which represented a spider on whose back was a human face 'trapped' in the centre of a filigree web. A set of ten backflaps, a nose-ornament incorporating a miniature gold and turquoise warrior figure, and various weapons were also included.

Besides the remains of a looted tomb, nine other burials were found whose contents suggested they accompanied lesser members of Sipán's elite. In addition to metalwork (notably copper headdresses), these contained such varied mortuary offerings as ceramic pan pipes, weapons, llama heads, headless llamas, shell-bead jewellery, pottery, sceptres and small ceramic masks. Perhaps the most important feature of these varied burials and their contents was that the excavated objects were those that appeared on Moche ceramics portraying scenes associated with rulership and its many ceremonial aspects.

As Walter Alva has observed, what emerges as most significant from these extraordinary discoveries is the way in which objects represent and embody the hierarchical relationships of Moche society. In life, the different ranks are shown in great detail on fine-line pottery, perhaps re-enacting cosmic myths as well as fighting (portrayed realistically, and perhaps metaphorically as deer hunts), taking prisoners, presenting them to the ruler, and humiliating and sacrificing them to the gods. In death, the elite are discovered buried with these same items of clothing and paraphernalia. Thus there is a strong, though not always straightforward, correlation between how the elite of Moche society saw themselves in relation to what we regard as the utterly distinct arenas of myth and history. Archaeology has revealed the existence of these correlations, though to what extent they reflect historical reality throughout the Moche area is much more difficult to assess.

Archaeology and art history combine in the investigation of the Moche, where excavations have yielded physical remains of people and their paraphernalia that appear the same as those items represented on fine-line painted scenes. Occasionally, as with the effigy vessels, fine-line pots portray real-life tasks, such as the inside of a dish which shows women weaving elaborate textiles on backstrap looms, a type which can still be seen in use today.

Sacrifice

In recent years, dramatic new discoveries have been made that throw intriguing light on the relationship between Moche human sacrifice, cosmology, religion and also, perhaps, the unique climatic event known as El Niño. Moche ceramics display many images of the imminent ritual decapitation of sacrificial victims which suggest a cut through the neck from front to back, and the subsequent drinking of the deceased's blood in a ceremonial goblet. In 1994, at the well-named site of Dos Cabezas ('Two Heads') in the Jequetepeque Valley, a unique discovery of eighteen decapitated heads was made. Nearby, and contemporary, were the remains of a man holding a ceramic head in one hand and a functional copper *tumi* knife in the other. The whole assemblage has been interpreted as the body of a real-life decapitator individual, perhaps the same one responsible for the eighteen heads lying nearby.

In the Moche Valley, excavations of the Huaca de la Luna have also yielded new insights into Moche sacrifical activities. Built between the sixth and seventh centuries AD, Plaza 3A and Platform II have yielded unexpected and still not fully understood human remains, almost certainly a series of layered sacrifices representing six ritual events and some seventy human bodies in the plaza, and four tombs in platform.

Excavation by Steve Bourget and his colleagues revealed that an older Moche cemetery had been partly removed in order to construct this plaza and platform, upon whose completion three children were buried, two of which were headless and may have been decapitated (alternatively, they may simply have been buried, their heads removed, after a natural death). One of the children was still grasping one of two small ceramic whistles in his right hand. Not long after this interment it seems there was a heavy downpour which washed a deposit of clay over part of the plaza, after which the childrens' burial space was surrounded by a wall of adobe bricks. At this point, there was nothing unusual in this discovery, as sacrifices were often made throughout the Americas to dedicate and sanctify new religious structures. However, comparison of the child burial with the two whistles and Moche ceramic iconography reveals a possible association between pottery images representing figures carrying (possibly dead female) children and whistling pots.

Further careful investigation revealed that on this same spot, five adults had later been sacrificed during a second downpour, and then more again after the liquid mud had hardened into clay. Holes had then been dug into the ground and filled with human remains and clay effigies of nude male figures each of which had a rope tightened around his neck. These figures were then ritually smashed. Sometime later, during another heavy rainfall, more people were killed again on the same spot and later, after the mud had again dried, still more were sacrificed. What is notable about this sequence of superimposed bodies is that they were all concentrated in a small area next to the possibly sacred rocky outcrop of Cerro Blanco, and their numbers increased at each event. Analysis of the bones indicates that all the bodies except those of the children were warriors captured in conflict. Interestingly, a bird-shaped whistle was found with these warrior remains, suggesting perhaps, and according to the excavator, a symbolic association between whistling and ritual death, whether of children or adults.

In a fortuitous discovery in one of the nearby platform tombs were found two items associated with the looted remains of a sixty-year-old male who may have been a priest-warrior. The first was a stirrup-spouted effigy pot depicting an elaborately garbed male holding a mace of the same kind shown on pottery depictions of warfare and of hunting both of deer and sea lions. Also found was a wooden mace which analysis revealed to have been drenched in human blood. This find suggests that the individual buried in the tomb may have used the mace interred with him to sacrifice some of the victims in the plaza below. It also supports the interpretation already mentioned that there was a connection in the Moche mind between hunting/sacrificing human warriors and deer (and probably also sea lions). Whatever the truth may be concerning this intriguing set of discoveries, the relationship between human sacrifice and torrential rain is suggestive of an association with the El Niño events that took place in the area during the late Moche era.

Empire

At its height, Moche influence extended from the Piura area in the north to the Huarmey Valley in the south and over offshore islands as well as the mainland valleys. The nature of Moche political control was subtle and regionally appropriate, with strong centralisation in the small valleys to the south, and a more co-operative approach in the populous larger valleys to the north. Archaeologists agree that Moche civilisation was an original and innovative state that managed to weld together large areas of Peru's northern and central coasts for the first time.

In the southern valleys, the Moche built large-scale architecture as a symbol of their imperial presence. Sites such as Pañamarca in the Nepeña Valley and Huancaco in the Virú Valley followed the designs of the Moche heartland, and administered trade, tribute and craftwork for the imperial centre. It seems likely that Moche control was spread militarily in many of these valleys, and that military and sacrifice scenes depicted on pottery reflect the activities of Moche warriors in these events. Such scenes suggest that Moche warfare was often concerned as much with gaining captives for sacrifice as with extending the borders of the state – in this sense at least making the Moche somewhat similar to the Classic Maya of Mesoamerica. However, as with the Maya, it is dangerous to assume that ritual motives were at the heart of conflict rather than an integral part of it.

In the northern valleys, the Moche appear to have adopted a more sophisticated divide-and-rule policy, retaining pre-existing local lords and their fragmented political groups, incorporating them into an overarching Moche political system, and thereby preventing any unified revolt against Moche presence and control. In many ways, this was a typical Andean political manoeuvre, ruling through local leaders who themselves gained added prestige by association.

The nature of Moche warfare and sacrifice as described above is in many ways a difficult issue to interpret. What is clear from the archaeological record is that Moche culture was an expansionist, imperialistic state during its height, between AD 200 and 550. The conquest and integration of other valleys, their local leadership regimes and their economic resources was a prime objective. Yet, simultaneously, the nature of Amerindian warfare throughout the Americas included strong ritual elements that blended into an ideology.

What we see on Moche ceramics and uncover in archaeological contexts are those aspects of warfare and sacrifice that emphasise the role of Moche leaders in making the most ideological capital out of real military confrontations. In other words, the propaganda bias of Moche iconography should not necessarily persuade us that Moche warfare was only or even mainly ritual in nature. Success in war brought material and ideological rewards for the victor – multidimensional benefits that were symbolically compressed and represented in art rather than indicating that Moche war was only waged for religious reasons to capture sacrificial victims.

Moche demise

Moche civilisation went into decline during the late sixth century AD – the transition between Moche Period 4 and Moche Period 5. This was not, however, a total or abrupt collapse, and did not happen in the same way for each of the valleys under Moche domination.

Various explanations have been offered to account for the stress on the Moche political system. The most recent theory is that some kind of environmental catastrophe struck the North Coast, such as an El Niño event which caused serious rainfall, flooding and disruption to canal-fed agriculture, food production and procurement, and political stability. Equally disastrous consequences would have followed an extended period of drought for which there is also evidence elsewhere in the Andes. Whether or not alternating droughts and floods were the combined cause of Moche decline, it is the case that large parts of the Cerro Blanco settlement area in the Moche Valley were covered over with wind-blown sand and soon abandoned.

A longer-established explanation is that of foreign intrusion, usually associated with the expanding Wari state. There is evidence of changing pottery styles to support Wari influence beyond its homeland of Ayacucho in the Andes. Although no remains of Wari-style architecture have been found in the Moche area – an indication, perhaps, that there was no military invasion *per se* – Wari iconography on ceramics and murals does appear, and excercises an influence over later artistic developments in the region. It may be that the southern coastal-valley frontier of the Moche empire was affected in some way by Wari encroachment nearby and that this led to destabilisation and Moche abandonment. A third possibility is that some form of internal stress affected, or contributed to, the Moche demise – perhaps a combination of ideological and political over-reach that disrupted the hitherto balanced system of expansion.

In the way of Andean (and wider Amerindian) cultural systems, any disruption to society could be seen in a religious light and may have serious political and ideological consequences. The religious nature of power is a fundamental characteristic of pre-Columbian (and native) American societies. It expresses itself in different ways – extraordinary cultural achievement when working well, and sometimes almost total collapse when put under pressure.

Whatever the cause of the Moche decline in the south, to the north a vast new (and apparently rapidly built) corporate centre was constructed at Pampa Grande in the Lambayeque Valley. While the population around the monumental architecture in the Moche Valley was a pale shadow of its former self, a new site was established over an earlier smaller village at Galindo on the north side of the Moche river. Galindo was a very different place from its predecessors, with an urban feel and discrete high-walled areas within which religious ceremonies were conducted replacing the more open and public platforms of earlier times. The nature of politics and ideology had clearly undergone drastic revision.

By about AD 750, both Galindo and Pampa Grande had collapsed, and with them the last true expression of classic Moche civilisation. In the years that followed, the influence of Wari was felt once again, though this time in the northern Moche area. Once more the presence is artistic rather than architectural or military, and Wari-associated ritual activities seem to have taken place at the old Moche Huaca de la Luna. It was perhaps from a creative synthesis of their ancient North Coast traditions and Wari influence that the descendants of the Moche would create the Sicán culture of the Lambayeque Valley and the imperial Chimú civilisation of the Moche Valley in the centuries to come.

NINE

Nasca

The Nasca culture was one of the most extraordinary in ancient Peru. It flourished in the valleys that cut across the arid south coast between AD 1 and 700. As with the North Coast Moche, the Nasca mainly belonged to the Early Intermediate Period (200 BC–AD 600), though continued on into following Middle Horizon (AD 600–1000). It is justly famous for its striking polychrome pottery, decorated with a wide range of real and mythical creatures, and its human trophy heads. The Nasca also created huge desert drawings or geoglyphs; these were of two types – earlier images of gigantic animals and, later, long lines (perhaps intended as ritual pathways), and geometric shapes, such as trapezoids and spirals.

Historically, there has been a confusing use of alternate spellings – Nasca and Nazca – with different investigators using one or the other at different times. Following the suggestion of Nasca specialist Helaine Silverman, the spelling Nasca will be used here when discussing the archaeological culture, and Nazca where it relates to geography, i.e. the region, town and river.

A more serious issue relates to the difficulties archaeologists have encountered in establishing a reliable chronology for the development of Nasca culture. For different reasons, especially the lack of reliable material from dwelling sites that can be subjected to radiocarbon dating, some of the phases are indistinct and sometimes overlapping: Nasca Period 1 (150 BC–AD 100); Nasca Period 2 (AD 100–200); Nasca Period 3, the height of Nasca culture (AD 200–400); Nasca Period 4 (AD 400–500); Nasca Period 5 (c. AD 525); Nasca Period 6 (AD 600–900); Nasca Period 7 (AD 576–696); and Nasca Period 8 (AD 830–c. 1000), and Nasca Period 9 (c. AD 1000–c. 1300).

Paracas and Nasca origins

Nasca culture developed out of the final phases of the preceding Paracas culture (*c.* 100 BC–AD 200). This precocious society takes its name from the Paracas Peninsula which juts out into the Pacific on the coast north of the Nazca region. During the 1920s, spectacular burials were excavated there by the Peruvian archaeologist Julio Tello. There were two occupation sites, Cerro Colorado and Arenas Blancas, and four cemeteries. The mortuary evidence permitted the identification of two different local cultures, the earlier Cavernas, with colourful painted pottery, and the later Necropolis/Topará, with monochrome ceramics but astonishingly coloured textiles decorated with equally dazzling embroidered images of humans and supernatural creatures.

The burial practices and material culture belonging to these two possibly contemporary societies are different. While all bodies were naturally mummified by the dry desert heat and preserved as mummy bundles, those belonging to Cavernas society were placed at the bottom of globular chambers cut into the bedrock. Those of the Necropolis/Topará society, by contrast, were simply placed among the ruins of abandoned dwellings. Despite the numbers of mummies discovered (over five hundred in all), and their rich grave goods – ranging from trophy heads to jewellery, Spondylus shell to slings – it has been the technical innovation and colourful decoration of the textiles that have received most attention from experts. Anthropomorphic beings, fish, plants, birds and felines all appear as richly embroidered images, indicating a vibrant animistic view of the world. It has been estimated that the textiles of each mummy bundle took between 5,000 and 29,000 hours to produce.

Despite being discovered on the Paracas Peninsula, the fullest picture of ancient Paracas culture comes from further inland, at sites located in the Ica, Pisco and Palpa Valleys. In the Ica Valley, Paracas objects are referred to as belonging to the Ocucaje style, and it is from this manifestation of Paracas culture that Nasca is most commonly thought to have developed.

The Paracas culture seems to have been influenced, at least in its iconography, by the ritual centre at Chavín de Huántar in the northern Peruvian Andes. Paracas, however, was an independent culture which selectively borrowed only some Chavín motifs, such as felines and birds, and integrated them into its own highly distinctive

Royal Moche burial from Sipán.
(© Author's collection)

Nasca mummy, well preserved by the
desert conditions. (© Author's
collection)

Entrance to underground freshwater puquio wells at Nazca. (© *Author's collection*)

The sunken plaza and temple at Tiwanaku. (© *Author's collection*)

Quechua woman and llama walking by the ruins of the temple-fortress of Sacsahuaman above Cuzco. (© *Author's collection*)

General view of the Inka mountain-top city of Machu Picchu. (© *Author's collection*)

material culture. Probably a major deity during early Paracas times was the so-called 'Oculate Being', a typically shamanic hybrid creature with human and feline elements and large prominent eyes, and often associated with human trophy heads. Ocucaje pottery is decorated with rows of eye-like motifs, and desert drawings (which first appeared during Ocucaje times) and petroglyphs show anthropomorphic creatures with staring eyes and rayed headdresses.

The end of the Paracas era at Ica, called Ocucaje Period 10, is seen as the immediate predecessor of Nasca Period 1. Archaeological and iconographic investigations indicate that the Nasca peoples were the same as their Ocucaje ancestors, using the same kinds of pottery, and decorating them with similar themes and motifs, such as the killer whale, felines and human trophy heads. Despite the apparent continuity of population, other cultural influences and developments inevitably left their mark. The early Nasca peoples changed elements of their predecessors' technology and production: pottery masks disappeared, and the practice of painting pots with one of thirteen different colours as a background slip before firing rather than afterwards was adopted. Clearly, for the Nasca potters, colour was a key element of decoration and perhaps suggests a prominent role for colours and shades in their cosmology. A striking Nasca innovation in pottery shape was the step fret vessel which featured also a double-spout-and-bridge handle.

Art, society and religion

Nasca society, its art and religion, were unique products of its desert and oasis-valley environment. Yet, like all other pre-Columbian American societies, its culture was also a result of social, historical and religious factors.

Nasca worldview, while typically Amerindian, reflected its own distinct characteristics and concerns, some of which are visible on its pottery – clearly its chosen medium for cultural expression. Agricultural fertility seems to have been a principal concern, not only in representations of different plants, but also in the more symbolically complex association of warfare and trophy-head hunting. For many indigenous American societies, headhunting, and the ritualised death of human sacrifice were an integral part of the recycling and renewal of life force, both physical and spiritual. This certainly seems to have been the case with the Nasca (see below).

It seems likely that the Nasca shared a generalised shamanic worldview with all pre-Columbian Andean peoples. This was characterised by beliefs in a spiritually animated universe, human-animal transformation, magical curing, animal sacrifices in acts of divination, and the taking of powerful hallucinogens to access the spirit realm. The discovery of over twenty headless guinea pigs at Cahuachi suggests curing and divination, and images of the powerfully hallucinogenic San Pedro cactus on pottery suggests its ritual use in shamanic seances.

Apart from this, evidence for the specific rituals of Nasca religion are ambiguous, a fact which has led to varying interpretations by different scholars. Some consider that they practised ancestor worship on the basis that some tombs seem to have been reopened after burial and the bodies and burial goods disturbed. While this might be the case, it is equally possible that, as elsewhere, prehistoric looting could have taken place, or even the deliberate removal of ancestral items to be re-used as sacred relics. It is often difficult to know whether pottery scenes which depict dancing and the dead represent a ritual surrounding burial, or a later ceremony which amounts to ancestor veneration.

As with Amerindian religion and worldview more generally, nature and supernature are not divided by hard and fast boundaries. Nasca pottery abounds with images of different kinds of birds, plants and animals though, significantly, many of these seem to have a symbolic association with other perhaps more mythical life forms. Among the natural animals which find their way into Nasca art are the killer whale, the pampas cat, falcons and foxes.

There are other more unusual figures that are also depicted on Nasca pottery, though whether these represented gods, shaman-priests dressed in elaborate costumes, or fantastical creations serving as visual metaphors for important Nasca principles is still debated. Perhaps the best known is the so-called 'Anthropomorphic Mythical Being', a human-like creature which has feline characteristics in much the same way as jaguar-shamans are described in more recent ethnographic South American societies. The 'Mythical Killer Whale', perhaps representing a maritime concept of predatory behaviour linked to fertility (i.e. the abundance of the sea and the regenerative quality of water), is shown with human trophy heads and knives.

Other, equally supernatural creatures are the 'Horrible Bird', an anthropomorphic raptorial bird, the 'Mythical Spotted Cat' based on the pampas cat but wearing a mouthmask, and the 'Jagged Staff God'. Each of these supernatural creatures can share elements of the other, suggesting the presence of a grammar of motifs, each of which carries a significance that can be recombined with others and shared between supernaturals. There are many other such creatures in the mythical zoo of the Nasca imagination and that also appear on pottery and textiles. While the supernatural world of the Nasca is realised in many scenes depicted on ceramics, they were almost certainly representative of beliefs which articulated Nasca religious and ceremonial life. Unusually, at least in terms of surviving items, it seems that musical instruments were also an important and integral part of Nasca ritual activities. Native Amerindian ideas of music, which incorporated beliefs concerning sacred breath, whistling and spiritual presence, add a strikingly non-Western dimension to the more unusual associations of music and dance in communal celebrations.

The frequency and variety of musical instruments depicted on Nasca pottery and found in archaeological sites (especially in tombs and offerings) indicate a central role for music in Nasca ceremonial life. Panpipes, trumpets and ceramic drums were all made from fired clay and painted in vivid colours. One unique item is a modelled representation of a family group dressed in their finery, accompanied by several dogs and playing and carrying panpipes. In excavations at the Great Temple at the Nasca centre of Cahuachi (see below) was found a cache of several hundred panpipes – all of which were broken, possibly ritually.

Due to their emphasis – perhaps obsession – with ceramic artistry, Nasca craftsmen expended little effort on other technological activities such as featherwork, stone-carving and metallurgy. Gold working, for example, never reached the heights of achievement that characterised the North Coast Moche, despite deposits being readily available in the area. It was hammered into thin strips and cut into various shapes such as face masks, nose-ornaments and decorative items attached to headdresses and clothing, some of which, such as the mouthmask, appear also on pottery images. Featherwork is occasionally found but rare, and stone carving would seem to have been restricted to either small stylised and sexless statuettes or somewhat more elaborate stone vases engraved with anthropomorphic figures with feline characteristics. In terms of achievement, the only rival to pottery, it seems, was the Nasca practice of creating giant designs on the vast open desert spaces (pampas) that separated their oasis-like valleys.

Geoglyphs, water and mountains

The thirty or so zoomorphic and countless geometric designs etched on to the sun-baked desert surface of the Nazca region – most notably the area known as the Pampa de San José between the Nazca and Palpa Valleys – are arguably one of the world's most famous and enduring archaeological enigmas. They have attracted the attention of a wide variety of investigators, some serious, others less so, and generated a bewildering array of bizarre explanations.

Nazca's desert drawings have been seen as evidence that the ancient Nasca people could fly, that Nazca was visited during prehistory by extraterrestial life-forms who inexplicably landed their intergalactic spacecraft on the cleared 'airstrips', and that they were seen in visions 'from above' during drug-fuelled flights of shamanic ecstasy. Other suggestions include the ideas that they were areas of large-scale textile production, or the dessicated remnants of agricultural fields and canals. While these theories give fascinating insights into our own society, they tell us little of why the ancient Nasca created these images, their development over time and the important meanings they clearly had.

For those who did not know where to look or how to 'see', i.e. anyone who was not a member of Nasca culture, the strange shapes on Nazca's deserts can be instantly recognised only from the air. It is for this reason that the geoglyphs first came to the world's attention during the 1920s and 1930s when commercial airlines began flying over the area. Although first discussed seriously by the Peruvian archaeologist Toribio Mejía Xesspe in 1927, it was the American scholar Paul Kosok who, by chance, saw the sun setting along one of the lines on the Pampa de San José at the winter solstice of 1941. This was the origin of the theory that the Nazca drawings were 'the largest astronomy book in the world', designed and laid out to measure and predict the movements of, and perhaps represent, the heavenly bodies. Exploring the theory of an astronomical and calendrical purpose for the Nazca lines became the life work of Maria Reiche, who spent decades walking, measuring and cleaning the great desert images.

Today, Reiche's investigations and her efforts to establish Nazca as a world-famous archaeological destination are justly acknowledged, and the desert drawings have UNESCO World Heritage status. The purely astronomical hypothesis has largely been discarded however.

With so many lines, plazas and geometric shapes criss-crossing the desert and superimposed with others over time, the chances of accidental alignments to stars, constellations and the sun are high and thereby prove little. The earlier (and much fewer) zoomorphic designs – including a giant spider, condor, killer whale and hummingbird – may have represented Nasca emblems and/or local magical animals (or animal constellations) associated with kinship, shamanism and mythology, but again, such associations are difficult if not impossible to prove. Perhaps the best hope of progress here lies in investigating possible correlations between these desert zoomorphs and their miniature counterparts painted on to Nasca pottery.

During the 1980s especially the astronomical hypothesis was replaced by several interrelated (and much more culturally informed) theories that saw a relationship between Nazca's lines and geometric shapes and the well-documented Andean ritual practice of constructing, maintaining and walking sacred lines (sometimes aligned to prominent mountains) as part of religious ceremonies associated with ancestor worship and fertility rites. Such interpretations also borrowed heavily from the well-documented (and much later) system of imaginary 'straight lines' called *ceques* that organised the ritual space of the Inka capital of Cuzco. These were related to water flow and were the focus of religious processions and sacrifices. These ideas were located much more securely in Andean worldview which saw the landscape as a living entity, mountains as the homes of all-powerful weather deities, and caves, lakes, freshwater springs and the Pacific Ocean as manifestations of the numinous – borderlands between earthly existence and the spirit realm.

The most recent theory draws in part on these new ideas but casts its explanation in a more scientific and pragmatic light. It suggests that there is indeed an association between the geoglyphs and water, but that it is based on correlations with subterranean water flow, aquifers, geological faults and the location of archaeological sites. This view sees the ancient Nasca people as possessing an intimate understanding of the local hydraulic regime, and building their villages, cemeteries, reservoirs and underground water-capturing filtration galleries (*puquios*), at points where geological faults brought water to (or near) the surface. Then, so the theory goes, they marked the location and flow of these underground water sources with geoglyphs on the surface.

This hypothesis was tested geologically and archaeologically at several locations, and appears to have yielded some positive correlations. Trapezoid-shaped geoglyphs were created over these faults and stone circles marked the points at which aquifers entered a valley. Zigzag designs are said to mark the waterless boundaries of aquifers and zoomorphic shapes announce a change in direction of sub-surface water flow. While this theory is not conclusive, and certainly not accepted by all Nasca experts, it does explain some associations and proposes a relationship between landscape, water and animal imagery that is in keeping with other better-documented Andean rituals that also incorporate these elements.

It is probable that over hundreds of years of prehistory, beginning with the preceding Paracas/Ocucaje culture, the Nasca people made geoglyphs of different shapes and sizes at different locations for a variety of practical and spiritual reasons, and that there is no single overall theory that can explain this diversity.

Trophy heads and headhunting

Although the practice of headhunting and the ritual treatment and display of human heads is widespread across the Americas, it appears that for Nasca society such activities held a special place. Most of our ideas about what Nasca trophy heads might have meant to the Nasca themselves come from projecting historically recent information back into the prehistoric past. Such information typically comes from the Jívaro Indians of Ecuador, although they, unlike the Nasca, removed the skull and thereby 'shrunk' the head. Ethnographic insights stress the spiritual purpose of headhunting and trophy collecting, whereby the powerful spiritual essence of the dead was symbolically captured and kept as magical protection against malign forces, and simultaneously advertised the warrior status of the victor.

While it can be misleading to read too much into Nasca trophy head hunting in the light of more recent activities, both the Jívaro and the Nasca ritually closed the eyes and mouth by sealing them shut with thorns, or by sewing them up. Ethnographically, this was to ensure that the power within did not escape through the two main sensory orifices of sight and speech. Whether this was also the case for the Nasca is unknown.

Trophy heads in Nasca society appear to have derived from the earlier Paracas culture, where images of human heads adorn their elaborate textiles. There is a case for head-taking to have occurred between different Nasca groups, rather than against a common non-Nasca enemy as previously supposed. Whether this was part of ritualised violence (well documented in recent times in the Andes) between otherwise friendly communities, or as a result of outright warfare between agonistic groups can only be guessed at. Sometimes trophy heads are found buried alongside complete bodies and treated in the same respectful way, and headless bodies sometimes have a piece of pottery or a gourd substituted for the missing head.

In Nasca society, trophy heads seem to have two distinct, albeit probably related aspects. In early Nasca times, it is likely that head-hunting was more religious and symbolic, appearing as quite rare real heads, and more commonly as pottery depictions associated with mythological beings, such as the 'Killer Whale' and the 'Horrible Bird', and as decorative motifs on bowls. It may be, as some experts believe, that this early manifestation of the trophy-head cult was related to ideas of ancestor worship and fertility which were probably an integral part of the rituals that took place at the great ceremonial centre of Cahuachi (see below).

In later Nasca times, after the demise of Cahuachi in about AD 400, a rise in conflict is apparent, as is a significant increase in the number of trophy heads found in excavations. While trophy heads probably did not lose their spiritual dimensions, it may be that now they reflect an increasingly secular, perhaps political and military significance, as they are shown in conflict situations on late Nasca pottery – carried by warriors, and attached to depictions of elaborately attired elite men – perhaps war leaders. It is also true that most Nasca trophy heads belong to young men of warrior age.

Trophy heads appear in art and archaeology throughout the life of Nasca culture. However, their presence can be misleading, as headhunting is a function of the political dynamic that shapes and drives a society as it changes through time. Headhunting is an inherently bloody and violent activity, imbued with many kinds of symbolism in pre-Columbian America. As Nasca society developed between early and late Nasca times, it must be acknowledged that the significance given to headhunting probably also changed, perhaps reconfiguring itself towards more secular political ends – although the spiritual dimension of politics in ancient Peru means that trophy heads were probably never simply trophies.

Cahuachi, the Nasca capital

Investigations by archaeologists Helaine Silverman and Guiseppe
Orefici at the great site of Cahuachi have revealed a large settlement
distinctly different from contemporary sites in other parts of Peru, as
well as from diverse smaller communities in the Nazca region.
Located in a probably sacred landscape amid wind-sculpted hills
and where subterreanean water emerges as a spring, Cahuachi's
temple-mound architecture appears physically and symbolically
aligned with some of the huge desert geoglyphs on the adjacent
pampa. Clearly, at some time in the past, the ritual activities that
defined Cahuachi's monumental architecture reached out on to the
desert, incorporating the still little-understood imagery scratched on
to the hard desert surface.

Cahuachi's location is not especially promising from the perspective of everyday living and economic activity. Water supply is
not particularly abundant, despite the proximity of the flood-prone
Nazca river; the soil is salt-ridden, and local windstorms scour the
area. Yet, at the beginning, Cahuachi was more in keeping with
other sites; during Nasca Period 1, there is evidence for extensive
occupation alongside early examples of monumental architecture,
such as the recently discovered 'Step Motif Temple'. Nevertheless,
some unknown factor in Nasca society led to an emphasis not on
developing or extending the site into an ancient city or even a well-
populated ritual centre such as Pachacamac on Peru's central coast,
but rather in privileging its ritual and ceremonial functions.

As a consequence, at its height during Nasca Period 3, Cahuachi
spread over 150 ha, but was never an urban phenomenon. Rather, it
had developed into a pilgrimage centre whose monumental architecture was probably produced by different groups coming together
at certain times of year to undertake commercial, ritual and,
probably, political activities. This view sees Nasca society not as an
hierarchically integrated state such as their contemporaries the
Moche on the North Coast, but rather as a chiefdom or confederacy
of chiefdoms who used Cahuachi, among other things, as a place to
create and maintain a peaceful co-existence.

It seems as if Cahuachi's many great temple mounds were made
piecemeal, inasmuch as they were not the result of human occupation, nor of a preconceived civic plan devised by one corporate elite
group. Rather, they were constructed by different groups of the

region who simply built around natural hills and mounds, thereby giving the impression of large-scale architectural undertakings. In this way, Cahuachi would have presented an impressive façade without the need for organised Moche-like labour forces and all the political support their mobilisation would have entailed. There are some forty ceremonial mounds of various sizes with adjacent plazas (presumably for public rituals).

Investigations have reinforced the impression of Cahuachi as an essentially empty ceremonial centre whose purpose was to be the focus of pilgrimage (and doubtless its many associated activites). Unlike contemporary sites elsewhere, Cahuachi has yielded comparatively little evidence of domestic refuse – the detritus of everyday life, such as domestic pottery and the animal bones from meals. There are few remains of guinea pigs for example, a normally ubiquitous food resource.

Nor has there been found, so far, any evidence for large-scale long-term storage or workshop areas for specialised craft production. However, it is likely that certain kinds of craftwork were carried on at Cahuachi but so far only tantalising details have emerged. There is evidence for an area that may have specialised in textile production, the remains of possible paintbrushes have been found and also pieces of red pigment, the latter two items suggestive of high-quality pottery production and decoration. The sheer quantity of obviously valuable and beautifully painted ceramics decorated with complex mythical-religious motifs found here indicates that at least some manufacturing could have been undertaken on site.

Despite the relative paucity of such everyday remains, the site is rich in the ritual paraphernalia that would be expected of occasional and temporary visitors, such as elaborate textiles, engraved gourds, sacrificed llama remains and an unusual cache of petrified wood that perhaps suggests its status as a sacred mineralised example of naturally occurring wood. At the so-called Great Temple, large quantities of high-quality pottery were found alongside feathers and the ceramic panpipes for which Nasca culture is well known. Probably equally a sign of ritual behaviour is the large amount of high-quality pottery that was discovered in pieces, perhaps an indication that the ritual smashing of ceramics was as much a part of Nasca religious behaviour as it was for the Tiwanaku and Wari civilisations.

The excavation of a temple mound known as Unit 19 illustrates the kinds of activity which took place in such structures. Across the mound were found elaborate pottery, textiles and pieces of ceramic panpipe. In a part of the mound called the 'Room of the Posts' it was apparent that there had originally been twelve wooden posts, eleven of which were of the characteristically twisted *huarango* tree, one of which had been cut smooth. In the centre of the room, circular depressions were cut into the floor, and careful examination of surviving walls revealed that the room had been replastered many times. Helaine Silverman interprets a clean layer of sand which covered the Room of the Posts as a much later (i.e. Nasca Period 8) ritual entombment into which later objects were placed, including whole pots and trophy heads. It seems that after the demise of Cahuachi, at least some of its buildings continued to be used as sites where local peoples congregated for ritual purposes.

It seems that Cahuachi's ritual purpose served a multitude of social ends. As a pilgrimage centre it was not only an expression of religious fervour, but also a ritual arena where local groups met to represent their local communities and probably also establish or reaffirm shared cultural values and the place of their community in the regional political hierarchy. The evidence suggests they dressed in their finery and brought sacrificial offerings of polychrome pottery, llamas, trophy heads and colourful textiles.

In this sense, Cahuachi was as much a political as a religious destination for the small communities spread over the Nazca region. Appearing to us as a religiously and ritually inspired place, to the Nasca peoples it was this and more – a sacred location where ethnic, social and spiritual identity were physically and symbolically renewed. The possibility that it served in some ways to integrate local groups and perhaps alleviate social tensions in a religious setting is supported by what occurred after its demise. At this time, there is archaeological and artistic evidence for an upsurge in armed conflict manifested most graphically by a dramatic increase in the number of trophy heads shown on pottery and deposited at the site. Cahuachi at this time, and for centuries to come, may have ceased to exercise social and political influence over Nasca society but clearly continued to be a sacred place where numerous burials were made. It may be that as the large-scale building activities ceased and Cahuachi was abandoned (in Nasca Period 4), cultural energies were transferred to the desert pampa and ever more ambitious geoglyphs (lines and plazas) were constructed.

The end of Nasca

The end of an identifiably Nasca culture occurred in about AD 700–800, during Nasca Period 8, or Loro as it is now called. The most striking difference between the Loro phase and its mainstream Nasca predecessors is the change in pottery. Highly polished and colourful pottery disappears and is replaced by thicker unpolished vessels, and the hitherto common panpipes and bridge-and-spout handle items also cease. Decoration too is radically different with the abandonment of mythical imagery and the appearance of geometric designs such as chevrons and zigzags, sometimes as abstractions of earlier forms such as the killer whale. By so-called Nasca Period 9, it is influence from the highland culture of Wari that is predominant, with several tons of Wari-style pottery fragments being discovered at the site of Pacheco nearby Cahuachi. By this time, pure Nasca culture had to all intents and purposes ceased to exist.

TEN

Wari and Tiwanaku

The Wari and Tiwanaku civilisations flourished during the so-called Middle Horizon (AD 650–1000) period of Andean prehistory. Wari (also spelt Huari) itself developed between c. AD 400 and 800 in the Ayacucho region of the central highlands of Peru. Its imperial influence spread throughout the Andes and along the adjacent Pacific coast, manifesting itself in different ways in these two regions. Wari innovations included roadbuilding, planned architecture, agricultural terracing, bronze working and the introduction of the uniquely Andean system of keeping (presumably) administrative records – the knotted string called *quipu*. At its height the city of Wari covered perhaps 4sq. km and had a population that may have numbered as many as thirty-five thousand.

Broadly contemporary, on the southern shores of Lake Titicaca in modern day Bolivia, the great city of Tiwanaku (also spelt Tiahuanaco) rose to prominence. Famous for its monumental architecture and sophisticated hydraulic engineering, it reached its zenith during the fourth century AD, extending over some 8sq. km with a population of between thirty thousand and forty thousand. It was the hub of an empire whose llama caravans connected vast areas of southern Peru and northern Chile. This chapter outlines the achievements of these two civilisations and illustrates their role in the rise of the Inka empire.

WARI

The origins of the Wari civilisation appear to have been with the Huarpa people (AD 100–600), famed for their abilities to produce terraces and canals in their wild homeland dominated by deep ravines and little available flat land suitable for agriculture. The Huarpa peope lived in scattered agricultural hamlets, and their capital of Ñawimpukuyo today overlooks the modern town of

Ayacucho. It is thought that the Huarpa people had long-distance contacts with the Nasca culture on Peru' south coast and also with the emerging Tiwanaku civilisation on Lake Titicaca's southern shores. It was this interaction which some experts believe stimulated Huarpa culture in ways which led to the development of the more sophisticated culture known today as Wari.

The city of Wari

The political centre of the Wari civilisation was the city of Wari itself, with a population calculated at between ten thousand and thirty thousand spread over some 4sq. km near the modern city of Ayacucho in the central southern Peruvian Andes. The earliest traces of habitation suggest the site had originally been settled by the Huarpa people. The site itself appears to have been terraced and to have had an elaborate system of underground drains to move water throughout the city. The early inhabitants had invested greatly in building a series of canals to irrigate the terraced fields that surround the city and were able to grow large quantities of maize and other crops on this previously under-exploited land.

The beginnings of Wari as a major political centre are associated with the appearance of the so-called Okros Style of pottery. During this period, the population centre at Ñawimpukuyo and other smaller Huarpa communities were abandoned and their populations moved to live at the nearby centre of Conchapata, and perhaps also at the more distant site of Wari.

A distinctive feature of ancient Wari was its system of massive walls that delineated compounds and would have made moving through the city a difficult undertaking. These high walls probably would have served to separate off one area from another and some archaeologists interpret this as an indication that Wari society was strongly segregated in nature, perhaps along lines of economic specialisation, kin, status or a combination of these.

The structures within the compounds had two or three storeys and were arranged around rectangular central patios, the buildings themselves having the appearance of long halls. The discovery of domestic refuse within indicated they were used as dwellings. One high-status compound, known as Cheqo Wasi, appears to have been the residence of high-ranking Wari individuals as indicated by the discovery during excavation of megalithic underground chambers formed of well-cut stone and containing human remains, and high-status goods made from gold, silver, lapis lazuli and the ritually important Spondylus shell. Many of these are exotic to the Wari region, and would have been the focus of long-distance trading activities. It seems likely that one feature of Wari as an urban phenomenon was the presence of specialist craftsmen working with these exotic raw materials alongside administrators and ritual specialists.

Society, art and religion

As Wari society developed out of the earlier Huarpa culture it seems as if its leaders became increasingly concerned with advertising their status by creating an art style which symbolised political, economic and presumably religious power. To this end, they selectively borrowed aspects of the art of the Nasca and Tiwanaku peoples.

Of the icons that Wari adopted from Tiwanaku and spread throughout the northern Andes, the most famous was the so-called 'Staff Bearer', often shown either as a human wearing a snarling feline face, or perhaps a mythical being with these age-old features of supernatural status. These figures decorated the extraordinary polychrome Wari pottery and, in a squeezed or stretched form, also adorned textiles. The related image of the Staff God, known best as the central figure on Tiwanaku's Gateway of the Sun, was also acquired by the Wari elite, though perhaps reinterpreted as a deity of agriculture and fertility.

Perhaps more unusual was the Wari borrowing of the typically Tiwanaku-style sunken ceremonial court in rectangular shape. One example, which seems to have been used for a century or so, between AD 580 and 660, was discovered buried beneath a later building at Wari. Archaeologists regard it as a religious building as it not only appears to have been kept clean, but its floors were regularly renewed with clay and coloured plaster. Whether this was, as in Mesoamerica and elsewhere, a kind of symbolic interment or had simply been built over is unknown, though its preservation indicates it was carefully built over. While much Wari art and religion were inspired by the beliefs and styles of Tiwanaku, it also had its own distinguishing features. One of these was the practice of ritually smashing the beautifully painted polychrome ceramics which, with their depictions of the so-called Wari rayed deity, were among the most expensive and prestigious examples of Wari material culture. While the Tiwanaku people also ceremonially smashed some of their high-status ceramics, for the Wari this activity involved drinking *chicha* beer stored in magnificent elaborately decorated pottery urns. The analysis of several excavated caches of these ceramics indicates they may have been specially made for these one-off ritual events.

One intriguing parallel between Wari and the later Inka is the discovery of Wari-period *quipus*, a record-keeping system of multi-coloured knotted strings. The *quipu* system was perfected by and is best known from the Inka period, when they were used by specialist bureaucrats known as the 'Keepers of the *quipu*'. Comparatively little is known of the few surviving Wari examples, other than that they are visually and technically different by virtue of having a coloured thread wrapped around the subsidiary strings which hang from the main cord.

Burial practices usually present archaeologists with insights into the nature of a culture's social structure, religious beliefs and ideological orientation. For the Wari period, information on burials is frustratingly incomplete due to prehistoric as well as more recent looting, and the practice of the Wari themselves of reopening ancestral tombs and adding and/or taking away body parts and other items. Available evidence indicates that the Wari buried their dead and caches of material culture beneath the floors of their buildings. Excavation reveals a variety of burial practices – indicative of a range of social statuses. Burials could be in simple earthen pits, rock cracks, or more elaborate stone-lined cists. They could hold one, two, or more individuals; sometimes an extra body was pushed in at a later date.

The most impressive unlooted burial so far found was perhaps the tomb of a local *curaca* (chief). It was discovered beneath the floor of a room, with the skeleton of a pregnant woman found just inside the tomb's entrance. Inside were fourteen other individuals including two fetuses in jars, pottery and items made from copper and greenstone. The archaeologists who excavated the tomb consider it possible that it was reopened and added to at least once.

Evidence from recent investigations at the site of Conchapata indicate that the structures known as 'mortuary rooms' held the remains of high-ranking individuals. Preliminary study of the damaged and incomplete skeletal remains suggest the main burials here were of elite men who were interred with a number of their wives and sometimes children. The occasional find of small gold items reinforces the impression that mortuary rooms were where the leaders of the community joined the company of immortal ancestors. Small holes in the slab covering the tomb may have been for communing with the spirits of the deceased or perhaps, on occasion, pushing through small offerings which were then found around the entrance when excavated. Although the Wari probably engaged in ancestor veneration, unlike the later Inka, they appear not to have mummified their dead leaders and paraded them around in public ceremonies, preferring to leave them in peace in their subterranean tombs.

As previously noted, Wari religion and ritual behaviour also saw the burying of smashed high-status ceramics in underground caches. These are painted with various figures as described above, though one, called the 'Front View Sacrificer', has recently been studied in depth. From both hands and both feet are suspended decapitated trophy heads which suggest ritual sacrifice. These figures are often shown in close proximity to a dome-shaped image which has been interpreted as the D-shaped building found at Wari sites such as Conchapata and Wari itself.

In recent years, many D-shaped structures have been identified and excavated, and many are associated with human remains, disarticulated skeletons and skulls, and on one occasion a cache of human trophy heads. It is thought that these D-shaped buildings are ceremonial precincts – temple locations for acts of human sacrifice, the remains of which are interred nearby, and the whole scene rendered in the iconography of the Front View Sacrificer on pottery.

Empire

Traditionally, the Wari have been seen as an imperial civilisation, spreading their culture and control over the Andes and adjacent Pacific coast through aggressive military actions and in many ways acting as precursors for the later Inka empire. Increasingly, as more archaeological investigations are undertaken, this view is being modified. Some experts now prefer to see alternative strategies at work, based perhaps on a mix of militarism and adaptive ideas in agriculture and economics. The nature of the Wari's relationship with Tiwanaku is often central to this issue.

Illustrating the hitherto universally accepted aggressive aspect of Wari, and its ambiguous relationship with Tiwanaku, is the strategically located and fortified site of Cerro Baúl. Initially it was considered that this was a Wari colony situated deep within Tiwanaku territory. This impression was reinforced by the fact that Cerro Baúl was a fortified site built atop a 600m high rocky outcrop in the Moquegua Valley and only approachable by a series of steep and easily defended switchback paths. Although there is evidence that Tiwanaku people lived nearby, the Wari created agricultural terraces and brought water to the citadel by a long canal. On the summit, around central patios they constructed typically Wari buildings in the remains of which were found smashed pottery and evidence of stone-bead production.

However, recent survey work during the 1990s suggests the possibility that this was perhaps an unpopulated or underpopulated area on the borderlands of the Tiwanaku sphere of influence, and that Cerro Baúl may simply have been a temporary control point for trade routes down to the south coast. Some archaeologists believe it was a Wari colony specifically designed to extract onyx for making elite jewellery. While some experts regard the evidence as pointing to the destruction of Tiwanaku settlements and the withdrawal of the Wari people, others see no real evidence for conflict. Yet, while the evidence for warfare remains ambiguous at Cerro Baúl, recently discovered polychrome pottery from the earlier levels of Conchapata show Wari warriors armed with battle-axes and bows and arrows kneeling on reed boats – presumably sailing on Lake Titicaca.

There is another view of Wari civilisation beyond its heartland and this is provided by looking at administrative centres rather than military locations. In these areas, it was not warfare that was the founding principle but rather the agricultural advances perfected and spread by the Wari people; irrigation canals, terracing, and the introduction of new high-yield crops clearly drew local peoples down from scattered villages at higher altitudes to congregate in Wari centres in low-lying flatland areas. In other words, the cultural landscape was redefined by Wari agricultural practices and new communities such as Jincamocco and Viracochapampa appeared. In these last two cases, and despite their proximity to other communities, there is no obvious evidence of militarism.

Such centres usually take the form of several rectangular enclosures with no defensive features. One of the largest and best investigated of these Wari administrative centres is that of Pikillaqta in the southern end of the valley of Cuzco. The site spreads over some 50ha, and still today has the remains of high walls, and large storage areas. It is thought to have functioned partly as a storehouse centre where food and other materials were kept in order to pay those who worked for the Wari state in this region. These workers probably lived in the numerous rooms that resemble an army barracks at the site. Excavation suggested some parts of the occupation area belonged to women who prepared food and drink (probably *chicha* beer) for the feasting that was such a feature of Wari social and ritual life.

At Conchapata, according to recent investigations during the late 1990s and early 2000, the site was dominated by elite architecture in the form of palaces. It originally covered over 20ha, and was traditonally thought to have faded as the city of Wari reached its zenith. Conchapata is especially famous for its Conchapata Style polychrome pottery which appears to take its inspiration from the art of Tiwanaku, especially the rayed deity holding two staffs and wearing an elaborate headdress similar to that portrayed as the central figure on the Gateway of the Sun at Tiwanaku.

Recent excavations have also revealed a number of large, beautifully painted ceramic urns and so-called face-neck jars which had been (presumably) ritually smashed then buried, though, significantly, not all were complete. These objects were decorated variously with the rayed deity, profile images of spotted felines, and horizontal anthropomorphic creatures with feline-like heads (or masks) carrying similarly feline-headed staffs. Most of the pottery dates to between AD 600 and 850, and so is contemporary with similarly decorated pottery from Tiwanaku.

These discoveries have enabled a more fine-tuned interpretation of Wari ceramics at the site. Not all are decorated with Tiwanaku style imagery and, even more important, the urns and face-neck jars are shapes which are not found at Tiwanaku. In other words, some of these newly found ceramics represent an identifiably independent pottery style. These have been seen as representing an intial pottery phase in local Wari style dating to *c*. AD 550 with more Tiwanaku-like examples dating to *c*. AD 850. Where both kinds appear together in later contexts, it may be that earlier pots were kept for centuries (or perhaps dug up) before being ritually smashed. If this was the case, then there was a sense in which Wari ancestor

Mythical animal and human heads painted on Conchapata pottery of the Wari culture. (© *Roxanne Saunders, after J. Ochatoma Paravicino and M. Cabrera Romero, 'Religious Ideology and Military Organization in the Iconography of a D-Shaped Ceremonial Precinct at Conchapata', in H. Silverman and W.H. Isbell (eds)*, Andean Archaeology II, *pp. 225–247, Fig. 8.9)*

veneration extended to 'scavenging' the power-laden bones of their long dead predecessors.

The archaeological evidence of pottery vessels made for drinking and serving suggests perhaps official feasting events which may have articulated a distinctive kind of social organisation for such centres. High-class Wari pottery is found alongside local imitations and also with local kinds of ceramics, and while buildings are never identical, they do conform to the Wari style. Archaeologists have interpreted this mix-and-match evidence as an indication that at such locations local people and their own leaders were living and working under Wari supervision. For the Wari, it seems, there was a variety of responses to the mosaic of local conditions, perhaps suggesting that Wari imperialism was a mix of militarism and economic reorientation.

This possibility seems to be supported by the evidence from the deserts of the Peruvian coast, where the advantages of Wari's sophisticated high-altitude agricultural revolution could not be applied. Despite this, Wari civilisation does seem to have exerted a profound influence on coastal civilisations, from Nasca in the south to the great shrine centre of Pachacamac on the central coast and north to the great cultures of the Moche and Lambayeque Valleys. This influence, however, was less technical than artistic and perhaps religious, as much of the evidence is in Wari-influenced imagery on pottery interred with the dead as grave goods. Particularly prominent in this respect is the so-called rayed deity. The presence of Wari artistic and religious motifs combined with the absence of their buildings and architecture creates a sense of ambiguity, and poses the so far unanswered question of what was the precise nature of Wari influence among coastal civilisations.

It has long been observed that Wari settlements appear located on or near much later Inka roads, suggesting perhaps that Inka highways merely followed original ones planned and built by the Wari to link their empire's administrative centres. However, while some Inka roads do follow earlier Wari ones, many do not and the two roadway systems reflect the different political and economic orientations of their respective empires. Neverthless, it is probably true that some aspects of Inka imperialism were but larger scale elaborations of previous Wari practices.

Although new evidence may alter the view, traditionally it is thought that Wari civilisation collapsed suddenly in about AD 800. The Ayacucho heartland ceased to enjoy extensive contacts with the rest of the Andes, and while Tiwanaku flourished for another two hundred years, the southern Peruvian Andes and adjacent coast seem to have entered a period of balkanisation with communities becoming inward looking, and probably poorer as well. As the situation in southern Peru deteriorated, the flag of pre-Columbian civilisation was taken up on the north coast with the emergence of the Sicán and later the Chimú civilisations.

TIWANAKU

The city by the lake

Tiwanaku civilisation embodied and symbolised two key elements of life in the Andes – stone and water. Located about 15km from Lake Titicaca's southern shore, next to a small river and possessing numerous springs, this monumental stone-clad city incorporated a sophisticated system of elaborate stone channels, conduits and drains designed, it seems, to display and control the ritual as well as actual flow of water. The ceremonial heart of the city, dominated by massive temple platforms and monolithic artworks, was itself surrounded by a great water-filled moat that perhaps made the city's core a symbolic reflection of the sacred Islands of the Sun in the middle of Lake Titicaca.

Although Tiwanaku's origins are not yet well known archaeologically, the city and the nearby lake feature repeatedly in cosmogonic creation myths of the region's local peoples. These legends, pieced together from the fragments of oral tradition collected by the Spanish, exist in different versions, some adapted for their own use by the later Inka. In one Inka version, the creator god Viracocha set out a new world order at his dwelling place at Tiwanaku, sending out the first man and wife from there to call forth Andean peoples from every feature of the landscape.

It was between AD 100 and 600 that the city grew to its maximum extent and included the magnificent ceremonial centre which has only recently begun to be scientifically investigated. There are two main periods in Tiwanaku's spectacular rise to power: Phase 3 is dated to AD 100–375, and Phase 4 to AD 375–600, this latter period representing the height of the city in terms of achievement and size. Period 5 lasts from AD 600 to 1000, and perhaps just slightly after. During most of this time, Tiwanaku became the single most impressive and important centre in the southern Andes, often described by such terms as centralised, hierarchical, and theocratic. At its height the city probably extended over some 8sq. km, within which the ceremonial core area was perhaps 16ha. Its population was in the region of 30,000 to 40,000, though the wider, so-called metropolitan district had perhaps as many as 365,000 people.

Three monumental constructions dominate Tiwanaku's sacred profile: the Kalasasaya, Pumapunku, and Akapana temple mound complexes. The Kalasasaya and Pumapunku are described as U-shaped rectangular platforms, open to the rising sun and having a typically Tiwanaku-style sunken court within. Both structures had a ceremonial entrance of a typically Tiwanaku-style monolithic stone doorway.

The earliest ceremonial structure, however, appears to be the so-called Semisubterranean Temple, which has predecessors at the earlier pre-Tiwanaku sites of Pukara and Chiripa. It is a large sunken plaza whose walls are adorned with small carved stone heads that have been inserted into the wall and which were probably replaced or renewed at various times. The whole structure may have been dedicated to a deity referred to as the 'Bearded Statue', a cult object which still stands in the sunken plaza in the shape of a roughly carved rectangular column depicting the features of a human being with prominent hands.

Nearby is the huge 15m high mound known as the Akapana. Long regarded as a natural hill, it is in fact the eroded and looted remains of an originally seven-stepped, stone-clad temple platform which may have been a symbolic miniature of the prominent sacred mountains that dominate the surrounding landscape. It is thought that the summit of the Akapana was designed with ideas of sacred geography in mind as it seems to be the only place on the low-lying valley floor where the distant snow-capped peaks of Mount Illimani and the glittering Lake Titicaca can be observed in a single glance. Investigation has revealed that this and other structures were closely associated with the ritual flow of water, and perhaps more generally the idea of sacred moisture. The Akapana's summit had a layer of green water-rounded gravel brought from nearby mountains, and stone drains to regulate water flow and perhaps produce fountains.

Recent excavations have yielded intimate insights into the practice of human sacrifice and the ways in which the philosophy of the Tiwanaku elite bound together religion, ritual death and material culture. One discovery was a cache of *keros*, distinctively shaped ceremonial beakers with a flared rim, used probably for ritual drinking and pouring libations. As was the practice at Wari, these vessels had been ritually smashed then carefully buried. Their decoration featured the same motif – decapitated human trophy heads. Nearby were the remains of sacrificial victims, many of whom had been decapitated, and a superbly carved stone image of a kneeling figure wearing a feline mask and holding a human trophy head. These burials appear contemporary, perhaps a single seventh century AD event that sanctified the Akapana mound. While indicating the practice of human sacrifice at Tiwanaku, they also play on age-old ideas of feline symbolism, masking and transformation, and dedicatory offerings of human life.

Adjacent to the Akapana, the Kalasasaya is another great ritual enclosure within which stands the impressive stone statue known as the Ponce Monolith. The figure appears framed by the great stone doorway that sits atop a monolithic stairway at the entrance to the enclosure. It has typically Tiwanaku-style rectangular eyes, a rectangular mouth and is shown holding a *kero* and a sceptre-like object. The Kalasasaya is bounded by massive walls and has elaborate water channels incorporated into its structure. Nearby, the building called the Putuni complex is now regarded as a palace built for Tiwanaku's ruling elite. Beneath it was laid an intricate sewage system and on the surface fresh spring water was channelled around the palace building. The excavation of an unlooted chamber tomb in the palace complex yielded the remains of a high-status woman accompanied by a miniature gold mask, a collection of obsidian chips and a collar of multi-coloured minerals including turquoise and lapis lazuli; in a side chamber were found a copper mirror and other metal items.

The third major architectural complex is the Pumapunku ceremonial platform. Built of andesite and sandstone masonry, this finest of all the city's great structures has a huge stone-built façade and several monolithic gateways. The lintel of one is carved with a typically long-tailed feline figure (perhaps a jaguar), complete with collar and leash. This masterpiece of stone carving perhaps suggests that, as with other Andean civilisations, jaguars, pumas and may be even the smaller ocelot were kept either as pets or more likely for ritual purposes.

Art and religion

Most experts consider that Tiwanaku art shares a common heritage in Andean mythology that was first represented by the culture that flourished at Chavín de Huántar between 800 and 400 BC. Motifs such as the 'Staff God', his helpers shown in profile, and anthropomorphic raptorial birds all appear at Tiwanaku as developments from earlier Chavín prototypes. While Chavín culture flourished centuries before Tiwanaku's great artistic designs appear, it is possible that the culture known as Pukara preserved and adapted older beliefs and images that were later taken up by the leaders of Tiwanaku. Pukara society (200 BC–AD 200) was a cosmopolitan culture and an urban phenomenon, spreading over some 4sq. km. Its population built monumental architecture including a sunken court, and its master craftsmen created a sophisticated style of stone carving.

Monumental art at Tiwanaku is dominated by the so-called Gateway of the Sun, a monolithic slab of andesite which, alongside the remains of Inka city of Machu Picchu, has become an international icon, emblematic of the archaeological grandeur of South America. The central figure on this monumental piece of stone sculpture is variously called the 'Staff God', 'Gateway God', or 'Rayed Deity'. It shows a squat anthropomorphic figure rendered face-on, with elaborate decoration around the eyes (sometimes interpreted as tears). He wears a headdress whose 'rays' feature feline heads and circles, a puma-ended belt, and a short tunic fringed with ambiguous miniature heads that could represent 'smiling felines' or perhaps grimacing human trophy heads (two definite trophy heads are suspended from the headdress). In each hand he grasps a staff, the ends of which finish in a beaked bird head (possibly that of a hawk).

This deity, thought by some to be a creator god or solar being, is approached on both sides by small winged figures with human, animal and bird heads. These figures – perhaps supernaturals or priests wearing masks – are depicted in profile. They wear smaller rayed headdresses and carry a single staff adorned with a zoomorphic head. Although rarely shown in illustrated general books on the site, the back of the gateway features two large and four small niches, though whether these originally supported a wooden superstructure or were simply the repositories of religious images is unknown. The Gateway of the Sun is only the best known of several such monolithic doorways at Tiwanaku, the second best known being the Gateway of the Moon.

Other monolithic statues are scattered around the civic centre of the site. One of the most famous is the so-called El Fraile ('The Friar'), a figure which is located in the south-west corner of the Kalasasaya. Purposefully carved from a block of stone with a vertical streak of lighter stone, it is a typically Tiwanaku-style front-facing figure with large staring eyes, and is depicted holding a *kero* and wearing a prominent belt.

Arguably the most impressive of all the city's freestanding monolithic statues, however, is that referred to as the Bennett Stela. Originally this stood as the focal point of the Semisubterranean Temple, surrounded – as if in homage – by a set of variously styled smaller sculptures and stelae. The Bennett Stela and most of the others have now been removed to a replica of the structure in Bolivia's capital La Paz.

As with the other statues, the Bennett Stela depicts a human figure holding a sceptre and *kero*, and dressed in typical Tiwanaku fashion. Its complex iconography has been reproduced as a roll-out drawing which in turn has led to several interpretations as to its symbolic meaning. One view sees the statue as encoding a twelve-month agricultural calendar based on observations of the moon and stars and on counting the number of engraved circles and running figures. Whether or not this is correct, it is a fact that flowering plants are depicted, as are llamas, images of maize and a *kero* for drinking maize beer (*chicha*).

Perhaps providing the most insight for the modern investigator are the images of the powerful hallucinogenic San Pedro cactus, still used by shamans today, and featuring also in the imagery of the earlier Chavín civilisation far to the north. When assessed in combination with the other ancient features of Andean culture, the presence of San Pedro on the Bennett Stela reinforces the view of the shamanic nature of Tiwanaku religion and cosmology. As with the later Inka and also the Aztec of Mesoamerica, it may be that the smaller statues represent ancestor images of other peoples conquered or peacefully incorporated into the Tiwanaku state, and that they were prominently displayed as symbolic hostages to the greater deity represented by the Bennett Stela.

Tiwanaku ceramics also carry the Staff God's image but usually only represent the head. Felines (pumas and jaguars), serpents and raptorial birds also are common motifs, as are the more hybrid creatures of myth. Some of the most beautiful of these ceramics are called *incensarios* (*incense burners*) though their actual function is unknown. They take the form of brightly painted goblets, typically decorated with long-tailed felines shown in profile and wearing elaborate headdresses. Some examples also have a feline head modelled on to the flared rim, the whole effect being that of the typical *kero* or ceremonial beaker.

Part of Tiwanaku religion undoubtedly was characterised by the ritual taking of hallucinogenic drugs. While such widespread practices were an integral part of pre-Columbian Andean worldview, in relation to the Tiwanaku they have left behind an important and diagnostic kind of material culture. The so-called snuff trays survive well in the dry conditions of the southern Andes and adjacent coast. They have been found with carved-bone snuffing tubes and it is probable that it was hallucinogenic powder known as vilca or yopó made from crushed seeds of the *Anadenanthera* plant that was inhaled. At the site of Niño Korin, a dry cave on the eastern slopes of the Andes, were discovered the remains of a shaman along with his magical paraphernalia used for curing – a snuff tray, snuffing tube, and even the remains of some of his curing plants. Coca chewing too was a common habit and some effigy keros and carved stone statues clearly show a human face chewing a wad of coca leaves.

Society and economy

It is likely that Tiwanaku was in some senses a multi-ethnic state, whose highest echelons were probably dominated by those of Aymara and Pukina ethnic affiliation, and who may have inter-married to form a ruling dynasty. It also seems likely that the official Tiwanaku language was the native tongue of one of these two groups and functioned in ways similar to the Quechua language of the later Inka empire. It has been suggested that, in typically Andean fashion, powerful ethnic lords – the chiefs known as *curacas* – who controlled the Aymara and Pukina societies somehow agreed to co-operate, producing an energetic and unified political power which led to the creation of the Tiwanaku state.

Tiwanaku had to be fed, and the scope of its architectural vision and prowess was matched by its transformation of large areas of surrounding altiplano into agriculturally productive land. The major means by which yields were increased and new land brought under cultivation was the large-scale creation and maintenance of ridged field systems, especially the 75sq. km of such constructions in the area known as the Pampa Koani.

Tiwanaku engineers displayed great ingenuity and persistence in controlling the seasonal flooding of the pampa by the lake and rivers, by planning, building, and maintaining canals and aqueducts, and canalising river courses. They did not simply pile up earth in long rows as raised or ridged fields but carefully thought out then constructed the fields with permeable foundations of variously sized boulders and stones upon which they deposited several metres of top quality soil brought in from elsewhere.

This well-planned integration of fields and drainage canals had heat-retaining qualities at this high altitude and permitted two or more crops a year in a region where normal rainfall agriculture could produce only one harvest. There is little doubt that this transformation of the agricultural landscape played a major role in supporting Tiwanaku's population. Ironically, this system is no longer used and the agricultural productivity of the area today is less than it was in AD 500. Administering this state-sponsored exercise were the two centres of Pajchiri and Lukurmata, both of which had smaller versions of the architectural features of the capital. Throughout Tiwanaku's hinterland were scattered smaller administrative centres and innumerable farms.

Empire and influence

Tiwanaku has been called an agro-pastoral state because of its dependence on large-scale intensive farming in the heartland and long-distance trading with far-flung colonies. By AD 600, this strategic mixed economy had combined with an aggressive foreign policy to produce what some experts refer to as a predatory imperial state. This appears to have been based on a variety of approaches which included military conquest, the foundation of large-scale colonies, the control of long-distance trade caravans, the establishment of client-tribute relationships with local rulers and, where appropriate, a stronger or weaker adherence to Tiwanaku's official state religion and ideology. This was not an empire on the Roman model, nor even identical to the succeeding Inka empire, but was rather a patchwork of variable responses to the multitude of far-flung ethnic groups and local conditions that came under Tiwanaku's influence.

Tiwanaku's presence beyond its heartland manifests itself as an ambiguous mix of militarism, economic exploitation, trade and artistic influence. At its height, Tiwanaku appears to have been the hub of a vast empire in the southern Andes and adjacent coastal regions. From high altiplano to steep river valleys and coastal desert oases such as San Pedro de Atacama, a network of llama caravans served Tiwanaku's administrative centres in a complex web of pan-Andean exchange.

Arguably one of the most impressive locations of such activity was the site of Qeremita by Lake Poopo, southeast of Tiwanaku. Located in a landscape of high-quality basalt much prized by Tiwanaku peoples for the production of tools and weapons, Qeremita still today shows evidence of high-density extraction and manufacturing in the mines themselves, and at the collection areas that served as points of departure for llama caravans that carried the stone to Tiwanaku communities throughout the region. These communities are of various kinds, a mix of local people and traditions and Tiwanaku people who controlled the caravan routes.

A spotlight is thrown on the relationships between local communities and smaller numbers of outsider groups from Tiwanaku at the site of Coya, which lies within the San Pedro de Atacama oasis, some 800km from Lake Titicaca. It is clear that while the two peoples lived alongside each other (probably intermarrying), and were buried together in one large cemetery, the distinctions of life were carried over into death. Ethnic identity, displayed in the colour, design and style of dress (including bags, belts, hats and tunics) was strictly observed post mortem by burying the dead in two distinct groups. While burials of locals contained items from the indigenous culture, those belonging to the Tiwanaku individuals had *keros*, hallucinogenic snuffing equipment and sometimes small lightweight gold items.

It may be, as in later Inka times, that the local *curaca* (chief) at San Pedro organised the extraction of mineral goods required for trade to Tiwanaku and received status, emblems, and perhaps even high-status women in return. Yet, such was the distance and the strength of local ethnic identity at San Pedro and other equally far-flung ethnic groups, that Tiwanaku probably never absorbed these communities wholesale into its empire. Rather, local peoples adapted and adopted selected aspects of Tiwanaku art and ideology for their own use, while benefiting from being locked, albeit temporarily, into the greater regional networks of trade and prestige.

In the Moquegua Valley, there is clear evidence of the conquest and incorporation of lower altitude, so called *yungas*, areas by the higher altitude altiplano civilisation of Tiwanaku. At the Moquegua Valley site of Omo, established between AD 600 and 700, the 7ha of main occupation indicate its importance not just by dense habitation, but also by the fact that it was the only centre outside the heartland which had monumental Tiwanaku-style architecture. This was a three-tiered temple platform built from adobe and stone, on whose summit was a sunken courtyard. A typical Tiwanaku-style head was all that remained of a large stone statue. Unusually, a small-scale model of the Omo platform carved in stone was also found.

Spread around this civic centre was a large area of densely packed housing and plazas, as well as several distinct burial grounds. There is pottery evidence for the large-scale brewing of alcohol (probably *chicha* beer), spindle whorls and coloured llama or alpaca wool to indicate textile production, and the shaping and polishing of Pacific Ocean shells (presumably for jewellery) that all speak of a diverse economy, albeit one based mainly on agriculture.

The end of Tiwanaku

Tiwanaku's demise seems to have begun in about AD 950 with a severe drought, possibly lasting for decades. The consequences of this might have included the diminishing of the large llama herds, increasing pressure on the water-dependent ridged field systems, and perhaps the movement of people away from the altiplano region to lower, less severely affected altitudes. The state appears to have responded well to earlier droughts by creating new ridged fields on the land exposed by the shrinking Lake Titicaca and laying fallow the increasingly stranded ones. But recent investigations suggest that the AD 950 drought was too severe to permit recovery.

For reasons not fully understood, the high-maintenance agricultural system fell into disuse, with the consequent loss of food which had enabled Tiwanaku to thrive. As the expensively reclaimed land fell into decay, population declined and the days of the great lakeside city were numbered. In more distant areas, there is evidence for a violent end to some Tiwanaku colonies, perhaps earlier than the collapse at Tiwanaku itself. At Omo, in about AD 800, the settlement was burned, irrigation canals disrupted and even the cemeteries desecrated, though whether this was the result of outsider action or internal uprising is not known.

It is not known either how Tiwanaku itself collapsed, although it has been inferred that changing climate and agricultural decline must have played a significant role. Alternatively, it may be that Tiwanaku's political system collapsed first and this led to the abandonment of the state-sponsored hydraulic regime. Certainly by AD 1000, the last vestiges of the once thriving Tiwanaku state had broken down, and the heartland had been de-urbanised if not depopulated.

Evidence suggests that local people fell back into a regional way of life, relocated themselves, and turned away from intensive agriculture and towards an increasingly pastoral life based on llama and alpaca herding. The Tiwanaku area continued to be inhabited, notably by the Aymara peoples and then the Inka, both of whom assimilated the vast ruins of the abandoned city into their own cultural landscapes and myths of origin.

However, it may have been the Inka, as South America's greatest imperial civilisation, that had the manpower, political will and ideological motivation partly to re-create Tiwanaku for their own ends. The presence of Inka artefacts across the site suggests that they may have been responsible for rearranging parts of it, moving the Gateway of the Sun and the Gateway of the Moon from their original places to their current and clearly 'out of context' locations. It was, after all, at Tiwanaku that Inka myth records how the creator deity Viracocha fashioned humankind from clays gathered from Lake Titicaca.

ELEVEN

Sicán and Chimú

In the great river valleys of Peru's north coast, the Sicán and Chimú civilisations flourished between about AD 800 and 1470. For many years, the astonishing architecture and artwork of the Sicán civilisation were referred to as the Lambayeque culture, after the valley in which its main monuments are found. The huge adobe temple platforms and stunning gold objects – from death masks to pairs of embossed-gold hands – were sometimes confusingly identified with the later imperial Chimú state which flourished in the Moche Valley to the south. Today, after decades of painstaking archaeological investigations by Izumi Shimada and his colleagues, a reappraisal has taken place and has been accepted by the archaeological community.

It now seems clear that in the Lambayeque and La Leche Valleys, the Sicán civilisation was a distinct cultural and political entity, beginning earlier than the Chimú culture which subsequently conquered it. Both civilisations shared a common past in the earlier Moche culture (see Chapter Eight) whose remains are also found in the area, and their immediate successors the Wari culture whose influence extended north along the Andes and adjacent Pacific coast from its central Andean centre of Wari in about AD 700 (see Chapter Ten). Both the Sicán and Chimú civilisations shared a characteristically north-coast orientation to the sea, engaged in inter-valley trade, promoted hydraulic agriculture in the form of irrigation canals and constructed large-scale adobe ceremonial buildings. Today, Sicán has reclaimed its place as one of pre-Columbian South America's most astonishing civilisations.

SICÁN

Sicán civilisation flourished between about AD 800 and 1375, at which time it was conquered by, and incorporated into, its southerly neighbour the Chimú state. Early Sicán culture began in about AD 800, but many of its traces are buried now beneath the remains of the later and more extensive Middle Sicán Period which developed about a century later. Nevertheless, one feature which did emerge during this early period was the zoomorphic face which blended human and bird characteristics and which appeared on pottery – this developed into the artistic motifs called the 'Sicán Deity' and 'Sicán Lord'. Archaeologists believe that it was during this early period that Sicán culture adopted some cultural features of the Wari civilisation.

Although problematic in their interpretation, there exist sixteenth- and seventeenth-century Spanish historical documents which seem to preserve an oral account of the founding of Sicán civilisation. They tell how a man known as Naymlap arrived off the coast of the Lambayeque Valley on a fleet of balsa-wood rafts which carried his family and royal court as well as a powerful greenstone idol. Among his courtiers are eight named officials each of whom had a specific responsibilty to his royal master. These include Llapchillulli who was Naymlap's dresser, Ninacola who looked after the throne and Fonga Sigde who, intriguingly, is responsible for scattering seashell dust in front of his lord. The latter official we will meet again.

Naymlap establishes a power base at a place called Chot, today identified with the archaeological site of Chotuna. A dozen of his descendants succeed to royal power in the area until the last ruler, known as Fempellec, interferes with the greenstone idol's sacred location, whereupon incessant rains, flooding and famine ensue. Fempellec is cast out by his own people, and the next major event is the conquest of the area by the Chimú.

Whatever the status or reliability of this story, archaeological evidence suggests that the fading of Wari as a cultural force soon led to a drastic reorientation in the coastal valleys north of the Moche river. Older Moche ideas combined with innovations to produce the confident theocratic state of the Middle Sicán Period. Between AD 900 and 1100, large numbers of huge adobe platforms were built especially in the Lambayeque Valley, and a huge cultural and ideological investment made in metallurgy, particularly in objects fashioned from arsenical copper and various gold and copper alloys. Large quantities of metal wealth were interred in newly developed shaft-tombs indicating a strict and hierarchical society. At the same time, Sicán culture forged new, or revitalised existing, trading relationships with far-flung areas to gain its precious raw materials, such as the sacred Spondylus shells from coastal Ecuador.

Society and religion

The main expression of Sicán religion would seem to be the common representations of the so-called Sicán Deity which most famously appears as a large face with comma-shaped eyes made out of sheets of hammered gold, but which can also be seen on textiles and pottery. The gold masks are often painted with imported red cinnabar, and accompanied their owner into the afterlife as funerary goods. Some experts believe this deity derived partly from previous Moche and Wari gods, and that the Sicán lords especially favoured the imagery of raptorial birds, as wings, talons and beaks also features as characteristics of the Sicán Deity.

In a long piece of vividly painted cotton textile found at the site of Sicán itself (also referred to as Batán Grande), the Sicán Deity is shown with a typical gold face-mask, holding up a severed trophy head in one hand and the typically Sicán ceremonial *tumi* knife in the other. Advancing towards him on both sides are a series of breaking waves, their feathered crests having zoomorphic faces, and within the body of which are images of fish. At one end of the waves is a representation of the sun as a Sicán-style face, and at the other is a crescent moon. This has suggested to some scholars that despite the focus here of symbols associated with the ocean and the heavens, the Sicán Deity may be an all-powerful god of everything, perhaps a cosmic lord of creation.

The shape of Middle Sicán society is indicated by their mortuary practices. The mass of ordinary people were buried in simple style beneath the floors of the houses and workshops where they had spent their lives. The idea of the dead and their spirits being ever-present for the living in this way, rather than separated off in a cemetery, tells us something of the conditions and beliefs of the common Sicán folk.

By contrast, the ruling classes were buried in deep burial chambers called shaft-tombs beneath large burial mounds. These chambers were of variable shape and often contained vast quantities of arsenical copper and high-class gold alloy items. To date, the most impressive unlooted burial of this type is called the Huaca Loro East Tomb, and was excavated by Izumi Shimada in 1991–2.

At the bottom of a shaft over 10m deep, crushed flat by the weight of earth on top, was found over a ton of grave goods accompanying one adult man, two women and two children. That Sicán rulers had created a cosmology based on the natural and supernatural symbolism of metals was clear from the discovery of layers of gold and gold-alloy regalia, 200kg of arsenical copper items and, perhaps most revealing of all, three piles of scrap *tumbaga* sheets along with several heaps of the ritually important Spondylus shell.

The remains of the main male burial were interred with metal jewellery including a death mask adorned with emeralds and amber, sets of golden ear spools, layers of shell and beads, and the signs of a now long since disintegrated cloak that originally had some two thousand thin gold squares sewn on to it. As Shimada himself observed, this vast haul represented not just incredible power wielded by the deceased, but also his ability to call on a wide-ranging trade network which supplied the exotic materials and embodied untold labour-hours in making such exquisite objects. Nearby was the Huaca Loro West Tomb, which revealed the remains of one man and twenty-three women, llamas or alpacas, indications of many rolls of cloth and *tumbaga*-plated pottery. Interestingly, the study of the physical remains of the occupants of both tombs suggests they were related.

These rich burials, and probably many others whose presence is suggested by geophysical investigations, indicate that the whole Huaca Loro temple-pyramid was a Middle Period Sicán centre built between AD 1000 and 1050. As with the Classic Maya temple-pyramids of Mesoamerica, they were focal points for ancestor worship and elaborate ceremonial, incorporating ideas of divine dynastic descent for those buried within. Other nearby mounds, thought possibly to have had similar functions for other elite segments of the society, are regarded as forming the sacred centre which Shimada calls the 'religious city of Sicán'.

This conglomeration of great adobe-brick temple-platforms was built around the so-called Great Plaza. Huaca Loro, La Ventanas, La Merced and other mound groups have been dated to between AD 900 and 1050 and were of a building style that permitted rapid construction. The mounds themselves are of two different kinds but both apparently possessed walls decorated with colourful murals depicting the Sicán Deity and other motifs. The political nature of Sicán civilisation has been interpreted as a kind of theocracy, with the great lords regarding themselves as the earthly embodiment of the Sicán Deity. The Sicán state was centred on the Lambayeque Valley, and was clearly successful at integrating the people of a number of lesser valleys and communities, tying their political leaders into a network of shared economic, political and ideological dimensions.

Arts and crafts

The material culture of the Middle Sicán Period was a vibrant expression of its vigorous cultural, religious and ideological confidence, stemming, as already observed, from a mix of previous Moche and Wari influences. Yet Sicán culture also defined itself independently. Its pottery, for example, eschewed the fascination with brightly coloured designs that so characterised Moche and Wari in favour of a virtual obsession with blackware. That the well-made, single-spouted Middle Sicán black ceramics were of high status can be seen from their wide distribution during this time – from Piura in the north to the great shrine of Pachacamac near modern Lima in the south.

Middle Sicán Period potters also elaborated an age-old ceramic production process known as paddle-and-anvil whereby the walls of raw and unfired vessels were given tensile strength by being struck with a wooden paddle on the outside while a stone was held on the inside as the anvil. Sicán master potters decorated their paddles (and thus the ceramics made with them) with small designs, either geometric or miniatures of such cultural images as *tumi* knives and various animals.

While Sicán pottery was a new departure from what had gone before, what crystallised and embodied the civilisation were its advances in metalworking. Hitherto, pure copper had been added to gold to make the *tumbaga* alloy, but Middle Period Sicán metalsmiths mastered the skill of using arsenical copper and thereby heralded what Shimada calls a 'Bronze Age' for the north coast. From a technological point of view, this development may have made metal items easier to cast and shape, as well as making them harder and more resistant to corrosion. It certainly led to a significant increase in the quantity of metal objects produced, such as *tumi* knives, headdresses and elaborate death-masks, often decorated with inlays of shell and semi-precious minerals.

In typically Amerindian fashion, the sacredness of such 'magical' technologies, and the supernatural transformative abilities they possessed, was illustrated by offerings of animals and pottery made during the construction and subsequent abandonment of smelting furnaces. Furthermore, the mystical qualities of the finished artefacts symbolised the powers of Sicán rulers who presumably claimed divine or semi-divine status and displayed this connection by the amount of shimmering metal regalia they wore during life and death. The sheer visual magnificence of the gold-alloy paraphernalia they wore in such great quantities must have had an impressive psychological impact not only on commoners, but the elites of other contemporary societies as well.

Sicán rulers presided over a creative explosion of outstanding metalworking, but it was also a multi-media tradition, incorporating semi-precious and precious minerals, several species of presumably sacred seashells, textiles, and exotic bird plumage. While some items were local, such as cotton textiles, other raw materials were obtained through an extensive trading system that plied the coastal strip and Andean Valleys north into modern-day Ecuador and Colombia. The presence in these distant areas of Sicán blackware pottery, and two kinds of arsenical copper segments called *naipes* and axe-monies, suggests that these objects formed part of the exchange mechanism by which Sicán rulers obtained their exotic luxury items. The multi-media skills of Sicán craftsmen working for their status-obsessed patrons perhaps created, or at least elaborated, a system of prehispanic trade networks that bound together northern Peru with other diverse cultures and regions on the northern Andes around AD 1000.

Perhaps the most intriguing of these trade connections involved the acquisition of the sacred Spondylus shell from the warm waters of Ecuador. The responsibility of Fonga Sigde to cast crushed Spondylus shell dust in his master's path may be taken to represent a constellation of duties that included obtaining and preparing the shells.

Recent innovative investigations have identified thirteen examples of Middle Sicán Period depictions of divers collecting Spondylus shells underwater, typically tied by a cord around their waist to the boat above. These images adorn gold ornaments, silver ear spools, textiles and a wooden bowl decorated with mosaic inlay. Clearly, the shell itself, its shiny brilliance when crushed, its associations with the sea, and perhaps also the difficulty of obtaining it were some of the reasons why it was chosen as a royal (and probably super-natural) symbol. That there was a symbolic connection, perhaps equivalence, between Spondylus shell and metalwork, is indicated by the finding of small metal items placed within a complete shell and buried as a unit. The presence of vast quantities of Spondylus shell dust in later Chimú burials has been interpreted as the Sicán practice having been imported to Chan Chan after the Chimú conquest.

The demise of Sicán

In about AD 1100, the culture that had worked so well for several hundred years went into steep decline. Significantly, this is seen most dramatically by the burning of the ceremonial buildings at Sicán itself. Yet, at the same time, ordinary non-monumental buildings and ways of life seemed to continue as before, extending into the so-called Late Sicán Period (AD 100–1350). As at the great metropolis of Teotihuacán in Mesoamerica, destruction seems to have focused on the buildings that symbolised the elite and their religio-ideological motif the Sicán Deity, which now disappears from material culture. Why this happened is unclear, although it is possible that it resulted from an internal revolt prompted by climatic changes the effects of which the elite were unable to predict or control.

With the demise of the religious centre at Sicán, the focus of political activity shifted to a new capital known as El Purgatorio (and sometimes as Túcume), situated at the junction of the Lambayeque and La Leche Valleys. Covering an area of over 200ha, the new centre was built around a central section known as La Raya. Construction at the site continued beyond the Sicán period into the new era dominated by the Chimú empire expanding from the south, and then the subsequent Inka period. The end of a politically independent Sicán state occurred in about AD 1375 with the arrival of the Chimú.

CHIMÚ

In about AD 1200, the Chimú civilisation emerged in the same Moche river Valley as the previous Moche civilisation, and became the most powerful state on Peru's north coast. The Chimú were a hierarchical and imperial society, ruled by god-like kings who created an extensive coastal empire, but who ultimately fell to the advancing Inka armies in about AD 1470.

Despite the prehistoric antiquity of Chimú civilisation's origins, there are several surviving Spanish historical accounts that have preserved an earlier oral tradition of the founding of the state. As with the accounts of Naymlap's founding of a royal dynasty in the Lambayeque Valley, some experts regard these as pure myth, while others consider a careful reading of them provides a useful outline of these early events.

A fragmentary document from the early seventeenth century relates how the founding figure, called Tacaynamo, arrived offshore of the mouth of the Moche river sailing a balsa-wood raft. It continues, telling how the Moche Valley is conquered by his son Guacricaur and grandson Ñançenpinco, the latter of whom also begins to conquer river valleys north and south of Moche. Between five and seven anonymous rulers follow until the ruler named Minchançaman appears who conquers new areas in the north before himself falling to the Inka armies of Tupac Yupanqui in about AD 1470 and is taken to Cuzco as a prisoner, whereupon a puppet ruler was installed at the Chimú capital of Chan Chan.

A literal reading of this account infers that the Chimú state was established in AD 1225, but like other later documents it seems that myth and history were interwoven with political expediency and ideology, and that this unique historical document is probably little more than propaganda. This in turn has led to scholarly disagreements and not a little confusion as to when the Chimú civilisation really began. Different archaeologists make different estimates ranging from *c.* AD 800 to *c.* 1100. Even scientific dating methods such as radiocarbon have so far been unable to establish an accurate sequence for the construction of the city's major buildings, the great compounds known as *ciudadelas*. The only generally accepted dating sequence is the agreement that the earlier compounds were built of flat bricks, while the later ones were constructed of tall bricks.

Chan Chan

In many ways, our knowledge of the Chimú is based on archaeological investigations of their capital – the great desert city of Chan Chan, located near the mouth of the Moche Valley. At its height,

Chan Chan sprawled over some 25sq. km, and had a population of between 25,000 and 30,000. Hence, it was the largest pre-Columbian city in South America at the time, though whether it was truly urban, or perhaps a city dedicated solely to servicing the needs of the royal elite is still a matter of debate. Interestingly, its resident population is small compared to the earlier, but similarly sized Mesoamerican city of Teotihuacán, which had around two hundred thousand inhabitants.

The heart of the city was composed of ten giant compounds, *ciudadelas*, that appear to have functioned as royal palaces during the lifetime of the rulers to whom they belonged, and as mausoleums dedicated to their cult after death. Archaeologists have examined also a number of lesser compounds identified as belonging to the elite, *barrios* (neighbourhoods) of specialist workers, and the remains of temple platforms presumably used for public ceremonial. Despite Chan Chan's overall size and evident sophistication, there appears to have been no city centre, no identifiable central core – only a ribbon-like development along a north–south axis that developed over time.

Nevertheless, there is a marked difference in the size of the capital and its outlying regional settlements, communities that presumably articulated its centralised political and economic control in far-flung areas. Typifying this is Manchan, a small administrative centre located in the Casma Valley several hundred kilometres south of Chan Chan. The lack of large buildings and storehouses at Manchan indicates that whatever wealth was generated in this region was funnelled straight back to the capital.

The *ciudadela* compounds, like most ancient Peruvian coastal buildings, were made of sun-baked mud bricks (adobes). The compounds vary in size, with floor areas ranging from 80,000sq. m to some 200,000sq. m. Most experts agree that the *ciudadelas* are an architectural expression of the deep social divisions of Chimú society, with their high walls up to 10m tall, and a single narrow entrance giving access to a labyrinthine interior composed of corridors, courts and passageways and, in some, a large, centrally located burial platform.

Investigations of these unusual interiors have given rise in the past to different interpretations as to their use – as storehouses, workshops and as the habitations of different segments of a royal family. However, today most archaeologists agree that they were probably built by succeeding Chimú emperors as their own personal palace-mausoleums, and that the complex internal divisions reflect a multitude of uses associated with the ideology of Chimú rulership, economic specialisation and social control.

The earlier and smaller *ciudadelas* are called Chayhuac, Tello and Uhle and these typically have storehouses whose total space was around 3,000sq. m. However, as time passed and the larger compounds known as Laberinto, Velarde and Gran Chimú were built, storage space doubled to 6,000sq. m, only to decline to 3,000sq. m with the last four compounds, known respectively as Rivero, Squier, Tschudi and Bandelier. In the later compounds also, a new kind of layout appears, based on a three-part division of internal space. This seems to have increased the overall storage area available. Although these storage areas were 'clean' when archaeologists investigated them, it seems likely they once contained craftwork such as cloth, metalwork, featherwork, pottery and perhaps other exotic items as well as perhaps food, gathered as tribute and representing the personal wealth of the royal family within whose compound it was stored.

Further insight into the almost obsessively hierarchical nature of Chimú society is provided by the architectural features of compounds known as *audiencias*. These are raised U-shaped platforms that take their name from their presumed function as places where Chimú administrators held audiences with those who came to pay tribute, and/or display their political and perhaps religious allegiance to the Chimú state. Sometimes, several hundred *audiencias* existed within a great *ciudadela*, whose artistic adobe friezes and apparently dedicatory human sacrifices interred beneath their floors suggested a typically Andean mix of politics, economics and religion.

At the centre of several large compounds have been found the remains of a great T-shaped burial structure which it is thought would have been the mausoleum of a deceased ruler and the centre of a royal cult administered by his extended family and retinue – presumably as much for their benefit as that of the spirit of the deceased. When archaeologists partially excavated the Huaca Las Avispas tomb platform they found the remains of almost a hundred young women presumably sacrificed during the ruler's funerary ceremony, rolls of cotton textiles, pottery and the sacred Thorny Oyster shell otherwise known as Spondylus.

There are different interpretations for the shape of the city in terms of the building and spacing of the *ciudadelas*. While the commonly accepted idea is that each new king built his own palace-mausoleum, another view is that Chan Chan's great *ciudadelas* were built in pairs, one each on the western and eastern halves of the city. This would accord well with typically Andean ideas about dual-kingship and the symbolic splitting of physical space into two halves or moieties, a practice followed by the later Inka in their capital at Cuzco.

Society

Chimú society was sharply ranked, its leaders probably regarded as divine or semi-divine beings, the social distance between rulers and ruled being expressed by the intimidating size and design of the *ciudadelas*. Supporting this hierarchical structure were those who made the goods which the elite then requisitioned and deployed as visual displays of their superior, and perhaps divinely sanctioned wealth and power. Some estimates suggest that over ten thousand full-time craft specialists lived and worked at Chan Chan, mainly engaged in metalworking and textile production. During the earlier period of the city's history, some of the higher-class specialist workers lived adjacent to the *ciudadelas*, probably working directly for the elite inhabitants within. Also in the central part of the city were two caravanserais, the final destination of long-distance traders and their llama caravans bringing in a variety of products such as coca, metal ingots and probably various foodstuffs.

By the end of Chan Chan's life, craft specialisation appears to have focused almost exclusively on production in two specially designated neighbourhoods on the city's boundaries, each of which had its own cemetery. These quasi-industrial suburbs had houses and workshops mingled together and seem to have been concerned mainly with producing everyday metalwork and textiles in a way which suggests the manufacture then assemblage of different components, with woodwork and shellwork being brought in from elsewhere.

Apart from the craftworkers, it seems that Chimú society used the typically Andean labour-tax system known as the *mita*, bringing in workers from surrounding areas to manufacture millions of adobe bricks and then using them to build the *ciudadelas* and elite compounds. Food and raw materials also were brought into Chan Chan from the hinterlands, probably by the llama caravans already mentioned. The impression gained by careful analysis of the nature of the Chimú political economy is one of a strictly monitored society whose elite kept tight control over all resources and then redistributed them as they saw fit.

The archaeological investigations of Chan Chan reveal a unique combination of factors that probably influenced the shifting of the city's population, or parts of it, from one area to another over time. This was based on the availability and supply of water, both for irrigated fields and everyday use. In the early stages, it seems that the focus of agricultural activity was on the north side of the city but that El Niño events and geological uplift upset the hyrdraulic regime, despite the construction of several large canals. The most impressive of these was the La Cumbre Canal which stretched some 70km, bringing water from the Chicama Valley to the fields of Chan Chan in the Moche Valley. Eventually, irrigation shifted to focus on the eastern side of Chan Chan, though water supply was a recurring problem towards the end of the city's independent life. Not only was there a lack of water, but sometimes also, a surfeit. Archaeologists believe they have identified the traces of a serious El Niño event with its associated flooding dating to between AD 1300 and 1350 which would also have seriously affected the dependable supply of water.

Arts and crafts

Chimú arts and crafts did not aspire to the individual excellence of its Moche or Middle Period Sicán predecessors. Reflecting the nature of its social, political and economic organisation, Chimú craftwork emphasised standardisation and mass production over artistic creativity.

Designs, shapes and decoration of ceramics were simple, stylised and seemingly endlessly repeated. Some motifs appear to have been based on Moche originals but changed over time to accord with Chimú styles. Other examples – often the most life-like ceramic representations – are believed to be Chimú revivals of earlier Moche pieces. What exactly this pre-Columbian retro style meant is unknown; perhaps it harked back to ancestral ideas and beliefs, the power of ceramic imagery to conjure new meanings for an ideologically reconfigured society where most pottery had perhaps ceased to carry a religious symbolic load.

Whatever the true reason for these revivals of Moche ceramic style, most typical Chimú pottery was black to dark grey in colour, usually made in moulds that divided into two parts and often with little attention paid to detail. Shapes were sometimes effigies of people or animals, with a handle – inherited from the Moche – of a typical North Coast stirrup-spout kind. Particularly notable are the so-called whistling pots, double-bodied vessels whose hidden interior design produced a distinctive sound when water (or perhaps originally *chicha* beer) was poured out. Given the multi-sensual nature of pre-Columbian Amerindian societies, where sound, touch and smell combine to represent spiritual qualities – if not to signify actual spirit presence – it is impossible to know whether whistling pots were just an amusement or held a deeper significance.

While Chimú pottery was not particularly well made, considerably more effort seems to have been put into kinds of material culture which could have been displayed in public – textiles (sometimes feathered) and metalwork. Ceremonial clothing and feather headdresses are intricately designed and coloured, adorned with shells, bird feathers and glittering metals which must have shimmered and tinkled as their wearer moved. These were elaborate multi-media creations, colourful and highly visible signs of social status and, perhaps, of ethnic identity. Chimú master weavers also made large-scale textiles as wall hangings, some measuring up to 10m long and 3m wide, and produced in llama or alpaca wool and cotton into which were woven (sometimes painted) colourful stylised images of humans, gods and animals such as birds, serpents and felines.

The Chimú evidently were master metalsmiths – a skill they shared with their northerly neighbours the Sicán people. In fact, after the AD 1375 Chimú conquest of the Sicán culture, many of its finest metalsmiths seem to have been taken to Chan Chan where they created Chimú-style objects that appear as hybrids of the two civilisations. Many items of metalwork once identified as Chimú are now recognised as being either Sicán or made by Sicán workers at Chan Chan.

Nevertheless, whatever their exact identity, Chimú-period metalworkers specialised in casting gold figures, often from alloys of gold and silver, and sometimes with copper and arsenic. They embellished these with such techniques as gilding and embossing, and then inlaid minerals such as turquoise and lapiz lazuli. Chimú metalworkers also employed the 'lost wax' technique to great effect; this involved the making of a model in wax which was then covered in clay and fired in a kiln – the wax then melted and ran out through several holes, whereupon gold was poured into the cavity. After cooling, the clay surround was removed, leaving a golden replica of the original wax shape. Gold or gold-alloy items were used to make a variety of bodily adornments, from elements decorating headdresses and clothing to jewellery such as bracelets, necklaces, earrings and nose ornaments. All were symbols of high social status, associating rank with the sacred qualities attributed to the raw materials from which the items were made, and their 'magical' production processes. The spiritual dimension of these items is hinted at also by the fact that many accompanied their deceased owner into the afterlife by being interred in the tomb as grave offerings.

Empire

The Chimú empire spread across large swathes of Peru's northern coastal valleys and deserts, and seems to have been the result of some two hundred years of expansion and consolidation. By far the most significant aspect of their imperial expansion appears to have been to the north, and involved the conquest and incorporation of the Jequetepeque Valley in about AD 1200. Some sources attribute this event to the Chimú general called Pacatnamú who ruled the area from the site of Farfán, where he built a Chimú-style *ciudadela* complete with a central burial platform. The impulse for this conquest may have been the disastrous aftermath of an El Niño event thought to have occurred in about AD 1100 and which destroyed the agricultural network adjacent to the northern part of Chan Chan and which led to a reconfigured policy based on conquest and the expropriation of resources from hitherto foreign (and politically independent) areas.

Further expansion took place in valleys north of Jequetepeque between AD 1350 and 1400. Typical Chimú material culture in architecture and pottery appears in the Lambayeque and La Leche Valleys at this time and political influence may have extended as far north as the area around Tumbes and Piura. Interestingly, and in some ways similar to what occurred in later Inka times, this increase in territorial expansion may have led to pressures on the Chimú elite's administrative abilities to control the empire. Changes in Chan Chan's architecture at the time indicate an increase in middle-level elite compounds which could best be accounted for by Chimú royalty bringing in non-Chimú individuals to help administer the expanding state.

As we have previously seen, much of this northern area was the heartland of the Sicán civilisation. The La Leche and Lambayeque Valleys were agriculturally rich, representing perhaps one third of all of ancient Peru's cultivated coastal area. Their tribute of foodstuff would have more than offset the decline in Chan Chan's own agricultural fortunes. Equally important was the fact that Sicán culture had developed an astonishingly advanced metallurgical tradition, their metalsmiths masters of working with arsenical copper and other precious metals. These specialists would now have been working for the imperial Chimú state, an interpretation supported by the apparent increase in the number of metalsmith workshops at the Sicán centre of Cerro Huaringa after the Chimú conquest.

It seems that the richness of these northern valleys reoriented Chimú society back in Chan Chan and, indeed, their whole imperial enterprise. The northern provinces probably doubled the wealth of the Chimú, not just by adding agricultural produce and expert metalwork, but by tapping into Sicán sources of raw materials and their trade networks up into the Andes. Conquered areas also yielded a supply of local rulers who were incorporated into the administrative apparatus of the Chimú state. The close-knit political and economic structures that formed the underpinning of Chimú state policy can be seen in the presence in conquered areas of typically Chimú features, such as the U-shaped *audiencias* and ceramics of Chimú style but locally made. Sometimes local people were moved from their own towns and villages and gathered together in newly built Chimú-style settlements. Again, as with the later Inka policy, the Chimú elite did not dismantle previous practices but simply brought them into the larger Chimú system.

At its height, between AD 1400 and 1450, the Chimú empire probably extended some 500km north–south along Peru's northern coast, from Tumbes in the north to the Chillón Valley in the south, though the nature of its political and military control was variable. Many valleys had their own cultures and material culture styles in architecture, pottery and textiles, and while Chimú control seems comprehensive in some valleys, it appears intermittent in others. In about AD 1470, the Inka empire caught up with the Chimú – its only imperial competitor – subjugated Chan Chan and, perhaps learning from the latter's example with Sicán, took its metalsmiths back to Cuzco.

TWELVE

Inka

The Inka empire was the last great pre-Columbian civilisation of South America, destroyed in its prime by Spanish conquistadors under Francisco Pizarro in 1532. While the scale of the Inka imperial achievement was unparalleled, the building blocks of their success were the accumulated cultural traditions, technological achievements, spiritual beliefs and worldviews not only of their contemporaries such as the Chimú, but of their predecessors, stretching back millennia into the Andean past.

MYTHS OF ORIGIN

For the Inkas, as with all native Andean peoples, mythology was a living reality, a way of seeing the world and of understanding and celebrating how things had come to be as they are. Mythology illuminated the mysteries of life and death, and the language used to recount individual myths was vivid and memorable. Recurring themes were the origins of human beings, the magical role of ancestors and the continued well-being and fertility of livestock, land and people.

In mythological accounts of their own origins, the Inka were influenced and inspired by the stories and traditions of their neighbours, as well as by the spectacular, though violent and unpredictable Andean world. Lake Titicaca was an important place in Inka mythology, and they built temples on the Island of the Sun in the middle of the lake. For the Inkas and the local Kolla peoples, Lake Titicaca was a cosmic 'place of emergence', a metaphor for spiritual rebirth with strong ties to the Pacific Ocean as the 'mother of fertility'.

Inka creation myths take many forms and appear in different versions. There is no single true account; each version preserves shadings of meaning and history that reflect the conditions under which it was created and later written down by the Spanish. The

half-Spanish, half-Inka chronicler Garcilaso de la Vega tells how the
world was at first nothing but mountains inhabited by uncivilised
and irreligious people who lived like wild beasts. They slept with
each other's wives, lived in caves, and preferred human flesh to
cultivating the land.

Garcilaso recounts how the sun pitied these creatures and sent
two of his children, a boy and a girl, to civilise them and instruct
them how to worship the sun as their god. The cosmic siblings
appeared on earth near Lake Titicaca and were told to thrust a
golden rod into the soil wherever they stopped to rest. Wheresoever
the rod sank easily into the earth, there they were to build the sacred
city of the sun. They were to feed, organise and protect the people
whom they civilised, and to treat them as their own beloved
children. In return, they would become the rulers and lords of all
whom they instructed.

At last, brother and sister arrived at Pacariqtambo, or the 'Inn of
the Dawn', and at the place called Huanacauri the golden rod
slipped easily into the soil. The pair gathered all the people they
could find, impressing them with their fine clothing and civilised life.
As numbers swelled, the heavenly pair were worshipped as living
gods and obeyed as rulers, and in this way, so Garcilaso says, the
great city of Cuzco became filled with people.

Another Inka creation myth relates how three brothers and three
sisters were the ancestors of the Inkas, and how they emerged into
the world from three caves at Pacariqtambo. One brother, Ayar
Cachi, made the others jealous by performing miraculous feats of
strength, hurling great slingstones and shaping the Andean
landscape. His brothers tricked him into returning to Pacariqtambo
where they sealed him up in the cave. Ayar Cachi escaped, and told
his brothers to wear golden earrings as a sign of their royal status.
At the mountain called Huanacauri, Ayar Cachi turned himself and
a brother into stone. The remaining brother, Manco Capac, then
founded the city of Cuzco on the site later occupied by the Temple
of the Sun God *Inti*.

In yet another myth, the supreme Inka deity Viracocha made
people out of clay, painting them with clothes whose colourful
designs distinguished one nation from another. He gave each group
its own language and customs, then blew his life-giving breath into
them. He sent them to earth and commanded they emerge from
caves, lakes and mountains. At each place they were to honour him

by making shrines for his worship. Heartened by his success, Viracocha then made light from the darkness – order from chaos – so that his creations could thrive. He made the sun, moon and stars rise into the sky from the Island of the Sun in Lake Titicaca. As the sun ascended, Viracocha called out, prophesying that the Inka and their leader Manco Capac would conqueror many nations. Viracocha gave Manco Capac a beautiful headdress and a great battle-axe as signs of his royal status among men. Manco then led his brothers and sisters into the earth from where they re-emerged into the daylight world at Pacariqtambo.

Inka creation myths served many purposes. They established the royal prerogatives of the ruling dynasty and offered dramatic and memorable accounts of the supernatural origins of the world. They explained how and why mountains, lakes, rivers and shrines were located in particular places and how they came to be full of supernatural power. In this way, Inka myths made use of age-old Andean ideas, especially beliefs in ancestor worship and transformation. The ability of culture heroes to change magically into rocks and stones or of these inanimate objects to adopt human form is a recurring and distinctively Andean theme.

RELIGION

Mythology and religion were never far apart in the pre-Columbian world. Adapting ancient beliefs and inventing new ones, the Inkas created a religion appropriate for empire, with an elaborate ritual calendar of festivals for the veneration of gods, the mummies of past emperors and the reigning monarch.

Inka mythology established that the land was alive, infused with spirituality, animated by the ancestors. Consequently, springs, lakes, rocks, caves, mountains and the tombs of ancestors were all sacred places known as *huacas*, and each could become the focus of religious activity. A common kind of *huaca* was the *apacheta*, a pile of small stones placed on mountain paths and at crossroads. Travellers could add another stone, offer coca leaves, deposit a seashell, or deliberately spill *chicha* (maize beer) as an offering to local spirits and Pacha Mama (Mother Earth).

At the opposite end of the scale, the largest *huacas* were the mountains themselves. Each was linked to the other in a system of sacred peaks which tied the empire together ideologically and spiritually as well as geographically. Overlooking Cuzco, the two prominent mountains Salcantay and Ausangate were considered brothers and the fathers of all mountains. This view of landscape as an animated sacred geography influenced the practical matters of everyday life. Granite blocks used to construct monumental buildings in Inka style were hence quarried from the flanks of what were believed to be living mountains. Temples, fortresses and palaces were all made from these sacred raw materials, and constructed in a fashion which defied the earthshaking tremors of the region.

The meshing of sacred and physical geographies is evident at Machu Picchu, perhaps the most famous Inka city and dominated by temples, palaces, houses, terraced fields, water conduits and fountains. At the city's centre, the carved stone pillar known as the Intihuatana or Hitching Post of the Sun may have served an astronomical purpose, though it might also have been associated with mountain worship, located at a point where sacred peaks were in alignment with the cardinal directions.

In Inka worldview, celestial phenomena were seen as closely linked to earthly events. The star group known as the Pleiades was called Collca (the granary), and considered the celestial guardian of seeds and agriculture. Inka priests used the Pleiades to calculate a lunar calendar and for divination in rituals of agricultural fertility and animal husbandry. In 1571, the Spanish chronicler Polo de Ondegardo observed that all terrestrial animals and birds had their celestial counterparts who were responsible for their fertility and well-being. For the Inka state, astronomical knowledge was critical in calculating two important religious festivals in Cuzco – the December and June solstices. The December solstice was Capac Raymi – the 'royal feast' – the main purpose of which was to initiate royal Inka boys into adulthood. Equally elaborate celebrations took place at the June solstice festival of Inti Raymi, dedicated to the sun god Inti.

A unique feature of imperial Inka religion tied earth to sky, spirituality to landscape and architecture, and ancestors to the living. This was the system of imaginary straight 'lines' radiating out from the Coricancha sun temple in Cuzco and known as *ceques*. They traversed the city, the valley of Cuzco, and reached out to the empire beyond, dividing land and space and imposing order on the lives of everyone. Each line had *huacas* along its length, with a total of some 328 *huacas* dotted along 41 *ceques* in the immediate area of the capital. Sometimes these *huacas* were royal tombs, while elsewhere they might be springs, caves, or rocky outcrops. Prayers, processions and sacrifices were associated with *huacas* and *ceques*.

The Inka had a pantheon of gods – powerful supernaturals who took the form of sky deities. While Viracocha reigned supreme over this pantheon, he was distant from everyday human affairs. Having set the universe in motion he retreated into the cosmic background and left day-to-day events to more active deities who presided over the heavens or dwelt atop snow-capped mountain peaks. They sent rain, hail, lightning, drought and earthquakes and had to be appeased if disaster was to be avoided.

Inti, the sun god, was the main one of these deities and the divine ancestor of Inka royalty. He was worshipped in his golden temple, the Coricancha, in the heart of Cuzco. His shimmering solar image was flanked by the mummies of dead emperors and surrounded by walls covered in hammered sheets of gold. Outside the temple was the sacred garden – a miniature landscape where every kind of life form known to the Inkas was modelled in gold, silver and precious jewels. Serpents, llamas, human beings and even the soil were all fashioned from these precious metals, and regarded as sacred prototypes for all earthly forms of life.

The weather god Ilyap'a was venerated for rain. He combined the sound of thunder with the power of thunderbolts and the flash of lightning. The Inkas saw rainstorms as Ilyap'a drawing water from the celestial river of the Milky Way which was kept in a huge water jug and released when he shattered it with a thunderbolt. Thunder was the crack of his slingshot, and lightning the sparkle of his brilliant clothing as he advanced across the sky.

The third-ranking deity was Mama Kilya the moon goddess, the sister-wife of Inti, and mother of the Inka race. This incestuous relationship was the sacred precedent for brother-sister marriage practised by the Inka emperor. Mama Kilya measured the passing time and regulated the festivals of the ritual calendar. During a lunar eclipse a great serpent or mountain lion was believed to be devouring Mama Kilya's celestial image, and the Inkas made as much noise as possible to scare it away. Mama Kilya's image in the Coricancha was flanked by mummies of previous Inka queens or *Coyas*, and her shrine was covered in silver – the colour of the moon in the night sky.

Many lesser gods also figured in Inka religion, including Cuichu, the rainbow, and a group of female supernaturals of whom the two most prominent were Pacha Mama the earth-mother, and Mama Coca, the sea-mother. All of these deities were served by a full-time priesthood, the highest office of which had a title which translates as 'slave of the sun'. Inka spirituality was not the sole preserve of priests however, and there were other lesser individuals who made sacrifices, interpreted oracles and cured illness.

The most famous group of individuals associated with Inka religion were the *acllas* or 'chosen women' – sometimes called the 'Virgins of the Sun'. These were young Inka maidens who served the cult of Inti, and tended the royal mummies as well as the present royal family. Selected for their physical beauty in their youth, they lived in convents called *aclla huasi*. Some prepared the clothing, food and drink for the emperor and for state occasions, while others took a vow of chastity in honour of Inti and guarded the sacred fire. Some *acllas* became royal concubines for the emperor, and could be given by him to foreign dignitaries to cement political marriage alliances.

Inka religious ritual was accompanied on almost every occasion by some kind of sacrifice. These were usually burnt offerings of maize cobs or coca leaves, and could be accompanied by the spilling of *chicha* on the ground for Pacha Mama. Animal sacrifices were also common, especially of llamas and guinea pigs. Most valuable were child sacrifices known as *capac hucha*, or 'royal obligation'. These were made on special occasions, such as times of war, famine, or the death of one emperor and the coronation of his successor. Buried alive or strangled, some two hundred children could be sacrificed when a new emperor came to power.

The *capac hucha* ritual also had political and ideological dimensions, as the sacrificed embodied and integrated ideas of sacred time and space in the imperial Inka vision of the world. Children of outstanding beauty were sent from the empire's villages to Cuzco, where they were honoured by the emperor, symbolically married, led in procession around the capital's great plaza, and then returned to their villages. After being welcomed back they were intoxicated with *chicha* and buried alive on the summit of a nearby mountain. These deaths were believed to restore spiritual well-being and maintained the balance of religious and political obligations between the far-flung corners of empire and Cuzco. In recent years, frozen mummies have been discovered on snow-capped Andean peaks and volcanoes, where they are accompanied by miniature human and animal figurines in gold, silver and coral-coloured seashell.

Such sacrifices were part of Inka religious practices that included the cult of royal mummies, and this in turn was a development of the ancient Andean tradition of ancestor worship. The Inkas believed that emperors never died. While their bodies might fail, their spirits infused their mummified remains, and could be fortified by acts of worship and sacrifice. Mummies were washed, fed and clothed by their own lineage groups (or *panaqas*). All royal mummies attended state occasions, where they sat in order of seniority, adding sanctity to the ruling families and authority to the living emperor.

SOCIETY

Inka society was strictly hierarchical, and this was both its strength and its weakness. The emperor, the Sapa (unique) Inka, ruled by divine right as the 'Son of the Sun'. He was revered as a living god, and his official wife was his full-blooded sister, the *Coya*. He had a harem of concubines made up of the most beautiful *acllas* or 'chosen women', whose royal offspring filled positions of power in the state administration. The male descendants of each emperor formed a royal *ayllu* or *panaqa* responsible for serving the emperor and guarding his wealth and estates.

The Sapa Inka was divine, his sacred body enveloped in elaborate ritual. His food, drink and clothing were specially prepared by the *acllas* and *mama cunas*, and every scrap of uneaten food, soiled clothing and even hairs from his head was burnt to prevent the possibility of sorcery. Entry into the imperial presence was strictly controlled, and all who sought an audience had to approach bearing a symbolic burden. Seeing the god-emperor's face was a great honour, and for most audiences he attended behind a screen. For those who did see him, the emperor sat on a low wooden bench on top of a raised platform (*usnu*), dressed in finely woven cloth, golden earrings and the royal fringe of red tassels around his forehead.

When the emperor died, his spirit lived on. His remains were preserved and the royal mummy placed in his palace which now became a mausoleum. He was treated as in life, and made grand visits to the mummies of other deceased emperors, or those friends who had outlived him. Such activities illustrate Inka views on death, but also served the ends of the deceased's *panaqa*, which was charged with perpetuating his memory and cult. In this way, they

NOBIENBRE
AIA·MARÇAI
quilla

la fiesta delos defuntos

Early seventeenth-century drawing by Guaman Poma showing a royal Inka mummy being paraded around Cuzco. *(© Author's collection)*

also ensured their own privileged positions in the power relations of imperial Inka society.

Beneath the Sapa Inka was the nobility, divided into 'Inkas by Blood', 'Inkas by Privilege' and *curacas*. The most powerful were the hereditary aristocracy who belonged to eleven royal *ayllus*. Early in Inka expansion, the emperor Pachacuti had been forced to increase the nobility to fill new offices of state. He did so by extending the privileges of Inka status to able and gifted individuals. These owed their promotion solely to the emperor and so were fiercely loyal, as were the *yana* – individuals in personal service to the emperor or state who had been elevated to high status. This meritocratic aristocracy ruled the empire, and were rewarded with insignia similar to those of the emperor – coloured headbands and the large earplugs which led to the Spanish calling them *orejones* (big ears).

The lower echelons of the nobility were the *curacas*, who filled administrative offices of state and also connected the imperial bureaucracy with older pre-Inka traditions of social obligations and ancestor worship. Native rulers of conquered peoples could become *curacas* though many were the hereditary chiefs of local communities. There were two *curacas* for each Inka *ayllu* – one for each of the two moieties, the symbolic halves into which traditional Andean societies were divided and which the Inka incorporated into their own social organisation.

Ayllus were the bedrock of Inka society and remain so today. An *ayllu* is a group of related individuals and families who share their labour, lands and herds and have a founding ancestor. Each is composed of lineages which belong either to the upper or lower moiety, and membership is traced through female lines for women and male lines for men. *Ayllus* hold rights to water, in springs, lakes and canals. *Curacas* managed the *ayllu*'s resources, oversaw the agricultural calendar, resolved disputes and provided *chicha* for ceremonial occasions. In return, their lands were tilled and herds tended. *Curacas* were organised in a decimal system: a *pacaka koraka* was a chief of 100 people, a *warañqa* of 1,000 and a *hono koraka* of 10,000.

Apart from long-established specialised groups such as the famous merchants from Chincha who traded highland copper for the ritually important Spondylus shell from coastal Ecuador, the lower levels of Inka society were composed of several kinds of commoners. While the highest were those who worked gold and silver, or were master potters or textile workers, the mass of unskilled labourers

were the *hatun runa*, farmers and herders, below whom were only
the *piña* or prisoners of war.

The success of Inka society as an imperial enterprise was partly a
result of an efficient bureaucracy organising a huge multi-ethnic
population and perfecting the record-keeping system of knotted
strings invented by the earlier Wari people and known as the *quipu*.
Some *quipus* were more than 10 feet long with 2,000 individual
strings, and were kept and 'read' by specialists known as *quipu
camayoc* or 'Keepers of the *quipu*'. These men, a human library of
Inka knowledge and traditions, were supported by the state. The
intricate code of their profession disappeared with them in the wake
of the conquest and the introduction of the Spanish language.

Inka society was organised around work – each person was classified according to physical strength, condition and their ability to
perform different activities. Children were called 'those who played',
but between the ages of nine and twelve, boys graduated to hunting
birds while girls picked flowers and dyed cloth. It was from this age
group that the empire's most beautiful girls were chosen to be the
human sacrifices known as *capac hucha*. Between eighteen and
twenty years old, young men were responsibile for guarding llama
and alpaca flocks, and could become the imperial messengers or
chasqui. Girls could now find themselves dedicated to the sun as
acllas. After a hard physical life, a commoner would undertake only
light work between sixty and seventy, and once over eighty little or
nothing was expected of those called the 'old deaf ones'.

Daily life for women centred on the home, where they prepared
food and spent much time spinning and weaving the family's
clothing. Men wore a long sleeveless tunic over a breechclout and a
large cloak in bad weather. They carried a small bag in which coca
leaves, tools and magic charms were kept. Women also dressed
conservatively, wearing long rectangular pieces of cloth fastened at
the shoulder with copper, silver or gold pins. As was to be expected
in such a multi-ethnic imperial society, clothing and hairstyles varied
from one part of the empire to another and were an effective form
of identification and social control.

Marriage was taken seriously by the Inkas as it had ritual and
economic as well as social importance. Marriage beyond the local
community was forbidden – partners had to be from the opposite
moiety of their own *ayllu*. The best partners were those with large
families because everyone was born with rights to land and water,

CŌTADOR·MAIOR·ITEZORERO
TAVANTIN·SVIO·QVIPOC
CVRACA·CON DOR·CHAVA

Early seventeenth-century drawing by Guaman Poma showing the Quipu Camayoc or 'Keeper of the Quipu'. (© *Author's collection*)

and thus the more relatives, the more wealth. Royal Inka men could marry their half-sisters, a gesture perhaps adopted from the emperor who always took a full-blooded sister as his principal wife. For the aristocracy, possession of many wives advertised a man's wealth and prestige, but the common man could usually afford only one partner. When he married he became a full member of the community with its attendant duties and obligations, and the couple were rewarded with enough land for a house and to support themselves.

Agriculture was the economic mainstay of the Inka empire. The Andes are one of the world's great centres of plant domestication, the vertical arrangement of its different ecological zones fostering innovation, exchange and trade. This key feature of Andean life became an important characteristic of the Inka economy. Cold high valleys produced varieties of potato and the grain quinoa, while at lower altitudes maize, chilli peppers and squash predominated. From the even lower hotter valleys came the sweet root acira, gourds and the sacred coca leaf. (The coca leaf was a stimulant which deadened feelings of hunger and thirst.) Although heavily dependent on vegetables, meat also figured in the Inka diet in the shape of deer and guanaco, as well as fish, llamas and the ubiquitous household guinea pigs. Llama meat and potatoes could be dried and stored.

The Inkas ate these foods in stews and soups, flavoured with herbs and chillis. Maize was especially versatile, and could be boiled, toasted, steamed or baked as a kind of bread, and made into *chicha* beer. While an everyday beverage, it was drunk to excess only on religious occasions. At the great festival of Inti Raymi, participants fasted for three days on a meagre diet of raw white maize, a few herbs and water. The night before the feast, Inka priests prepared llamas for sacrifice and gathered food as offerings to the sun. *Acllas* made huge quantities of maize dough as a sacred food.

Every aspect of daily life was strictly controlled, and there were rules and regulations for everyone and every occasion. Laws had religious sanction, and so civil disobedience was sacrilege as well as social offence. The smallest infringements of the law were harshly punished by hanging, stoning, and being pushed off cliffs. Nevertheless, the Inkas recognised class differences, and the educated upper classes were punished more severely than commoners; adultery meant death for a noble, but only torture foraa commoner.

In death, special ceremonies saw relatives dressed in black and women cutting their hair in mourning rituals that could last a year in the case of the nobility. The dead person's belongings were burnt and the body wrapped in cloth and buried. For the aristocracy, funerals sometimes involved secondary wives and servants being sacrificed to accompany their master, and offerings of food and drink being regularly made at the tomb. These Inka practices were part of the age-old tradition of ancestor worship in the Andes.

EMPIRE

Before about AD 1400, little had distinguished the Inkas from many other small groups living in the valley of Cuzco, though, much later, the Inka emperors rewrote these humble beginnings. In about AD 1438, the powerful Chanca people attacked and defeated the Quechuas who were allies of the Inkas. When the Chanca finally attacked them, many Inka nobles advised the elderly Inka leader Viracocha to abandon Cuzco. Two sons, Yupanqui and Roca, refused to leave, fortified the city and repulsed the Chanca attacks. They also created a powerful myth that magical stones had turned into men to help them defeat the enemy. Yupanqui was crowned the new Inka ruler and took the title Pachacuti or 'cataclysm'.

This official version probably conceals a more complicated story of political intrigue and factionalism. Nevertheless, Pachacuti emerged victorious and began on the path to empire. The new ruler was an extraordinary and talented man – a brilliant general and a gifted administrator. The Inka empire was his vision and creation, and he was fortunate in having an equally talented son in Tupac Yupanqui. Together they forged the empire known as Tawantinsuyu or 'Land of the Four Quarters' that extended from Ecuador in the north to Argentina and Chile in the south.

The size and efficiency of Inka armies proved irresistible from the coastal deserts to Lake Titicaca, though rebellions were frequent and reconquests necessary. As he grew older, Pachacuti handed over the armies to Tupac Yupanqui, and concentrated on overhauling the empire's administration. He began rebuilding Cuzco, transforming it into an imperial capital.

Tupac Yupanqui reinforced the areas previously won and pushed the northern frontier towards Quito. He then marched west, conquering the land between the highlands and the coast, stopping only long enough to voyage out into the Pacific on a large sea-going balsa-wood raft. His next move was to outmanoeuvre and defeat the last great independent kingdom of Peru – the Chimú empire of the north coast, then sweep south bringing the whole of coastal Peru into the empire. These brilliant victories have led to Tupac Yupanqui being dubbed the Alexander the Great of South America.

In 1471, Pachacuti stepped down after thirty-three years as Sapa Inka. Tupac Yupanqui inherited the throne and immediately launched new military expeditions into the eastern tropical rain-forests, put down another rebellion of the Kolla people of Lake Titicaca, and conquered large parts of north-west Argentina and Chile, where he established the southern boundary of the empire by the banks of the River Maule. In some fifty years, and with astonishing speed, Pachacuti and Tupac Yupanqui had created the largest empire ever seen in the Americas.

Tupac Yupanqui died in 1493 and was succeeded by his son Huayna Capac. The new emperor seemed endlessly to be engaged in putting down revolts, and repulsed an invasion by the Chiriguano people from Argentina. The Chiriguano had a strange hostage – a Spaniard named Alejo García who had been captured on the Atlantic coast. García was the first and only European to see the Inka empire at the height of its power. Huayna Capac established a new northern boundary for the empire at the Ancasmayo river near the modern border between Ecuador and Colombia.

Huayna Capac died unexpectedly in 1527. Just before his death he heard of strangers from the sea – an early sighting of Francisco Pizarro, the eventual conqueror of the Inka empire, on an earlier voyage of exploration. The emperor's sudden death left a power vacuum. His official son Huascar should have taken the throne, but while recognised by the Cuzco nobility the succession was contested by Atahualpa, a son of one of Huayna Capac's concubines in Quito. Huascar had official backing and held most of the empire, but Atahualpa had command of most of the army and two seasoned generals, Quisquis and Chalcuchima. In five years of disastrous civil war, Atahualpa's generals outwitted and outfought Huascar's army and captured Huascar himself. It was in the northern town of Cajamarca in 1532 that Atahualpa received news of his final victory, but this was accompanied by the reappearance of the strangers – the Spanish conquistadors of Francisco Pizarro.

The success of the Inka empire was due in equal measure to their skill in administration as to their prowess on the battlefield. Organising a mosaic of ethnic groups, languages and religious traditions was social engineering on a grand scale. Unlike the Classic Maya or Aztecs of Mexico, Inka military strategy had religious and ideological components aimed at increasing the empire's size, prestige and wealth, rather than at acquiring prisoners for sacrifice.

The political mechanisms created by the Inkas drove their empire forward. When an emperor died the empire was bequeathed to his successor, but the income from the lands he had conquered was retained by his *panaqa* or male descendants. The new emperor had to acquire his own wealth by conquering new lands that became the source of wealth for his *panaqa* when he died. Also, as the empire expanded so did the number of local lords whose continued loyalty had to be bought with regular gifts of food, clothing, women, gold and silver. The Inka empire was locked into an unsustainable cycle of conquest.

The Inka army was composed of levies from all able-bodied male citizens – peasant farmers whose labour tax or *mita* was rendered as periods of military service. They were reinforced by special units such as archers from the tropical rainforests and spear throwers from the coast. They wore quilted cotton tunics and fought with spears, slings, battle-axes and war clubs. War drums were made of human skin and some warriors wore necklaces of human teeth. Battlefield tactics were primitive, however, and the Inka relied on superior numbers to overwhelm opponents.

Hand in hand with military force went subtle and intimidating diplomacy. Once the Inka decided on an area to conquer they invited native leaders to join the empire peacefully and become 'Inkas by Privilege'. If this failed, Inka armies were marched to a nearby strategic point and last-minute offers were made. If these were rejected, the Inka gods were invoked and their priests read the signs of entrails of sacrificed llamas. If the auguries were good then fighting began.

The empire that resulted from such tactics was called 'the Land of the Four Quarters' or Tawantinsuyu. The largest quarter was Collasuyu and stretched over the mountains and coast to the south, Antisuyu was the smallest part to the north-east, Cuntisuyu included all areas to the southwest, and Chinchasuyu incorporated the mountains and coast to the north. Each quarter, or *suyu*, was governed by a royal prefect and was divided into provinces under an imperial governor. Mobilising their vast resources of manpower, the Inkas transformed the landscape through large-scale terracing, road-building, bridge construction and hydraulic engineering. These projects possessed religious and ideological dimensions as terrace systems produced maize not only for food but to make huge quantities of *chicha* beer given free to the people during religious festivals.

The arteries of Tawantinsuyu were the 30,000km of imperial roads built and maintained by local people under Inka supervision. They crossed rivers and gorges with suspension bridges in the mountains, and were wide avenues on the coasts. Along their lengths were regularly spaced way-stations and storehouses called *tambos* in which supplies of food, drink, weapons and clothing were kept. These roads were only for official business, the emperor and his armies, and the imperial runners or *chasqui*, who ran in relays up to 250km a day.

Beyond their heartland, the Inkas imposed administrative centres on subject peoples. These were built in the impressive and psychologically intimidating polygonal Inka style, and were designed to replicate in miniature the capital at Cuzco. One such centre was Huánuco Pampa, which housed a small number of Inka administrators but whose size – four thousand buildings spread over 200ha – suggests that several thousand people could have been accommodated during elaborate state-sponsored festivals. Huánuco Pampa had a great central plaza, a palace for Inka Tupac Yupanqui, an area for cooking and feasting, and an *aclla huasi* where the 'chosen women' brewed *chicha* beer and made clothing for local Inka officials. Five hundred storehouses were also built nearby.

More famous is the mountain-top city of Machu Picchu, rediscovered only in 1911. Never found (or damaged) by the Spanish, it was built by Pachacuti first as a fortress then redesigned as a royal estate. The quality of the architecture and workmanship is impressive, as seen in the sophisticated system of water channels and fountains that still work today. The architectural highlights include the semi-circular 'observatory', the cave known as the 'Royal Mausoleum', and the carved stone block of the Intihuatana or 'Hitching Post of the Sun'.

A masterstroke of Inka political organisation was the instigation of a system whereby local populations were transferred wholesale from one place to another. These people were called *mitmaq*, and by moving thousands of families at a time the Inkas secured their borders, ensured stability and removed the focus of insurrection. *Mitmaq* colonists could be moved thousands of miles from their native areas yet retained their traditional costumes and their own leaders. They propagated Inka values and fostered the adoption of the official language of Quechua.

In the complex and cleverly administered Inka state, money was unknown. Food, clothing and housing were provided by the *ayllus* under government control. Taxes were levied but paid in goods and services such as the *mita* labour tax. Unless excused by the emperor, all able-bodied men contributed to *mita* service – whether in the fields, maintaining the imperial highways and infrastructure, or serving in the army. For agricultural workers, *mita* service was divided into three kinds. First to be cultivated was land allotted to the state religion and local gods and which supported the priest-hood. Next to be worked was the emperor's land whose yields supported the Cuzco aristocracy and fed the armies. Last to be tended was land which belonged to the local community. The sheer scale of the *mita*'s success as an organisational system is visible today in the vast terraces which cover large areas of the Andes.

All roads in Tawantinsuyu led to Cuzco, the great city at the sacred heart of empire and the focus of religious and political activity. Cuzco was the embodiment of Inka myth, history and cosmic identity – the place where earth, sky and rivers met. It was laid out in the shape of a giant puma, the predatory feline that was the royal symbol of the Inka. Overlooking the city was the temple-fortress of Sacsayhuaman with its massive zig-zag walls. Cuzco and its royal lineages were divided into two sacred halves or moieties, upper or *hanan* Cuzco, and lower or *hurin* Cuzco.

The most important temple was the Coricancha or 'House of the Sun', whose inner walls were lined with sheets of gold. Flanked by the palace-mausoleums of earlier emperors was the great plaza dominated by a ceremonial platform – the centre of creation. The floor of the plaza was covered with sand brought from the Pacific coast as a symbolic statement of the far-reaching power of the Sapa Inka, and linked Cuzco with the sea as the 'mother of fertility'. Cuzco was the mirror of heaven – its layout, monumental buildings and royal inhabitants were all organised by the principles of religion and ideology.

The Spanish Conquest

The Spanish conquistador Francisco Pizarro arrived at the edge of the Inka empire at Easter 1532, and found it wracked by years of civil war. In September, he advanced to the mountain town of Cajamarca where he was met by a 30,000 strong Inka army. On Saturday

16 November 1532, Pizarro hid his soldiers and cavalry in the buildings of the town and ambushed the Sapa Inka who, confident in his superiority, paid him a visit with an unarmed entourage.

The Spaniards slaughtered the Inkas and took Atahualpa prisoner. The unexpected victory had several benefits for Pizarro. He had captured the enemy leader in his first military action. In addition, Atahualpa was an absolute ruler whose orders would be obeyed even though he was held captive. Also, the Inka emperor had surrounded himself with a bodyguard not of soldiers but of his most important counsellors and officials – the administrators of the empire. Now, all were dead. Atahualpa had misjudged the newcomers and the most powerful ruler in the Americas had been captured by a handful of brave but reckless adventurers.

The Sapa Inka soon realised that the Spanish were greedy for gold and silver. He offered to fill the room in which he was kept prisoner once with gold, then twice over with silver within two months. Pizarro accepted this astounding offer and soon llama caravans were making their way to Cajamarca laden with the ransom. As each load of priceless objects arrived they were broken so that more could be squeezed into the chamber. Six months later, the great treasure was melted down into ingots – 11 tons of gold and 26,000lb of silver – stamped and weighed, then distributed to every Spanish soldier according to rank.

Once the booty had been allocated, arguments began about Atahualpa's fate, and it was judged too dangerous to honour their word and set him free. On the evening of Saturday 26 July 1533, Atahualpa was put to death. He should have been burnt at the stake but was offered a more civilised death by garotting if he converted to Christianity. In Inka belief, the body had to remain intact so it could be mummified and join past emperors as a deified ancestor. Maybe for this reason Atahualpa agreed to convert, but after strangulation his body was burnt anyway and given a Christian burial. Not long after, his remains were spirited away, mummified, and hidden in the surrounding mountains.

Atahualpa's death left the empire open and defenceless. Pizarro moved quickly, taking advantage of the splits between Huascar's faction in Cuzco and Atahualpa's supporters. A member of Huascar's royal line, Tupac Huallpa, became Pizarro's puppet ruler, and accompanied by the new emperor and his entourage, Pizarro finally left Cajamarca and marched south towards Cuzco. Tupac

Huallpa died mysteriously en route whereupon Pizarro appointed an Inka prince called Manco to replace him. After one last fruitless battle with the Spanish the remainder of Atahualpa's men under the general Quisquis retreated north to Quito and Pizarro and his conquistadors finally entered Cuzco.

The Spaniards immediately indulged their appetite for treasure, sacking the city, stripping its golden temples and plundering tombs. They robbed the Coricancha, and melted down its priceless artworks. But even this did not satisfy their greed and they soon set about ravaging the country, torturing and burning alive those whom they thought might reveal the whereabouts of more treasure. They also abused the *acllas* with Pizarro himself, though not a young man, setting a precedent by taking a teenaged Inka princess and having an illegitimate daughter by her.

After several years of abuse and humiliation, Manco escaped to the mountains and joined a gathering army which had been raised in secret. This new Inka force surrounded Cuzco and the 200 Spaniards within. The Inka soon attacked, fighting their way through the city's narrow streets, and within a few days were in almost total control. The Spanish sent fifty horsemen out of the city and with the help of Amerindian allies recaptured the great temple-fortress of Sacsayhuaman overlooking Cuzco. The Inka seige of their own imperial capital continued for another ten months, and Spanish rescue missions were wiped out, but the Inka army could not break back into the city. In April 1537 the siege was lifted.

Manco remained defiant at the town of Ollantaytambo north of Cuzco, but soon retreated to the distant forests of Vilcabamba and established a base at Vitcos. A punitive expedition by the conquistador Rodrigo Orgóñez came close to capturing the fugitive emperor and so the Inkas built the new city of Vilcabamba even deeper in the jungle. For six years the small Inka kingdom at Vilcabamba was left in peace as the Spanish factions fought among themselves. Pizarro and his former ally-turned-enemy Diego de Almagro were killed and control of Peru was taken by the Spanish Crown after the victory of a royal army over the remnants of Almagro's supporters. Tragically, even these internal Spanish squabbles spelled disaster for Manco who was murdered by five of Alamagro's men to whom he had given sanctuary at Vilcabamba.

Resentment against the Spanish grew among the native people of the Andes. After many attempts, the Spanish lured one of Manco's

sons from Vilcabamba but in typical Inka fashion another son, Titu
Cusi Yupanqui, ruled in his place and so the Spanish gained nothing.
Yupanqui died of natural causes in 1571 and was succeeded by his
brother Tupac Amaru. In June 1572, the new Spanish viceroy
Francisco de Toledo marched north and captured Tupac Amaru in the
forests near Vilcabamba. The expedition returned to Cuzco dragging
the emperor behind them in chains, along with a golden statue of Inti
and the sacred mummies of Manco Inka and Titu Cusi Yupanqui.

Like Atahualpa before him, Tupac Amaru converted to Christianity but was tried and sentenced to death. On the day of his execution, grieving Inkas gathered on the hills surrounding Cuzco and
watched as Tupac Amaru was decapitated and all the city's church
bells began to toll. So ended the final act in the tragedy which
engulfed the successors of Pachacuti and Tupac Yupanqui.

LEGACY OF CONQUEST

The Inka empire collapsed under the weight of Spanish military
victories, maltreatment of the natives, and the effects of European
disease. The Inkas and other indigenous groups did not disappear
from history, however. In the years following 1532, the Spanish
created a colonial society within which a mosaic of native peoples
accommodated themselves in a variety of ways to the new social,
economic and religious conditions. Changes could be dramatic, as
with Viceroy Toledo's forced regrouping of 1.5 million natives into
600 communities, a process which facilitated Spanish administration
but dismantled many traditional social structures that had survived
the trauma of the conquest.

In the hard years that followed, native Andean ideas and beliefs
meshed with Christian ones and produced a hybrid or syncretic view
of the world that owed as much to the pre-Columbian past as it did
to the new Spanish order. As with all conquests, the defeated influenced the victors as much as the victors changed the defeated. This
can be seen most clearly in the ways in which native Andeans
retained their worldview but infused it with elements from Christian
theology and European society.

Typical of this was the natives' reaction to their harsh treatment
by the Spanish which saw them searching for signs that their new
masters would soon be driven out. Natural disasters, such as the
volcanic eruption near Arequipa in 1600 and the Cuzco earthquake

of 1646, were interpreted in this way. More subversive were native messiahs like the 'Christ of Tacobamba' who advocated drinking *chicha* and eating the hallucinogenic San Pedro cactus, and countless shamans who proclaimed themselves Saint James the Apostle or the Virgin Mary. These events were part of a wider sense of insurrection which climaxed around 1780 with the appearance of the native leaders Tupac Amaru II and Tupac Catari.

While these overt rebellions failed to shake Spanish control, other kinds of resistance proved more effective. Native peoples often affected to adopt Christianity while in reality preserving ancient beliefs. In the mid-1600s, a clandestine ritual took place in the town of San Pedro de Hacas. During the Christian festival of Corpus Christi, devotees talked to the ancient *huacas* in an attempt to convince them that despite their forced devotions to Catholic saints, the festival was really in honour of them. They then scattered coca leaves in the town plaza, sang, chanted, remembered the deeds of their sacred mummies and drank until dawn. When the Spanish discovered these pagan rites they burnt the mummies, but the villagers gathered up the resulting ashes and made them into a new kind of holy relic which they called the 'burned fathers'.

Typical of the post-conquest mixing of pre-Columbian and Christian ideas and values was the way in which native artists blended Spanish styles of religious painting with their own native ones to create something new. In seventeenth-century Cuzco, elements of Inka iconography were freely combined Catholic imagery by native artists to form the School of Cuzco which flourished between 1688 and 1800. Here, images of jewels, feathers and elaborate gold-leaf played a prominent role, and Christ and the Virgin Mary were associated variously with Inka deities such as Inti, Mama Coya and Pacha Mama.

Exemplifying the work of these artists is the so-called Virgin of the Andes, in fact a series of stunning and colourful seventeenth- and eighteenth-century paintings of the Virgin Mary in various guises. In such masterpieces as 'The Virgin Mary of the Mountain of Potasiama' and 'Our Lady of Lake Titicaca', the European style of painting represents the virgin in the shape of a mountain and incorporates flowers, feathers, colours and motifs of pre-Columbian origin. Such artworks clearly draw on ideas of anthropomorphic sacred landscapes and identify Christian figures with their Inka predecessors.

Roman Catholic festivals such as Corpus Christi were especially fertile ground for native Andeans to express and legitimate their new status. Particularly notable was the way colonial Inka chiefs recombined and displayed old Inka symbols in their new regalia. Feathered collars, gold chestplates, crowns and standards that incorporated the image of the rainbow, and coats of arms that included the sun and moon were all hybrid statements through which Andean elites recreated themselves with old ideas in the style of European heraldry.

Beyond Cuzco, in the rural hinterland of the old Inka empire, traditional celebrations also became syncretic events. The festival of Qollur Rit'i ('Snow Star') originated as an Inka ritual focused on the appearance of the Pleiades star group. This ancient ceremony was Christianised in 1780, and became identified with Corpus Christi. During the modern festivities, pilgrims climb to the base of a nearby glacier, and at dawn, as sunlight hits the snowfield, they pray to mountain deities. They descend bearing crosses and carrying chunks of sacred ice on their backs – part of a ritual which guarantees fertility and rebirth during the coming year.

Today, traces of the Inka past are still found in the Andes. At the Quechua village of Misminay, near Cuzco, modern inhabitants regard animal constellations and the Milky Way as exerting a powerful influence on local mythology and cosmology, as well as on important cycles of earthly fertility. The Vilcanota (Urubamba) river is seen as an earthly reflection of the Milky Way, and together they are responsible for the recycling of water from earth to sky, whence it eventually falls again to earth as rain.

Modern visitors to Peru are overwhelmed by the splendours of Inka civilisation built in a harsh and breathtaking landscape. Through their arts, crafts and economic activity, Native Andean peoples are re-establishing (and recreating) themselves in the new globalised tourist economy. Cuzco's streets have regained Inka names, and in countless markets, colourful textiles and pottery are sold alongside fertility charms, maize, coca and potatoes. In subtle ways, the souvenirs sold at such places are hybrid fragments of an Inka past that now travel far beyond the borders of Tawantinsuyu.

It is perhaps the ultimate irony that after five hundred years, the descendants of the Inkas are only now benefiting from the architectural wonders created by their ancestors.

Glossary of Terms

MAYA

Ahau	Term for lord
Bacabs	Four gods who supported the four quarters of the sky
Balam	Jaguar (*Panthera onca*), America's largest feline, and the sacred animal of Maya royalty and warriors
Balche	Intoxicating drink made from fermented honey and the bark of the balche tree. Consumed on ritual occasions
Ceiba	Ceiba or silk-cotton tree (*Ceiba pentandra*). As the great cosmic tree it stands in the centre of the earth, penetrating all three levels – its roots in the underworld, its trunk in the earthly world and its top piercing the sky. It is called *yaxche* in Maya
Cenote	Called *tz'onot* in Maya, cenotes were underground water sources in the limestone geology of the Yucatan, and were formed when the cavern roof collapsed
Chilam	High-ranking Maya priests of the Yucatan, famous in late Post-classic times for writing down their prophecies known today as the Books of Chilam Balam ('Books of the Jaguar Priest')
Copal	Called *pom* in Maya, copal was a naturally occurring resin obtained from conifer trees and burnt as a purifying incense during rituals
Corbelled arch	Typical lowland Classic Maya architectural feature, also known as the 'false arch' as it lacks a keystone
Gucumatz	Creator deity in the Popol Vuh of the Quiché Maya. Identified as the equivalent of the Aztec Quetzalcoatl and Yucatec Maya *Kukulkán*
Haab	The Maya solar calendar of 360 days plus 5 unlucky days
Halach uinic	The ruler or supreme lord of a Yucatecan Maya city
Huipil	Typical Mayan woven-cotton blouse
Kinich Ahau	Name of the Sun god, literally 'sun-faced'
Kukulkan	Yucatec Maya term for 'feathered serpent', the equivalent to the Aztec Nahuatl name Quetzalcoatl
Lacandon	Maya group who wear white shifts and their hair long
Moan bird	Symbol of the aged God L, associated with the underworld, whose prototype was the Yucatecan screech owl
Nacom	Maya war chief
Pop	Maya word for mat, the seat and symbol of authority, some-times interpreted as 'royal throne'
Popol Vuh	The eighteenth-century AD Book of Council of the Quiché Maya of highland Guatemala
Puuc	Name of a range of low hills in the Yucatan; name given to Maya architectural style typified by the city of Uxmal

Putún	Maya group from Tabasco and Campeche regions, also called the Chontal Maya
Sacbé	Maya name signifying 'white road', given to great ceremonial causeways that connected different parts of a city, and often different cities in the Yucatan
Tun	The period of 360 days
Tzeltal	Maya linguistic group of Chiapas, Mexico
Tzolkin	Maya sacred calendar of 260 days
Tzotzil	Maya linguistic group of Chiapas, Mexico
Uayeb	Five 'unlucky days' at the end of the solar year of 360 days. For the Postclassic Maya it was a time of great ritual importance since they believed it was when the evil of the underworld escaped into the earthly world
Uinal	Maya month of 20 days

AZTEC

Acatl	Reed
Altepetl	Aztec name for a city-state and surrounding territory
Amanteca	Professional featherworkers
Atl-atl	Spear-thrower
Calmecac	Aztec school for children of the nobility
Calpulli	Group of between 100 and 200 families which served as an administrative unit or neighbourhood in cities
Chichimec	Semi-civilised hunting and gathering peoples from northern Mexico
Chinampa	Raised field, usually made from mud dredged up from lake or swamp beds
Cihuacoatl	Literally 'Snake Woman', most important office in the Aztec state second only to the emperor
Coatl	Snake, as in Quetzalcoatl – 'feathered snake'
Codex	Name given to indigenous Mesoamerican painted books that date either from the pre-Columbian period, or the colonial period
Cuauhtli	Eagle
Macehualtin	Commoners
Metate	Stone slab used to grind maize (corn); usually paired with the mano or cyclindrical grinding-stone
Nahuatl	Name of the Aztec language
Ocelotl	Jaguar
Patolli	An Aztec gamblers' game of chance similar to pachesi
Pipiltin	The lower rank of Aztec nobility
Pochteca	Full-time Aztec traders
Pulque	Alcoholic drink made from the fermented sap of the maguey plant
Tecuhtli	Noble, who served as a high-ranking official

Telpochcalli	Aztec school for commoner children
Teocalli	Literally 'God House'; common name for temple
Teotl	Literally 'deity', conceptually the spiritual power that animated gods and the universe
Tlachtli	The Aztec rubber ball-game
Tlatoani	Literally 'the speaker', a title of city-state rulers. The Aztec emperor was Huey Tlatoani, 'Great Speaker'
Tollan/Tula	Literally 'place of reeds', a metaphorical term applied to any populous and sophisticated city; also the name of the capital of the Toltecs
Tonalpohualli	Literally the 'count of days', the 260-day ritual calendar used in divination and whose codex form was the *tonalamatl* (sacred book)
Tzompantli	Skull-rack
Xochitl	Flower

INKA

aclla	A 'chosen woman'
aclla huasi	House of the 'chosen women'
Apu	Inka lord, or ruler of one of the empire's four administrative regions
ayllu	Lineage group or kin-based community
Cacique	Spanish term for *curaca*
Camayoc	An official or craftsman
Capac	Wealthy or influential person
Capac hucha	Human sacrificial victim
Ceque	Sacred lines of spiritual power radiating out of the Coricancha (Temple of the Sun) in Cuzco
Chasqui	Official Inka messenger
Coya	Inka queen or high ranking woman
Cumbi	Fine woollen cloth
Curaca	Amerindian chief, principal chief of a village
Huaca	Sacred place or thing, which could be a mountain, spring, or mummy bundle
Mama cuna	Literally 'mothers', women who had taken a vow of chastity and dedicated themselves to the Inka religion, sometimes called the Virgins of the Sun
Mita	System of labour tax
Mitmaq	People sent by the Inkas to colonise newly conquered areas and aid integration into the empire
Moiety	Symbolic half or division into which Inka society was divided
Ñusta	The emperor's daughter or a young woman of noble Inka birth
Pachacamac	Pre-Inka oracle site and pilgrimage centre on Peru's central coast, later integrated into the Inka empire
Panaqa	Royal *ayllu* of male descendents

Quipu	System of multi-coloured knotted strings used to record information and possibly historical events and songs
Quipu camayoc	The Keeper of the Quipu, the administrative record keeper
Sapa Inka	Great Inka, i.e. the emperor
Sinchi	War chief
Suyu	Region or division, a quarter, as in Tawantinsuyu
Tambo	Way station/storehouse or inn sited along an Inka highway
Tawantinsuyu	Literally 'the Land of the Four Quarters', the Inka name for their empire
Ushnu	Stone throne used by the emperor on ceremonial occasions
Yana	Servant, often directly responsible to the emperor

Bibliography

Finding one's way through the tens of thousands of books and articles that have been published on pre-Columbian America can be a daunting and frustrating task. The aim of this bibiliography, therefore, is to provide a comprehensive, balanced and up-to-date guide to what I consider the most important and accessible publications on the prehistoric archaeology of ancient Middle and South America. There is a vast specialist literature in many languages spread across many international publications, much of it difficult for non-specialists to obtain. Here, I have focused on books published in English, although where necessary I have included chapters in edited volumes and articles in academic journals. There is also the occasional publication in Spanish. Many of the books listed below are edited volumes within which are numerous specialist chapters, and all have their own detailed bibliographies, as do the journal articles. Keen readers will have no problem finding their way to several lifetimes' reading on almost any culture, theme, or topic mentioned in this book.

General

Adams, R.E.W. and MacLeod, M.J. (eds), *The Cambridge History of the Native Peoples of the Americas, Volume II, Mesoamerica Parts 1 and 2*, Cambridge University Press, 2000

Benson, E.P. (ed.), *Death and the Afterlife in Pre-Columbian America*, Washington, DC, Dumbarton Oaks, 1975

——, *Birds and Beasts of Ancient Latin America*, Gainesville, University Press of Florida, 1977

—— (ed.), *The Sea in the Pre-Columbian World*, Washington DC, Dumbarton Oaks, 1977

Bercht, F., Brodsky, E., Farmer, J.A. and Taylor, D. (eds), *Taíno: Pre-Columbian Art and Culture from the Caribbean*, New York, The Monacelli Press, 1997

Berrin, K. (ed.), *The Spirit of Ancient Peru*, Thames & Hudson, 1997

Brotherston, G., *Book of the Fourth World: Reading the Native Americas Through their Literature*, Cambridge University Press, 1994

Bruhns, K.O., *Ancient South America*, Cambridge University Press, 1994

Carrasco, D. (ed.), *Oxford Encyclopaedia of Mesoamerican Cultures*, 3 vols, Oxford University Press, 2000

Coe, M.D., *Mexico*, Thames & Hudson, 2002

Conrad, G.W. and Demarest, A.A., *Religion and Empire: The Dynamics of Aztec and Inca expansionism*, Cambridge University Press, 1984

Descola, P., *In the Society of Nature: A Native Ecology in Amazonia*, Cambridge University Press, 1994

Edgerton, S.Y., *Theaters of Conversion: Religious Architecture and the Indian Artisans in Colonial Mexico*, Albuquerque, University of New Mexico Press, 2001

Emmer, P.C. (ed.), *General History of the Caribbean: Volume II, New Societies: The Caribbean in the Long Sixteenth Century*, London, UNESCO and Macmillan, 1999

Hill Boone, E. and Cummins, T. (eds), *Native Traditions in the Postconquest World*, Washington DC, Dumbarton Oaks, 1998

—— and Mignolo, W.D. (eds), *Writing Without Words: Alternative Literacies in Mesoamerica and the Andes*, Durham, NC, Duke University Press, 1994

Joyce, R.A. *Gender and Power in Prehispanic Mesoamerica*, Austin, University of Texas Press, 2000

Keatinge, R.W., *Peruvian Prehistory*, Cambridge University Press, 1988

Levenson, Jay A. (ed.), *Circa 1492: Art in the Age of Exploration*, Washington DC National Gallery of Art, and New Haven, Yale University Press, 1991

McEwan, C. (ed.), *Pre-Columbian Gold: Technology, Style and Iconography*, British Museum Press, 2000

——, Barreto, C. and Neves, E., *Unknown Amazon*, British Museum Press, 2001

Miller, M.E., *The Art of Mesoamerica from Olmec to Aztec*, Thames & Hudson, 1986

—— and Taube, K., *The Gods and Symbols of Ancient Mexico and the Maya*, Thames & Hudson, 1993

Olsen, D.A., *Music of El Dorado: The Ethnomusicology of Ancient South American Cultures*, Gainesville, University Press of Florida, 2002

Roosevelt, A. (ed.), *Amazonian Indians from Prehistory to the Present*, Tucson, University of Arizona Press, 1994

Saloman, F. and Schwarz, S.B. (eds), *The Cambridge History of the Native Peoples of the Americas, Volume III, South America, Parts 1 and 2*, Cambridge University Press, 1999

Saunders, N.J., *People of the Jaguar: The Living Spirit of Ancient America*, Souvenir, 1989

—— (ed.), *Ancient America: Contributions to New World Archaeology*, Oxford, Oxbow Books, 1993

—— (ed.), *Icons of Power: Feline Symbolism in the Americas*, Routledge, 1998

—— and Montmollin, O. de (eds), *Recent Studies in Pre-Columbian Archaeology*, 2 vols, Oxford, British Archaeological Reports International Series 421, 1988

Smith, M.E. and Masson, M.A. (eds), *The Ancient Civilizations of Mesoamerica – A Reader*, Oxford, Basil Blackwell, 2000

Steward, J.H. (ed.), *Handbook of South American Indians*, 7 vols, Washington DC, Smithsonian Institution/U.S. Government Printing Office, 1946–59

Stone-Miller, R. (ed.), *To Weave for the Sun: Ancient Andean Textiles*, Thames & Hudson, 1994

Sullivan, L.E., *Icanchu's Drum: An Orientation to Meaning in South American Religions*, Macmillan, 1988

Townsend, R.F. (ed.), *The Ancient Americas: Art from Sacred Landscapes*, Chicago, University of Chicago Press, 1991

Von Hagen, A. and Morris, C., *The Cities of the Ancient Andes*, Thames & Hudson, 1998

Chapter One

Allaire, L., 'Archaeology of the Caribbean' in F. Salomon and S.B. Schwartz (eds), *The Cambridge History of the Native Peoples of the Americas: Volume III, South America, Part 1*, Cambridge University Press, 1999, pp. 668–733

Arens, W., *The Man Eating Myth: Anthropology and Anthropophagy*, New York, Oxford University Press, 1979

Bedini, S.A. (ed.), *The Christopher Columbus Encyclopedia*, 2 vols, New York, Simon & Schuster, 1992

Boucher, P.B., *Cannibal Encounters: Europeans and Island Caribs 1492–1763*, Baltimore, MD, Johns Hopkins University Press, 1992

Bray, W. (ed.), *The Meeting of Two Worlds: Europe and the Americas 1492–1650*, The British Academy, 1994

Brecht, F., Brodsky, E. Farmer, J.A. and Taylor, D. (eds), *Taíno: Pre-Columbian Art and Culture from the Caribbean*, New York, The Monacelli Press, 1997

Columbus, C., *The Four Voyages of Christopher Columbus*, Harmondsworth, Penguin, 1969

Crosby, A.W., *The Columbian Exchange: Biological and Cultural Consequences of 1492*, Westport, Conn., Greenwood Press, 1972

Dacal Moure, R. and Rivero de la Calle, M., *Art and Archaeology of Pre-Columbian Cuba*, Pittsburgh, University of Pittsburgh Press, 1996

Deagan, K. and Cruxent, J.M., *Columbus's Outpost among the Taínos: Spain and America at La Isabela, 1493–1498*, New Haven, Conn., Yale University Press, 2002

Denevan, W. (ed.), *The Native Population of the Americas in 1492*, Madison, University of Wisconsin Press, 1976

Gerbi, A., *Nature in the New World: From Christopher Columbus to Gonzalo Fernandez de Oviedo*, tr. J. Moyle, Pittsburgh, University of Pittsburgh Press, 1985

Greenblatt, S. (ed.), *New World Encounters*, Berkeley, University of California Press, 1993

Hulme, P. and Whitehead, N.L., *Wild Majesty: Encounters with Caribs from Columbus to the Present Day*, Oxford, Clarendon Press, 1992

Johnson, K., *The Fragrance of Gold: Trinidad in the Age of Discovery*, School of Continuing Studies, University of the West Indies, St Augustine, Trinidad, 1997

Keegan, W.F., *The People who Discovered Columbus: The Prehistory of the Bahamas*, Gainesville, University Press of Florida, 1992

Las Casas, B. de, *A Short Account of the Destruction of the Indies*, Harmondsworth, Penguin, 1992

Lovén, S., *Origins of the Tainan Culture, West Indies*, Göteborg, Elanders, 1935

Oliver, J.R., 'Gold Symbolism among Caribbean Chiefdoms: Of Feathers, Çibas, and *Guanín* Power among Taíno Elites', in, C. McEwan (ed.), *Pre-Columbian Gold: Technology, Style and Iconography*, British Museum Press, 2000, pp. 196–219

Pané, Fray Ramón, *An Account of the Antiquities of the Indians*, ed. José Juan Arrom, Durham, NC and London, Duke University Press, 1999

Rouse, I.B., *The Tainos: Rise and Decline of the People who Greeted Columbus*, New Haven, Conn., Yale University Press, 1992

Sale, K., *The Conquest of Paradise*, Macmillan, 1992

Sauer, C.O., *The Early Spanish Main*, Berkeley, University of California Press, 1969

Saunders, N.J., 'Biographies of brilliance: pearls, transformations of matter and being, *c.* AD 1492', *World Archaeology* 32 (2) (1999), pp. 243–57

——, *An Encyclopædia of Caribbean Archaeology and Traditional Culture*, Oxford, ABC-Clio, 2005

—— and Gray, D., 'Zemís, trees and symbolic landscapes: three Taíno carvings from Jamaica', *Antiquity* 70 (270) (1996), pp. 801–12

Stevens-Arroyo, A.M., *Cave of the Jaguar: The Mythological World of the Taínos*, Albuquerque, University of New Mexico Press, 1988

Sued-Badillo, J. (ed.), *General History of the Caribbean: Volume 1, Autochthonous Societies*, London and Paris, UNESCO and Macmillan, 2003
Wilson, S.M., *Hispaniola: Caribbean Chiefdoms in the Age of Columbus*, Tuscaloosa, University of Alabama Press, 1990
—— (ed.), *The Indigenous People of the Caribbean*, Gainesville, University Press of Florida, 1997

Chapter Two

Arqueología, *Olmecs* (special edition), Mexico City, Arqueología Mexicana, n.d.
Art Museum, The, *The Olmec World: Ritual and Rulership*, Princeton, Princeton University Press/The Art Museum, 1996
Benson, E.P., *The Olmec and their Neighbors*, Washington DC, Dumbarton Oaks, 1981
—— (ed.), *Dumbarton Oaks Conference on the Olmec*, Washington DC, Dumbarton Oaks, 1968
—— and de la Fuente, B. (eds), *Olmec Art of Ancient Mexico*, Washington DC, National Gallery of Art, 1996
Bernal, I., *The Olmec World*, Berkeley, University of California Press, 1969
Brush, C.F., 'Pox Pottery: Earliest Identified Mexican Ceramic', *Science* 149 (1965), pp. 194–5
Byers, D.S., *Prehistory of the Tehuacán Valley*, 5 vols, Austin, University of Texas Press, 1967
Clark, J.E. and Blake, M., 'The Power of Prestige: Competitive Generosity and the Emergence of Rank Societies in Lowland Mesoamerica', in E. Brumfiel and J. Fox (eds), *Factional Competition and Political Development*, Cambridge University Press, 1994, pp. 17–30
—— and Pye, M.E. (eds), *Olmec Art and Archaeology in Mesoamerica*, New Haven, Conn., Yale University Press, 2000
Coe, M.D., *America's First Civilization: Discovering the Olmec*, New York, American Heritage Publishing, 1968
——, 'Olmec Jaguars and Olmec Kings', in E.P. Benson (ed.), *Cult of the Feline*, Washington DC, Dumbarton Oaks, 1972, pp. 1–12
—— and Diehl, R., *In the Land of the Olmec*, 2 vols, Austin, University of Texas Press, 1980
Diehl, R.A., 'The Precolumbian Cultures of the Gulf Coast', in R.E.W. Adams and M.J. MacLeod (eds), *The Cambridge History of the Native Peoples of the Americas, Volume II, Mesoamerica Part 1*, Cambridge University Press, 2000, pp. 156–96
Drucker, P., Heizer, R.F. and Squier, R.J., *Excavations at La Venta Tabasco, 1955*, Smithsonian Institution Bureau of American Ethnology Bulletin 170, Washington DC, U.S. Government Printing Office, 1959
Flannery, K.V. (ed.), *The Early Mesoamerican Village*, Academic Press, 1976
—— (ed.). *Guilá Naquitz: Archaic Foraging and Early Agriculture in Oaxaca, Mexico*, New York, Academic Press, 1986
Fowler Jr, W. (ed.), *The Formation of Complex Society in Southeastern Mesoamerica*, Boca Raton, Fl., CRC Press, 1991
Gillespie, S., 'Llano del Jícaro: An Olmec Monument Workshop', *Ancient Mesoamerica* 5 (1994), pp. 223–42
Grove, D., 'The Formative Period and the Evolution of Complex Culture', in J.A. Sabloff (ed.), *The Handbook of Middle American Indians, Supplement 1: Archaeology*, Austin, University of Texas Press, 1981, pp. 373–91

——, *Chalcatzingo: Excavations on the Olmec Frontier*, Thames & Hudson, 1984
—— (ed.), *Ancient Chalcatzingo*, Austin, University of Texas Press, 1987
——, 'The Preclassic Societies of the Central Highlands of Mesoamerica', in R.E.W.
  Adams and M.J. MacLeod (eds), *The Cambridge History of the Native Peoples
  of the Americas, Volume II, Mesoamerica Part 1*, Cambridge University Press,
  2000, pp. 122–55
—— and Joyce, R.A. (eds), *Social Patterns in Pre-Classic Mesoamerica*, Washington
  DC, Dumbarton Oaks, 1999
Hirth, K.G. (ed.), *Trade and Exchange in Early Mesoamerica*, Albuquerque,
  University of New Mexico Press, 1984
Joralemon, D., *A Study of Olmec Iconography*, Studies in Pre-Columbian Art and
  Archaeology 7, Washington DC, Dumbarton Oaks, 1971
Justeson, J.S. and Kaufman, T., 'A Decipherment of Epi-Olmec Hieroglyphic
  Writing', *Science* 259 (1993), pp. 1703–11
Nicholson, H.B. (ed.), *Origins of Religious Art and Iconography in Preclassic
  Mesoamerica*, Berkeley, University of California Press, 1976
Porter, M.N., *Tlatilco and the Pre-Classic Cultures of the New World*, Viking Fund
  Publications in Anthropology 19, New York, 1953
Sanders, W.T., Parsons, J.R. and Santley, R.S., *The Basin of Mexico: Ecological
  Processes in the Evolution of a Civilization*, New York, Academic Press, 1979
Sharer, R. and Grove, D. (eds), *Regional Perspectives on the Olmec*, Cambridge
  University Press, 1989
Soustelle, J., *The Olmecs: The Oldest Civilization in Mexico*, Norman, University
  of Oklahoma Press, 1985
Taube, K., 'The Olmec Maize God: The Face of Corn in Formative Mesoamerica',
  RES: Anthropology and Aesthetics 29–30 (1996), 39–82
Voorhies, B., *The Chantuto People: An Archaic Period Society of the Chiapas
  Littoral, Mexico*, Papers of the New World Archaeological Foundation 41,
  Provo, 1976
Zeitlin, R.N. and Zeitlin, J.F., 'The Palaeoindian and Archaic Cultures of
  Mesoamerica', in R.E.W. Adams and M.J. MacLeod (eds), *The Cambridge
  History of the Native Peoples of the Americas, Volume II, Mesoamerica Part 1*,
  Cambridge University Press, 2000, pp. 45–121

Chapter Three

Bernal, I., 'Archaeological Synthesis of Oaxaca', in R. Wauchope (ed.), *Handbook
  of Middle American Indians*, vol. 3, Austin, University of Texas Press, 1965
Blanton, R.E., *Monte Albán: Settlement Patterns at the Ancient Zapotec Capital*,
  Academic Press, 1978
Blanton, R.E., Feinman, G.E., Kowaleski, S.A. and Nicholas, L.M., *Ancient
  Oaxaca*, Cambridge University Press, 1999
Calloway, C.H., 'The Church of Nuestra Señora de la Soledad in Oaxaca, Mexico',
  PhD dissertation, University of Maryland, Ann Arbor, Mich., University
  Microfilms, 1989
Caso, A., *Las estelas zapotecas*, Monografías del Museo Nacional de Arqueología,
  Historia y Etnografía, Mexico City, Talleres Gráficos de la Nación, 1928
——, 'Sculpture and Mural Painting of Oaxaca', in R. Wauchope (ed.), *Handbook
  of Middle American Indians*, vol. 3, Austin, University of Texas Press, 1965, pp.
  849–70
—— and Bernal, I., *Urnas de Oaxaca*, Memorias de Instituto Nacional de
  Arqueología e Historia, II, Mexico City, Secretaría de Educación Pública, 1952

——, —— and Acosta, J.R., *Le Céramica de Monte Albán*, Memorias de Instituto Nacional de Arqueología e Historia, 13, Mexico City, Secretaría de Educación Pública, 1967

Chance, J.K., *Conquest of the Sierra: Spaniards and Indians in Colonial Oaxaca*, Norman, University of Oklahoma Press, 1989

Flannery, K.V. (ed.), *The Early Mesoamerican Village*, New York, Academic Press, 1976

—— and Marcus, J. (eds), *The Cloud People: Divergent Evolution of the Zapotec and Mixtec Civilisations*, Academic Press, 1983

Marcus, J., 'Archaeology and Religion: A comparison of the Zapotec and Maya', *World Archaeology* 10 (1978), 172–89

——, 'Zapotec Writing', *Scientific American* 242 (1980), 50–64

——, 'Zapotec Chiefdoms and the Nature of Formative Religions', in R. Sharer and D. Grove (eds), *Regional Perspectives on the Olmec*, Cambridge University Press, 1989, pp. 148–97

—— and Flannery, K.V., 'Ancient Zapotec Ritual and Religion', in C. Renfrew and E. Zubrow (eds), *The Ancient Mind: Elements of Cognitive Archaeology*, Cambridge University Press, 1994, pp. 55–74

——, *Zapotec Civilization*, Thames & Hudson, 1996

——, 'Cultural Evolution in Oaxaca: The Origins of the Zapotec and Mixtec Civilizations', in R.E.W. Adams and M.J. MacLeod (eds), *The Cambridge History of the Native Peoples of the Americas, Volume II, Mesoamerica Part 1*, Cambridge University Press, 2000, pp. 358–406

Paddock, J. (ed), *Ancient Oaxaca*, Stanford, Calif., Stanford University Press, 1966

Parmenter, R., *Four Lienzos of the Coixtlahuaca Valley*, Washington DC, Dumbarton Oaks, 1982

Romero Frizzi, M. De Los A., 'Indigenous Mentality and Spanish Power: The Conquest of Oaxaca', in J. Marcus and J.F. Zeitlin (eds), *Caciques and their People: A Volume in Honor of Ronald Spores*, Anthropological Papers, Museum of Anthropology No. 89, Ann Arbor, University of Michigan Press, 1994, pp. 227–44

——, 'The Indigenous Population of Oaxaca from the Sixteenth Century to the Present', in R.E.W. Adams and M.J. MacLeod (eds), *The Cambridge History of the Native Peoples of the Americas, Volume II, Mesoamerica Part 2*, Cambridge University Press, 2000, pp. 302–45

Scott, J.F., *The Danzantes of Monte Albán*, 2 vols, Washington DC, Dumbarton Oaks, 1978

Smith, M.E., *Picture Writing from Ancient Southern Mexico: Mixtec Place Signs and Maps*, Norman, University of Oklahoma Press, 1973

Spores, R., *The Mixtec Kings and their People*, Norman, University of Oklahoma Press, 1967

Whitecotton, J.W., *The Zapotecs: Princes, Priests, and Peasants*, Norman, University of Oklahoma Press, 1977

Winter, M., *Oaxaca: The Archaeological Record*, Mexico City, Minutiae Mexicana, 1990

Chapter Four

Acosta, J.R., *El palacio de Quetzalpapalotl*, Mexico City, Instituto de Antropología e Historia, 1964

Barbour, W., 'The Figurines and Figurine Chronology of Ancient Teotihuacan, Mexico', unpublished PhD dissertation, Department of Anthropology, University of Rochester, Newe York, 1976

Berlo, J.C., *Teotihuacan Art Abroad: A Study of Metropolitan Style and Provincial Transformation in Incensario Workshops*, British Archaeological Reports, International Series 199, Oxford, 1984

—— (ed.), *Art, Ideology, and the City of Teotihuacan*, Washington DC, Dumbarton Oaks, 1992

Bernal, I. (ed.), *Teotihuacan: Descubrimiento, reconstrucciones*, Mexico City, Instituto de Antropología e Historia, 1963

Berrin, K. (ed.), *Feathered Serpents and Flowering Trees: Reconstructing the Murals of Teotihuacan*, San Francisco, The Fine Arts Museum of San Francisco, 1988

—— and Pasztory, E. (eds), *Teotihuacan: Art from the City of the Gods*, Thames & Hudson, 1993

Cabrera, Castro, Sugiyama, R.S. and Cowgill, G., 'The Temple of Quetzalcoatl Project at Teotihuacan', *Ancient Mesoamerica* 2 (1991), 77–92

Cowgill, G., 'State and Society at Teotihuacan, Mexico', *Annual Review of Anthropology* 26 (1997), 129–61

Cowgill, G., 'The Central Mexican Highlands from the Rise of Teotihuacan to the Decline of Tula', in R.E.W. Adams and M.J. MacLeod (eds), *The Cambridge History of the Native Peoples of the Americas, Volume II, Mesoamerica Part 1*, Cambridge University Press, 2000, pp. 250–317

Diehl, R. and Berlo, J.C. (eds), *Mesoamerica after the Decline of Teotihuacan: A.D. 700–900*, Washington DC, Dumbarton Oaks, 1989

Heyden, D., 'Caves, Gods, and Myths: World View and Planning in Teotihuacan', in E.P. Benson (ed.), *Mesoamerican Sites and Worldviews*, Washington DC, Dumbarton Oaks, 1981, pp. 1–39

Kolb, C.C., *Marine Shell Trade and Classic Teotihuacan, Mexico*, British Archaeological Reports International Series 364. Oxford, 1987

Kubler, G., *The Iconography of the Art of Teotihuacan*, Studies in Pre-Columbian Art and Archaeology 4, Washington DC, Dumbarton Oaks, 1967

Langley, J.C., *Symbolic Notation at Teotihuacan: Elements of Writing in a Mesoamerican Culture of the Classic Period*, British Archaeological Reports International Series 313, Oxford, 1986

Linné, S., *Archaeological Researches at Teotihuacan, Mexico*, Ethnographic Museum of Sweden Publication 1, Stockholm, 1934

Matos Moctezuma, E. *Teotihuacan, the City of the Gods*, New York, Rizzoli, 1990

Miller, A.G., *The Mural Painting of Teotihuacan* Washington DC, Dumbarton Oaks, 1973

Millon, R., 'Teotihuacan: City, State, and Civilisation', in J. Sabloff (ed.), *Supplement to the Handbook of Middle American Indians*, Austin, University of Texas Press, 1981, pp. 198–243

——, Drewett, B. and Cowgill, G. (eds), *Urbanization at Teotihuacan, Mexico. Vol. 1. The Teotihuacan Map*, Austin, University of Texas Press, 1973

Pasztory, E., *The Iconography of the Teotihuacan Tlaloc*, Studies in Pre-Columbian Art and Archaeology 15, Washington DC, Dumbarton Oaks, 1974

——, *The Murals of Tepantitla, Teotihuacan*, New York, Garland Press, 1976

——, *Teotihuacan: An Experiment in Living*, Norman, University of Oklahoma Press, 1997

Séjourné, L., *Arquitectura y pintura en Teotihuacan*, Mexico City, Siglo XXI, 1966

Spence, M., 'Obsidian Production and the State in Teotihuacan', *American Antiquity* 46 (4) (1981), 769–88

Storey, R., *Life and Death in the Ancient City of Teotihuacan: A Modern Paleodemographic Analysis*, Tuscaloosa, University of Alabama Press, 1992

Sugiyama, S., 'Burials Dedicated to the Old Temple of Quetzalcoatl at Teotihuacan, Mexico', *American Antiquity* 54 (1) (1989), 85–106

Taube, K.A., 'The Teotihuacan Spider Woman', *Journal of Latin American Lore* 9 (2) (1983), 107–89

——, 'The Temple of Quetzalcoatl and the Cult of Sacred War at Teotihuacan', *Res: Anthropology and Aesthetics* 21 (1992), 53–87

Von Winning, H., *La iconografía de Teotihuacan: Los dioses y los signos*, 2 vols, Mexico City, Universidad Nacional Autónoma de México, 1987

Chapter Five

Adams, R., *Río Azul: A Classic Maya City*, Norman, University of Oklahoma Press, 1998

Bassie-Sweet, K., *From the Mouth of the Dark Cave*, Norman, University of Oklahoma Press, 1991

Benson, E.P. and Griffin, G.G. (eds), *Maya Iconography*, Princeton: Princeton University Press, 1988

Boone, E.H. (ed.), *Ritual Human Sacrifice in Mesoamerica*, Washington DC, Dumbarton Oaks, 1984

Brady, J.E. and Prufer, K.M., 'Caves and Crystalmancy: Evidence for the Use of Crystals in Ancient Maya Religion', *Journal of Anthropological Research 55 (1999), 129–44*

Bricker, V.R., *The Indian Christ, The Indian King: The Historical Substrate of Maya Myth and Ritual*, Austin, University of Texas Press, 1983

Coe, M.D., *Breaking the Maya Code*, Thames & Hudson, 1992

——, *The Maya*, 5th edn, Thames & Hudson, 1993

——, *The Art of the Maya Scribe*, Thames & Hudson, 1997

Farriss, N., *Maya Society under Colonial Rule*, Princeton: Princeton University Press, 1984

Fash Jr, W.L., *Scribes, Warriors, and Kings: The City of Copán and the Ancient Maya*, Thames & Hudson, 1991

Folan, W.J., Kintz, E.R. and Fletcher, L.A., *Coba: A Classic Maya Metropolis*, Academic Press, 1983

Freidel, D.A. and Sabloff, J.A., *Cozumel: Late Maya Settlement Patterns*, Academic Press, 1984

Freidel, D.A., Schele, L. and Parker, J., *Maya Cosmos: Three Thousand Years on the Shaman's Path*, New York, William Morrow, 1993

Hammond, N. (ed.), *Social Process in Maya Prehistory*, Academic Press, 1977

——, 'The Maya Lowlands: Pioneer Farmers to Merchant Princes', in R.E.W. Adams and M.J. MacLeod (eds), *The Cambridge History of the Native Peoples of the Americas, Volume II, Mesoamerica Part 1*, Cambridge University Press, 2000, pp. 197–249

Houston, S., *Hieroglyphs and History at Dos Pilas: Dynastic Politics of the Classic Maya*, Austin, University of Texas Press, 1993

Jones, G.D., *Maya Resistance to Spanish Rule*, Albuquerque, University of New Mexico Press, 1989

Looper, M.G., *Lightning Warrior: Maya Art and Kingship at Quirigua*, Austin, University of Texas Press, 2003

McAnany, P., *Living with the Ancestors: Kinship and Kingship in Ancient Maya Society*, Austin, University of Texas Press, 1995

Marcus, J., *Emblem and State in the Classic Maya Lowlands: An Epigraphic Approach to Territorial Organisation*, Washington DC, Dumbarton Oaks, 1976

Martin, S. and Grube, N., *Chronicle of the Maya Kings and Queens*, Thames & Hudson, 2000

Miller, Mary Ellen, *The Murals of Bonampak*, Princeton, Princeton University Press, 1986

——, *Maya Art and Architecture*, Thames & Hudson, 1991

Orellana, S., *The Tzutujil Mayas: Continuity and Change, 1250–1630*, Norman, University of Oklahoma Press, 1984

Reents-Budet, Dorie, *Painting the Maya Universe: Royal Ceramics of the Classic Period*, Durham, NC, Duke University Press, 1994

Robicsek, F., *The Smoking Gods: Tobacco in Maya Art, History, and Religion*, Norman, University of Oklahoma Press, 1978

Roys, R.L., *The Book of Chilam Balam of Chumayel*, Norman, University of Oklahoma Press, 1967

Sabloff, J.A., *The New Archaeology and the Ancient Maya*, New York, Scientific American Library, 1990

Scarborough, V., 'Ecology and Ritual: Water Management and the Maya', *Latin American Antiquity* 9 (2) (1998), 135–59

Schele, L. and Freidel, D., *A Forest of Kings: The Untold Story of the Ancient Maya*, New York, William Morrow, 1990

—— and Mathews, P., *The Code of Kings*, Thames & Hudson, 1998

—— and Miller, M.E., *Blood of Kings: Dynasty and Ritual in Maya Art*, Fort Worth, Kimbell Art Museum, 1986

Sharer, R., *The Ancient Maya*, Stanford, Stanford University Press, 1994

Taube, K.A., *The Major Gods of Ancient Yucatan, Studies in Pre-Columbian Art and Archaeology 32*, Washington DC, Dumbarton Oaks, 1992

Tedlock, D., *Popol Vuh: The Mayan Book of the Dawn of Life*, New York, Simon & Schuster, 1985

Thompson, J.E.S., *Maya History and Religion*, Norman, University of Oklahoma Press, 1970

Chapter Six

Berdan, F., *The Aztecs of Central Mexico: An Imperial Society*, New York, Holt, Rinehart & Winston, 1982

—— and Anawalt, P., *The Essential Codex Mendoza*, London, University of California Press, 1997

Bray, W., *Everyday Life of the Aztecs*, Batsford, 1968

Brotherston, G., *The Painted Books of Mexico*, British Museum Press, 1995

Burkhart, L.M., 'Pious Performances: Christian Pageantry and Native Identity in Early Colonial Mexico', in E.H. Boone and T. Cummins (eds), *Native Traditions in the Postconquest World*, Washington DC, Dumbarton Oaks, 1998, pp. 361–81

Díaz del Castillo, B. ,*The Conquest of New Spain*, Harmondsworth, Penguin, 1976

Diehl, R., 'Tula', in J.A. Sabloff (ed.), *Supplement to the Handbook of Middle American Indians*, Austin, University of Texas Press, 1981, pp. 277–95

Carrasco, D., *To Change Place: Aztec Ceremonial Landscapes*, Niwot, University of Colorado Press, 1991

Clendinnen, I., *Aztecs: An Interpretation*, Cambridge University Press, 1991

Cline, S.L., 'Native Peoples of Colonial Central Mexico', in R.E.W. Adams and M.J. MacLeod (eds), *The Cambridge History of the Native Peoples of the Americas, Volume II, Mesoamerica Part 2*, Cambridge University Press, 2000, pp. 187–222

Cowgill, G., 'The Central Mexican Highlands from the Rise of Teotihuacan to the Decline of Tula', in R.E.W. Adams and M.J. MacLeod (eds), *The Cambridge*

History of the Native Peoples of the Americas, Volume II, Mesoamerica Part 1,
    Cambridge University Press, 2000, pp. 250–317
Davies, N., *The Aztecs*, Macmillan, 1973
——, *The Toltecs until the Fall of Tula*, Norman, University of Oklahoma Press,
    1977
Diehl, R., *Tula, The Toltec Capital*, Thames & Hudson, 1983
—— and Berlo, J.C. (eds), *Mesoamerica after the Decline of Teotihuacan A.D.
    700–900*, Washington DC, Dumbarton Oaks, 1989
Edgerton, S.Y., *Theaters of Conversion: Religious Architecture and the Indian
    Artisans in Colonial Mexico*, Albuquerque, University of New Mexico Press, 2001
Gillespie, S., *The Aztec Kings: The Constitution of Rulership in Mexican History*,
    Tucson, University of Arizona Press, 1989
Gruzinski, S., *Painting the Conquest: The Mexican Indians and the European
    Renaissance*, Paris, Flammarion, 1992
——, *The Conquest of Mexico: The Incorporation of Indian Societies into the
    Western World, 16th–18th Centuries*, Cambridge, Polity Press, 1993
Hassig, R., *Aztec Warfare: Imperial Expansion and Political Control*, Norman,
    University of Oklahoma Press, 1988
Hill Boone, E. (ed.), *The Art and Iconography of Late Postclassic Central Mexico*,
    Washington DC, Dumbarton Oaks, 1982
—— (ed.), *The Aztec Templo Mayor*, Washington DC, Dumbarton Oaks, 1987
León-Portilla, M., *Aztec Thought and Culture*, Norman, University of Oklahoma
    Press, 1978
——, *The Broken Spears: The Aztec Account of the Conquest of Mexico*, Boston,
    Beacon Press, 1990
Matos Moctezuma, E., *The Great Temple of the Aztecs*, Thames & Hudson, 1988
—— *Aztecs*, Royal Academy of Arts, 2002
Pasztory, E., *Aztec Art*, New York, H.N. Abrams, 1983
Saunders, N.J., 'The Day of the Jaguar: Rainmaking in a Mexican Village',
    Geographical Magazine 55 (1983), 398–405
——, 'A Dark Light: Reflections on Obsidian in Mesoamerica', *World Archaeology*
    33 (2) (2001), 220–36
Smith, M., *The Aztecs*, Oxford, Basil Blackwell, 1996
Thomas, H., *Conquest: Montezuma, Cortés, and the Fall of Old Mexico*, New
    York, Simon & Schuster, 1993
Todorov, T., *The Conquest of America*, New York, Harper & Row, 1984
Townsend, R., *The Aztecs*, Thames & Hudson, 1993

Chapter Seven

Benson, E.P. (ed.), *Dumbarton Oaks Conference on Chavín*, Washington DC,
    Dumbarton Oaks, 1971
Bird, J.B. and Hyslop, J., *The Preceramic Excavations at Huaca Prieta, Chicama
    Valley, Peru*, American Museum of Natural History Anthropological Papers 62
    (1), 1985
Burger, R.L., *The Prehistoric Occupation of Chavín de Huántar, Peru*, Berkeley,
    University of California Press, 1984
——, 'Unity and Heterogeneity within the Chavín Horizon', in R.W. Keatinge (ed.),
    Peruvian Prehistory, Cambridge University Press, 1988, pp. 99–144
——, *Chavin and the Origins of Andean Civilization*, Thames & Hudson, 1995
Conklin, W.J., 'Chavin Textiles and the Origins of Peruvian Weaving', *Textile
    Museum Journal* 3 (92) (1971), 13–19

Cordy-Collins, A., 'Chavin Art: its Shamanic Hallucinogenic Origins', in A. Cordy-Collins and J. Stern (eds), *Pre-Columbian Art History*, Palo Alto, Calif., Peek Publications, 1979, pp. 353–62

Donnan, C.B. (ed.), *Early Ceremonial Architecture in the Andes*, Washington DC, Dumbarton Oaks, 1985

Feldman, R., 'From Maritime Chiefdom to Agricultural State in Formative Coastal Peru', in R. Leventhal and A. Kolata (eds), *Civilization in the Ancient Americas: Essays in Honor of Gordon Willey*, Cambridge, Mass., Peabody Museum of Archaeology and Ethnology, 1983, pp. 289–310

Grieder, T., Bueno, A., Smith Jr, C. Earle and Malina, R. *La Galgada, Peru: A Preceramic Culture in Transition*, Austin, University of Texas Press, 1988

Kano, C., *The Origins of the Chavin Culture*, Studies in Pre-Columbian Art and Archaeology 22, Washington DC, Dumbarton Oaks, 1979

Lathrap, D., *The Upper Amazon*, Thames & Hudson, 1970

——, Collier, D. and Chandra, H. *Ancient Ecuador: Culture, Clay and Creativity 3000–300 BC*, Chicago, Field Museum of Natural History, 1975

McEwan, C., Barreto, C. and Neves, E. *Unknown Amazon*, British Museum Press, 2001

Moseley, M., *The Maritime Foundations of Andean Civilization*, Menlo Park, Calif., Cummings Publishing, 1975

—— and Watanabe, L., 'The Adobe Sculpture of Huaca de Los Reyes', *Archaeology* 2 (1974), 154–61

Quilter, J., *Life and Death at Paloma: Society and Mortuary Practices in a Preceramic Peruvian Village*, Iowa City, University of Iowa Press, 1989

Roosevelt, A. (ed.), *Amazonian Indians from Prehistory to the Present*, Tucson, University of Arizona Press, 1994

——, *Moundbuilders of the Amazon*, Academic Press, 1991

Rowe, J.H., *Chavín Art: An Enquiry into its Form and Meaning*, New York, The Museum of Primitive Art, 1962

Willey, G., *Prehistoric Settlement Patterns in the Viru Valley, Peru*, Washington DC, Smithsonian Institution, 1953

—— and Corbett, J., *Early Ancon and Early Supe Culture*, Columbia Studies in Archaeology and Ethnology 3, 1954

Chapter Eight

Alva, W. and Donnan, C.B., *Royal Tombs of Sipán*, Los Angeles, Fowler Museum of Cultural History, 1994

Bawden, G., *The Moche*, Oxford, Basil Blackwell, 1996

Benson, E.P., *The Mochica: A Culture of Peru*, Thames & Hudson, 1972

——, *A Man and a Feline in Mochica Art*, Studies in Pre-Columbian Art and Archaeology 14, Washington DC, Dumbarton Oaks, 1974

——, 'Death-associated Figures on Mochica Pottery', in E.P. Benson (ed.), *Death and the Afterlife in Pre-Columbian America*, Washington DC, Dumbarton Oaks, 1975, pp. 105–44

Bourget, S., 'Children and Ancestors: Ritual Practices at the Moche Site of Huaca de la Luna, North Coast of Peru', in E.P. Benson and A.G. Cook (eds), *Ritual Sacrifice in Ancient Peru*, Austin, University of Texas Press, 2001, pp. 93–118

Cordy-Collins, A., 'Blood and the Moon Priestesses: Spondylus Shells in Moche Ceremony', in E.P. Benson and A.G. Cook (eds), *Ritual Sacrifice in Ancient Peru*, Austin, University of Texas Press, 2001, pp. 35–54

Donnan, C.B., *Moche Art and Iconography*, Los Angeles, Latin American Studies Publications, University of California, Los Angeles, 1976
——, *Moche Portraits from Ancient Peru*, Thames & Hudson, 2004
—— and Mackey, C.J., *Ancient Burial Patterns of the Moche Valley, Peru*, Austin, University of Texas Press, 1978
—— and McClelland, D., *The Burial Theme in Moche Iconography*, Studies in Pre-Columbian Art and Archaeology 20, Washington DC, Dumbarton Oaks, 1979
——, *Moche Fine Line Painting: Its Evolution and its Artists*, Los Angeles, UCLA Fowler Museum of Cultural History, 1999
Jones, J., 'Mochica Works of Art in Metal', in E.P. Benson (ed.), *Pre-Columbian Metallurgy of South America*, Washington DC, Dumbarton Oaks, 1979, pp. 53–104
Pillsbury, J. (ed.), *Moche Art and Archaeology in Ancient Peru*, Washington DC, Washington Studies in History of Art, 2002
Quilter, J., 'The Moche Revolt of the Objects', *Latin American Antiquity* 1 (1990), 42–65
Shimada, I., *Pampa Grande and the Mochica Culture*, Austin, University of Texas Press, 1994

Chapter Nine

Aveni, A.F., *Between the Lines: The Mystery of the Giant Ground Drawings of Ancient Nasca, Peru*, Austin, University of Texas Press, 2000
—— (ed.), *The Lines of Nazca*, Philadelphia, Pa., The American Philosophical Society, 1990
Browne, D., Silverman, H. and García, R., 'A Cache of 48 Nasca Trophy Heads from Cerro Carapo, Peru', *Latin American Antiquity* 4 (3) (1993), 274–94
Clarkson, P., 'The Archaeology and Geoglyphs of Nazca, Peru', unpublished PhD dissertation, University of Calgary, 1985
Dwyer, E. and Dwyer, J.P., 'The Paracas Cemeteries: Mortuary Patterns in a Peruvian South Coastal Tradition', in E.P. Benson (ed.), *Death and the Afterlife in Pre-Columbian America*, Washington DC, Dumbarton Oaks, 1975, pp. 145–61
Hadingham, E. *Lines to the Mountain Gods: Nazca and the Mysteries of Peru*, New York, Random House, 1987
Johnson, D.W., Proulx, D.A. and Mabee, S.B., 'The Correlation between Geoglyphs and Subterranean Water Resources in the Rio Grande de Nazca Drainage', in H. Silverman and W.H. Isbell (eds), *Andean Archaeology II, Art Landscape, and Society*, New York, Kluwer Academic, 2002, pp. 307–32
Kosok, P. and Reiche, M., 'The Mysterious Markings of Nazca', *Natural History* 56 (1947), 200–7, 237–8
Kroeber, A.L. and Collier, D., *The Archaeology and Pottery of Nazca, Peru*, ed. P. Carmichael, Walnut Creek, Calif., Altamira, 1998
Lumbreras, L.G., *Formulación de los lineamientos para la elaboración de un Plan de Manejo de Las Líneas de Nasca: Vol. 1, Contexto Arqueológico*, Lima, UNESCO/Lluvia Editores, 2000
Morrison, T. and Hawkins, G.S., *Pathways to the Gods: The Mystery of the Andes Lines*, Book Club Associates, 1979
Orefici, G., *Nasca: arte e societá del popolo dei geoglifi*, Milan, Jaca Books, 1993
—— and Drusini, A., *Nasca: Hipótesis y Evidencias de su Desorrollo Cultural*, Lima, CISRAP, 2003
Paul, A. (ed.), *Paracas Art and Architecture: Object and Context in South Coastal Peru*, Iowa City, University of Iowa Press, 1991

Proulx, D.A., 'Ritual Uses of Trophy Heads in Ancient Nasca Society', in E.P.
  Benson and A.G. Cook (eds), *Ritual Sacrifice in Ancient Peru*, Austin, University
  of Texas Press, 2001, pp. 119–36
Reiche, M., *Mystery on the Desert*, Stuttgart, Offizindruck AG, 1968
Reinhard, J., *The Nazca Lines: A New Perspective on their Origin and Meaning*,
  Lima, Los Pinos, 1987
Schreiber, K. and Lancho, J., 'The Puquios of Nasca', *Latin American Antiquity* 6
  (3) (1995), 229–54
Silverman, H., *Cahuachi in the Ancient Nasca World*, Iowa City, University of Iowa
  Press, 1993
—— and Proulx, D., *The Nasca*, Oxford, Basil Blackwell, 2002

Chapter Ten

Cordy-Collins, A., 'Fonga Sigde, Shell Purveyor to the Chimu Kings', in M.E.
  Moseley and A. Cordy-Collins (eds), *The Northern Dynasties: Kingship
  and Statecraft in Chimor*, Washington DC, Dumbarton Oaks, 1990,
  pp. 393–417
Heyerdahl, T., Sandweiss, D.H. and Narvaez, A. (eds), *Pyramids of Túcume: The
  Quest for Peru's Forgotten City*, Thames & Hudson, 1995
Holstein, O., 'Chan Chan, Capital of Great Chimu', *Geographical Review* 27
  (1927), 36–61
Keatinge, R.W., 'Chimu Rural Administrative Centers in the Moche Valley', *World
  Archaeology* 6 (1974), 66–82
—— and Conrad, G.W., 'Imperialist Expansion in Peruvian Prehistory: Chimu
  Administration of a Conquered Territory', *Journal of Field Archaeology* 10 (3)
  (1983), 255–83
Klymyshyn, A.M.U., 'The Development of Chimu Administration in Chan Chan',
  in J. Haas, T. Pozorski and S. Pozorski (eds), *Origins and Development of the
  Andean State*, Cambridge University Press, 1987, pp. 97–110
Mackey, C.J. and Klymyshyn, A.M.U., 'Construction and Labor Organization in
  the Chimu Empire', *Ñawpa Pacha* 19 (1981), 99–114
Moseley, M., 'Chan Chan: Andean Alternative to the Pre-Industrial City?', *Science*
  187 (1975), 219–25
—— and Cordy-Collins, A. (eds), *The Northern Dynasties: Kingship and Statecraft
  in Chimor*, Washington DC, Dumbarton Oaks, 1990
—— and Day, K.C. (eds), *Chan Chan: Andean Desert City*, Albuquerque,
  University of New Mexico Press, 1982
—— and Mackey, C.J., *Twenty-Four Architectural Plans of Chan Chan, Peru*,
  Cambridge, Mass., Peabody Museum Press, Harvard University Press, 1974
Ortloff, C.R., Moseley, M.E. and Feldman, R.A., 'Hydraulic Engineering Aspects of the
  Chimu Chicam-Moche Intervalley Canal', *American Antiquity* 47 (3) (1982), 572–95
Pozorsky, T.G., 'The Las Avispas Burial Platform at Chan Chan, Peru', *Annals of
  the Carnegie Museum* 48 (8) (1979), 119–37
Ravines, R (ed.), *Chan Chan: Metrópoli Chimú*, Lima, Instituto de Estudios
  Peruanos, 1980
Rowe, A.P., *Costumes and Featherwork of the Lords of Chimor: Textiles from
  Peru's North Coast*, Washington DC, The Textile Museum, 1984
Rowe, J.H., 'The Kingdom of Chimor', *Acta Americana* 6 (1948), 26–50
Shimada, I. *Cultura Sicán: Dios, Riqueza y Poder en la Costa Norte del Perú*, Lima,
  Banco Continental, 1995
——, 'The Late Prehispanic Coastal States', in L.L. Minelli (ed.), *The Inca World:*

The Development of Pre-Columbian Peru, A.D. 1000–1534, Norman, University of Oklahoma Press, 2000, pp. 49–110
—— and Griffin, J.A., 'Precious Metals in Middle Sicán', *Scientific American* 270, no. 4 (1994), 60–7
—— and Merkel, J.F., 'Copper Alloy Metallurgy in Ancient Peru', *Scientific American* 265 (1991), 80–6
——, 'A Sicán Tomb in Peru', *Minerva* 4 (1) (1993), 18–25

Chapter Eleven

Albarracin-Jordan, J., *Tiwanaku: Arqueología regional y Dínamica Segmentaria*, La Paz, Editores Plural, 1996
Bandelier, A., *The Islands of Titicaca and Koati*, New York, The Hispanic Society of America, 1910
——, 'The Ruins at Tiahuanaco', *Proceedings of the American Antiquarian Society* 21 (1911), Part 1
Bennett, W.C., 'Excavations at Tiahuanaco', *Anthropological Papers of the American Museum of Natural History* 34 (1934), 359–494
——, *Excavations at Wari, Ayacucho, Peru*, Yale University Publications in Anthropology 49, New Haven, Conn., 1953
Bermann, M., *Lukurmata: Household Archaeology in Prehispanic Bolivia*, Princeton, Princeton University Press, 1994
Browman, D., 'New Light on Andean Tiwanaku', *American Scientist* 69, no. 4 (1981), 408–19
Conklin, W.J., 'The Information System of Middle Horizon Quipus', in A.F. Aveni and G. Urton (eds), *Ethnoastronomy and Archaeoastronomy in the American Tropics*, New York, New York Academy of Sciences, 1982, pp. 261–82
——, 'Huari Tunics', in E. Hill Boone (ed.), *Andean Art at Dumbarton Oaks*, Washington DC, Dumbarton Oaks, 1997, pp. 375–98
Cook, A., 'Aspects of State Ideology in Huari and Tiwanaku Iconography: the Central Deity and the Sacrificer', in D.H. Sandweiss (ed.), *Investigations of the Andean Past*, Cornell University, Latin American Studies Program, Ithaca, NY, 1983, pp. 161–85
——, 'The Stone Ancestors: Idioms of Imperial Attire and Rank among Huari Figurines', *Latin American Antiquity* 3, no. 4 (1992), 341–63
——, *Wari y Tiwanaku: Entre el Estilo y la Imagen*, Lima, Pontifica Universidad Católica del Péru, 1994
——, 'Huari D-Shaped Structures, Sacrificial Offerings, and Divine Rulership', in E.P. Benson and A.G. Cook (eds), *Ritual Sacrifice in Ancient Peru*, Austin, University of Texas Press, 2001, pp. 137–64
Czwarno, R.M., Meddens, F.M. and Morgan, A. (eds), *The Nature of Wari: A Reappraisal of the Middle Horizon Period in Peru*, British Archaeological Reports International Series 525, Oxford, 1989
Goldstein, P.S., 'Tiwanaku Temples and State Expansion: A Tiwanaku Sunken-Court Temple at Moquegua, Peru', *Latin American Antiquity* 4, no. 1 (1993), 22–47
Isbell, W.H., *The Rural Foundations for Urbanism*, Illinois Studies in Anthropology 10, Urbana, University of Illinois Press, 1977
——, *Mummies and Mortuary Monuments*, Austin, University of Texas Press, 1997
—— and Cook, A., 'A New Perspective on Conchapata and the Andean Middle Horizon', in H. Silverman and W.H. Isbell (eds), *Andean Archaeology II: Art, Landscape, and Society*, New York, Kluwer Academic, 2002, pp. 249–306
—— and McEwan, G.F. (eds), *Huari Administrative Structure: Prehistoric*

Monumental Architecture and State Government, Washington DC, Dumbarton Oaks, 1991

Kolata, A.L., *The Tiwanaku: Portrait of an Andean Civilization*, Oxford, Basil Blackwell, 1993

—— (ed.), *Tiwanaku and its Hinterland: Archaeology and Paleocology of an Andean Civilization. 1 Agroecology*, Washington DC, Smithsonian Institution Press, 1996

Lynch, T.F., 'Camelid Pastoralism and the Emergence of Tiwanaku Civilization in the South Central Andes', *World Archaeology* 15, no. 91 (1983), 1–14

Menzel, D., 'New Data on the Huari Empire in Middle Horizon 2A', *Ñawpa Pacha* 6 (1969), 47–114

Oakland, A., 'Tiwanaku Textile Style from the South Central Andes, Bolivia and North Chile', unpublished PhD dissertation, University of Texas, Austin, 1990

Ortloff, C.R. and Kolata, A.L., 'Climate and Collapse: Agro-Ecological Perspectives on the Decline of the Tiwanaku State', *Journal of Archaeological Science* 20 (1993), 195–221

Ponce, C., *Tiwanaku: Espacio, Tiempo y Cultura: Ensayo de Sintesis Arqueológica*, La Paz, Academia Nacional de Ciencias, Publicación 22, 1972

Posnansky, A., *Tihuanacu, the Cradle of American Man*, New York, J.J. Agustin, 1945

Protzen, J.-P., and Nair, S., 'The Gateways of Tiwanaku: Symbols or Passages?', in H. Silverman and W.H. Isbell (eds), *Andean Archaeology II: Art, Landscape, and Society*, New York, Kluwer Academic, 2002, pp. 189–224

Reinhard, J. 'Underwater Archaeological Research in Lake Titicaca, Bolivia', in N.J. Saunders (ed.), *Ancient America: Contributions to New World Archaeology*, Oxford, Oxbow, 1992, pp. 117–43

Schaedel, R.P., 'Congruence of Horizon with Polity: Huari and the Middle Horizon', in D.S. Rice (ed.), *Latin American Horizons*, Washington DC, Dumbarton Oaks, 1993, pp. 225–62

Schreiber, K., *Wari Imperialism in Middle Horizon Peru*, Anthropological Papers of the Museum of Anthropology, University of Michigan, No. 87, Ann Arbor, 1992

Seddon, M.T., 'Ritual, Power, and the Development of a Complex Society: The Island of the Sun and the Tiwanaku State', unpublished PhD dissertation, Department of Anthropology, University of Chicago, 1998

Stanish, C., *Ancient Titicaca: The Evolution of Complex Society in Southern Peru and Northern Bolivia*, Berkeley, University of California Press, 2003

Wassen, H. A., *Medicine-Man's Implements and Plants in a Tiahuanacoid Tomb in Highland Bolivia*, Gothenburg, Goteborgs Etnografiska Museum, 1972

Chapter Twelve

Ascher, M. and Ascher, R., *The Code of the Quipu: A Study in Media, Mathematics, and Culture*, Ann Arbor, University of Michigan Press, 1981

Bauer, B.S., *The Sacred Landscape of the Incas: The Cusco Ceque System*, Austin, University of Texas Press, 1998

—— and Dearborn, D.S.P., *Astronomy and Empire in the Ancient Andes*, Austin, University of Texas Press, 1995

—— and Stanish, C., *Ritual and Pilgrimage in the Ancient Andes*, Austin, University of Texas Press, 2001

Bingham, H., *Machu Picchu: A Citadel of the Incas*, New York, Hacker Books, 1970

Cieza de León, P. de, *The Incas of Pedro de Cieza de León*, Norman, University of Oklahoma Press, 1959 [1553]

Classen, C., *Inca Cosmology and the Human Body*, Salt Lake City, University of Utah Press, 1993

Cobo, B., *History of the Inca Empire*, Austin, University of Texas Press, 1983 [1653]

——, *Inca Religion and Customs*, Austin, University of Texas Press, 1990 [1653]

D'Altroy, T.N., *Provincial Power in the Inca Empire*, Washington DC, Smithsonian Institution Press, 1993

Damian, C., *The Virgin of the Andes: Art and Ritual in Colonial Cuzco*, Miami Beach, Grassfield Press, 1995

Dean, C., *Inka Bodies and the Body of Christ*, Durham, NC, Duke University Press, 1999

Garcilaso de la Vega, *Royal Commentaries of the Incas and General History of Peru*, Austin, University of Texas Press, 1987 [1609]

Guaman Poma de Ayala, F., *El primer crónica y buen gobierno*, 3 vols, eds, J.V. Murra and R. Adorno, Mexico City, Siglo XXI, 1980

Hemming, J., *The Conquest of the Incas*, Harmondsworth, Penguin, 1983

Hyslop, J., *The Inca Road System*, New York, Academic Press, 1984

——, *Inca Settlement Planning*, Austin, University of Texas Press, 1990

Kendall, A., *Everyday Life of the Incas*, Batsford, 1973

MacCormack, S., 'Demons, Imagination, and the Incas', in S. Greenblatt (ed.), *New World Encounters*, Berkeley, University of California Press, 1993, pp. 101–26

Morris, C. and Thompson, D.E., *Huánuco Pampa: An Inca City and its Hinterland*, Thames & Hudson, 1985

Moseley, M.E., *The Incas and their Ancestors*, Thames & Hudson, 1992

Patterson, T.C., *The Inca Empire: The Formation and Disintegration of a Pre-Capitalist State*, Oxford, Berg, 1991

Quilter, J. and Urton, G. (eds), *Narrative Threads: Accounting and Recounting in Andean Khipu*, Austin, University of Texas Press, 2002

Reinhard, J., 'Sacred Peaks of the Andes', *National Geographic* 181, no. 3 (1992), 84–111

——, 'Peru's Ice Maidens', *National Geographic* 189, no. 6 (1996), 62–81

Rostworowski de Diez Canseco, M. *History of the Inca Realm*, Cambridge University Press, 1999

Rowe, J.H., 'Inca Culture at the Time of the Spanish Conquest', in J.H. Steward (ed.), *Handbook of South American Indians 2*, Washington DC, Smithsonian Institution Press, 1946, pp. 186–330

Silverblatt, I., *Moon, Sun, and Witches: Gender Ideologies and Class in Inca and Colonial Peru*, Princeton, Princeton University Press, 1987

Spalding, K., *Huarochiri: An Andean Society under Inca and Spanish Rule*, Stanford, Calif., Stanford University Press, 1984

Urton, G., *At the Crossroads of the Earth and Sky: An Andean Cosmology*, Austin, University of Texas Press, 1981

——, *The History of a Myth: Pacariqtambo and the Origin of the Incas*, Austin, University of Texas Press, 1990

Wachtel, N., *The Vision of the Vanquished*, Brighton, Harvester Press, 1977

Index